The Fo

For Wa..........
Sons of Norway.

18 Feb. 2000
Peter Tjernagel Hartvol

A Gift to Washington Lodge
from Carra Johnson Callies

The

American Land & Life

Series

Edited by Wayne Franklin

The Follinglo Dog Book

A Norwegian Pioneer Story from Iowa

Peder Gustav Tjernagel

Foreword by Wayne Franklin

Prologue & Epilogue by Peter Tjernagel Harstad

UNIVERSITY OF IOWA PRESS IOWA CITY

University of Iowa Press,

Iowa City 52242

Copyright © 1999

by the University of Iowa Press

All rights reserved

Printed in the United States of America

Design by Richard Hendel

http://www.uiowa.edu/~uipress

Printed on acid-free paper

Library of Congress Cataloging-in-Publication Data

Tjernagel, Peder Gustav, 1864–1932.

The Follinglo dog book: a Norwegian pioneer story from

Iowa / by Peder Gustav Tjernagel; foreword by Wayne

Franklin; prologue and epilogue by Peter Tjernagel Harstad.

p. cm. — (American land and life series)

ISBN 0-87745-679-8, ISBN 0-87745-678-x (pbk.)

1. Tjernagel, Peder Gustav, 1864–1932—Childhood and

youth. 2. Pioneers—Iowa—Scott Township (Hamilton

County) Biography. 3. Norwegian Americans—Iowa—

Scott Township (Hamilton County) Biography.

4. Tjernagel, Peder Gustav, 1864–1932—Family.

5. Dogs—Iowa—Scott Township (Hamilton County).

6. Farm life—Iowa—Scott Township (Hamilton County).

7. Frontier and pioneer life—Iowa—Scott Township

(Hamilton County). I. Title. II. Series.

F629.S397T57 1999

977.7'52—dc21 99-25337

99 00 01 02 03 C 5 4 3 2 1
99 00 01 02 03 P 5 4 3 2 1

Contents

Foreword *by Wayne Franklin*, vii

Prologue *by Peter Tjernagel Harstad*, xv

Preface, xi

Milla, 1

Fido, 12

Fido the Second, 24

Tige, 31

Chip, 61

Carlo, 136

Carlo the Second, 140

Carlo the Third, 141

Chip the Second, 145

Chip and Hector, 150

Chip and Kate, 153

Noble, Sheppo, and Chip, 156

Chip the Third, 159

Epilogue *by Peter Tjernagel Harstad*, 161

Foreword

WAYNE FRANKLIN

The Follinglo Dog Book both *is* and *is not* a book about dogs. Part of its charm is that under a title seemingly meant to appeal to younger readers, it offers instead a kind of family epic straight from the American heartland. The canines certainly are here: yes, from Milla to Chip the Third, we encounter a procession of winning if unfortunate creatures who, along with their immigrant owners, led a hard life on the nineteenth-century American frontier. With some jocular exaggeration, the epic is said to be theirs even though it is not. The epic belongs instead to the hardy race of the Tjernagels and the Follinglos, Norwegian pioneers who made their way to Iowa and then made Iowa their home. If you pick up this book thinking it will offer a good read about canine experiences, you will find yourself reinformed by the way it unfolds. You might as well think of picking up Ford Madox Ford's sad novel of betrayal, *The Good Soldier*, expecting a fictional account of Verdun. More on the hard part of the canines' lives later. For now, let it be noted that the animals actually provide a clock for measuring the human action in this narrative.

From the 1860s, when the Norwegian pioneers left their temporary quarters in the Fox River country of Illinois, to the 1960s, when (as will be seen in Peter Tjernagel Harstad's fine extension of the saga) disaster struck their world, the Tjernagels passed five generations on their farm north of Des Moines. In the record of their time there one may read a chronicle of the State of Iowa, the Midwest region, and the nation. They passed over the Mississippi and moved across the Iowa prairie in what was still the age of wooden equipment and animal power, then witnessed each successive revolution on the land, from mechanization to steam power to gas and diesel tractors, and on to that strangely modern device that brought the disaster of 1968. I find a neat emblem of such changes in one of the buildings that the author of the epic erected on Follinglo Farm. It was modeled after a traditional

Norwegian structure, a granary, of which one may see examples at the museum of Norwegian American folklife, Vesterheim, in the northeast Iowa town of Decorah. But this granary, actually used as a seed house, was made of poured concrete and wood, a modern innovation that attracted wide attention at the time of its construction in 1916. The Tjernagels did not merely follow along in the tracks of American modernization on the farm. They clearly relished the movement and, Peter Tjernagel Harstad makes clear, were widely celebrated in the popular rural press for their forward-looking innovations.

It is unusual to have an *inside* account of this process. Most agricultural history is written about farm families rather than by them, but when Peder Gustav Tjernagel sat down in 1909 at the age of forty-four to write out his family history for his children, he accomplished much more than he modestly intended. With humor, human understanding, and sensitivity, he inscribed a family account of rare insight, and it has been cherished by the family, which saw a private edition into print three decades ago. But Tjernagel did much more. He told the story of European peasant migration to North America as it seldom has been told by an insider. And he told as well a human story of even broader appeal. In the adaptation of these people to the vastly changed conditions of their life — in the passage from coastal Norway to the American heartland but also from an ancient way of life to a modern one — Peder Gustav reached, without ever losing his cozy jocularity, a level of history he probably never intended to.

In this last sense, there may seem to be few books of his era or later to which to compare *The Follinglo Dog Book*. Yet, although he probably would have vehemently denied or even been ignorant of the fact, Peder Gustav was working within a broader cultural context when he penned it. In many corners of America at the time, the local colorists were seeking to capture in prose and poetry — as their counterparts were on artist's paper and canvas — the peculiar surfaces of regional life. To some extent, the whole effort was a nostalgic indulgence. But that was especially true of the "outsider" productions of the local color school. When Sarah Orne Jewett composed *The Country of the Pointed Firs* in the 1890s, she turned her attention away from her own Maine town of South Berwick on the Piscataqua River, some miles upstream from Portsmouth, New Hampshire, and sought out an isolated coastal zone where the customs and values of the surviving residents were markedly out of sync with modern national assumptions. Moreover, she introduced as her surrogate in the book an educated Boston schoolteacher, the quintessential outsider, who looks on Dunnet Landing with sympathetic but necessarily distant eyes. Similar patterns can be distinguished in the work of other writers from the period. Willa Cather, a migrant from Virginia to the plains of Nebraska, resembled Jewett's schoolteacher, and when she wrote about immigrant life in her adopted home she focused on the ethnic Bohemian communities, whose peasant origins, strange language, and peculiar customs formed a clear contrast with the ways of life that Cather's contemporaries — such as the slightly older Edith Wharton — were chronicling among the Anglo elite elsewhere in the nation.

If there is anything exotic about the Tjernagels as they are recalled by one of their own — and in the voice of Peder Gustav's grandson, Peter Harstad, by another of their own — the exotic note is something the reader brings to the book. Peder Gustav did not sentimentalize or for the most part make heroes out of his contemporaries and ancestors. Store Per, the near-legendary figure one meets in these pages, may be an exception, but beyond that individual Peder Gustav looked at the others close-up. And while he may have used his humor to change the proportions of their experience a bit, he mostly saw things well and wrote about them as only an insider can. In this regard, the book that his own tale most reminds me of is a peculiar product of a somewhat earlier writer in a quite different world. That is *The Story of an Old Farm*, a New Jersey memoir and family history written a couple of decades prior to *The Follinglo Dog Book* by Andrew J. Mellick Jr. Mellick, a modestly educated descendant of prerevolutionary German immigrants to New Jersey, produced a remarkable account of his family's past, supported by a sense of the natural and cultural landscape of the region and a feeling for human nature that gives the book even today a broad appeal. Unlike so many family historians, Mellick was able to understand not only the inner workings of his clan but also where they all fit into the larger patterns of their community's experience. And he wrote with a felicity akin to that of Peder Gustav Tjernagel, in a prose that, if not exactly "finished" in a strictly literary sense, is nonetheless distinctive. Both authors have an unmistakable voice. With another body of material of which they remind me — the exceptional archive produced by former residents of the forcibly depopulated Blasket Islands off Ireland's Dingle peninsula — they share the capacity to illuminate zones of our human past that have been all but foreclosed by the electronic universe of today.

That point in a sense may bring us back to those canines, from Milla on. At a time when sheep have been cloned, mechanical dogs have been invented and marketed, and elaborate machines are slowly sneaking up on our own cherished ability to think, there is something wrenchingly corporeal about Milla and the other creatures that weave in and out among the Tjernagels of the first generations on the prairie. Some readers may be distressed at what seems like mistreatment of various kinds visited on the animals. Tige, for instance, was ruthlessly shot by a hunter who happened to be on the spot and had a gun and "out of pure meanness" used it. "Poor Milla" herself, innocent of any wrong except for being in heat, at last was shot on purpose because of the crowds of noisy dogs that drove her hardworking family crazy with their racket night after night. And so on. Animal rights are important rights in our contemporary estimation, as well they should be, but we ought to be honest enough to recognize a few things about our own values, as well as about those of other people in other places or at other times. As is often the case, a history of the terms we use can be illuminating. The word "pet" would seem to be of such transparency that it would hardly repay scrutiny. However, its original use — and some other meanings clustered about its core — can shed light on this subject. The word, intriguingly enough, originally referred not specifically to canines and felines and birds (let alone skinks, geckos, or boas) or other animals specifically raised for the special role we assign our own pets today but rather to lambs that, instead of being raised for slaughter or at least for shearing, were taken into the farmhouse and

Foreword

"petted," both physically coddled and emotionally fussed over. They were also called "cades" or "cade lambs," a term of obscure origin that implied they had been rejected by their mothers or were orphaned and had to be given such special, exceptional attention. The same term frequently was extended to cover other, similar animals, such as foals that never were allowed to suckle their dams but instead were brought up indoors. All such animals were abstracted in a sense from the biological and economic context within which they normally would have had their very being.

Like most farm and domestic animals, of course, sheep are the artifacts of our long intervention in the globe's fauna, and Dolly is the latest example of that intervention rather than a radical departure from our tinkering past. In any case, from its first use to refer to such lambs exempted from their expectable fate, the term "pet" came to be used for animals that had less distinct economic functions, at least in the orbit of European culture, animals whose sole raison d'être came to be that they essentially did nothing material and provided no material benefit to people. But in fact most so-called pet species originally had economic value for the people who created, kept, and employed them. Dogs and cats, never routinely eaten in Europe or in Euro-America, gained from that taboo, perhaps, an easier transition to the purely decorative uses they may be said to have today. But canines of the many kinds we have perfected, from the terriers to the shepherds, the pointers to the hounds, always helped people produce or defend food even if they were not themselves deemed fit to be eaten. Felines, by the same token, were prized for their ability to control rodent populations and chase birds from crops rather than for their cozying up under the pressure of a loving hand. Only when sufficient numbers of Europeans and Euro-Americans moved off the land and had no more need for sheepherding allies in the pasture or rat-hunting agents in the barn was it possible for that singularly modern creation, the house pet, to be invented. And all such animals, it might be argued from a long view of human history, are cades, castaways, flukes. If we were more dispassionate in assessing our own foibles we might confess that the whole business is curious. I often reflect, when I see a cat catch and play with some creature smaller than itself, which generally hops around and won't run off, that the desire to train a pet is all about domination rather than love. But that is another story.

It is not, though, the story of the canines of Follinglo Farm. These were working animals, even if their only function was to be the dog on the place. "No well regulated household could be without a dog in the early days," Peder Gustav himself explains. "Even if he could not do anything else, he could report when the tin peddler turned into the yard." Here Peder Gustav's customary humor takes over, for he adds: "Each respectable farm place was supposed to furnish its reasonable amount of barking, so as to break the monotony, especially during the long winter evenings." Below his humor, though, is the reality that such animals served as sentient security systems for remote houses in an era before rural (or urban) electrification. Today the security light and the high-tech alarm and its central monitoring station hook-up perform the canine's old jobs, while the canine sleeps inside, protected like all the other inmates by those substitutions. Cast off by the advance of our material civilization, the cade is pampered. Indeed, herds of other beasts are raised to be slaughtered so that such nonworking creatures can thrive. We cause some animals to be killed so that we can give others what we routinely, unflinchingly call a "special treat."

Peder Gustav does not cloak the realities of his own world in such evasions. Yes, the animals did not always receive fair play. But this was a universe in which, in cities as well as out on the farms, childhood diseases were seldom kind to the vulnerable members of our own species either. And it was a universe in which expedients we take for granted, such as readily available and fairly sophisticated veterinary care, simply were beyond the reach of most people and their animals. A number of the Follinglo Farm canines were put to death to curtail their suffering — only with regard to such exceptional animals as Noble, who "died a natural death" (having been crippled with rheumatism), was this usual violent remedy unnecessary. Could Milla be spayed? Technically, yes, since that procedure has long been known. But in practical terms it likely was not really available. In the period when the Tjernagels and Follinglos migrated to Iowa, some local governments in this country routinely charged double taxes on what tax assessors typically termed "sluts," suggesting that there was a disincentive to keeping such unneutered animals. But if that was so, what happened to female pups? One can only imagine. And in view of Milla's fate, perhaps we need to recall that modern laws about the confinement of canines (and now in some communities, felines as well) are just that — modern. Peder Gustav portrays the dogs attracted by Milla as descending on Follinglo Farm from as far as fifty miles or more. In an era before rabies vaccination, not successfully accomplished until after Pasteur's demonstration in 1885, such packs of strange canines lingering about the farm night after night not only were an annoyance. They were a positive threat to the other animals, including not just livestock but also one's own dogs and bitches, and the children and adults.

A taboo is a powerful psycho-social implement. In the case of the canines of Follinglo Farm, we should not allow our own potentially strong susceptibility to a few modern taboos to deflect our attention from the extraordinary account of life on the land that Peder Gustav Tjernagel, and his grandson, have collaboratively produced. If there are animals barking in the night as we read, that is as it should be. The world is never as tidy as our notions of it, but it is real in a way that notions cannot be. In this book, Follinglo Farm is added to the modest territory of literature's real places.

Prologue
Of Time, Place, People, & Text

PETER TJERNAGEL HARSTAD

Peder Gustav Tjernagel (pronounced chair-nah-gull), the author of *The Follinglo Dog Book* and my maternal grandfather, was the first child of European ancestry born at Follinglo Farm. He lived his entire life there from the last year of the American Civil War (1865) until the stock market bottomed during the depths of the Great Depression (1932).[1]

Follinglo Farm is located in the center of Iowa on north/ south-running Interstate 35, which divides both Iowa and the nation into two nearly equal parts. It is at mile marker 127 in Section 30 of Scott Township, Hamilton County, four miles northeast of Story City. Except for a small area where the last glacier left deposits of sand and gravel, the acres that make up this farm are among the most fertile in the world.

I never met Grandfather because he died three years before I was born. But I am named after him and have been curious about him as long as I can remember. I have walked the fields that he tilled, milked cows from bloodlines that he developed, visited buildings and rooms that he built, handled items that he made out of wood, viewed pictures of him, read his writings, and spent time with his next of kin. Even as a child I asked relatives to share Tjernagel lore. They did, including versions of stories in this book. But no text of *The Follinglo Dog Book* was available to my immediate family while I was growing up.

Grandfather told the history of Follinglo Farm and its people in a unique and engaging manner — by the regimes of the farm dogs. He developed the technique while telling bedtime stories to his children. As a farmer, he knew the rhythms of the earth and the plants and animals it supported. Year-round, the rooster proclaimed each new day. Cows dropped their calves each spring and gave milk morning and evening. The seasons brought times to sow, cultivate, harvest, and rest. At 42 degrees north latitude and in the interior of the continent, even the land rests, tucked under a blanket of snow. Springtime paints the countryside in delicate shades of green. When the oak leaves grow to the size of squirrels' ears it is time to plant the corn. After haying and grain harvest, the corn tassels, develops ears, towers, and turns darker shades of green. Grandfather's brother Nehemias, a world traveler, often told the Tjernagels of Follinglo Farm that nothing was more beautiful than a field of ripening corn.

For the last third of the nineteenth century and the first third of the twentieth, Grandfather, with increasing efficiency, harvested corn and fed it to swine destined for market or the Tjernagel smokehouse. But there was more to Peder Gustav's life than the production of farm commodities. His transition from youth to manhood coincided with the passing of the virgin prairie and the rise of commercial farming in central Iowa. These are main themes of *The Follinglo Dog Book*. In its totality (foreword, prologue, dog book, and epilogue), this volume may also be read as an account of Grandfather's life and a history of Follinglo Farm and its people.

Grandfather thought differently in some areas than do his living descendants. He deserves to be understood on his own terms. His way of thinking about time serves as an example. Before young Peder Gustav went out on the lonely prairie to herd cattle, his father, a Norwegian seaman, taught him to read the angle of the sun to determine when it was time to eat lunch and when it was time to drive the cattle home. Grandfather did not see a clock until his father purchased one and brought it to the farm during the reign of Fido the Second. Great-grandfather had a ritual of setting his clock by the way the sun's rays struck the floorboards of his house. Watching him do this is one of my mother's most vivid girlhood memories.

When the Tjernagels of Follinglo Farm dug systematically into the prairie soil to tile and drain their fields they unearthed evidence of geologic time. Teeth, tusks, and skeletal material from extinct animals accumulated in the sitting room of the farmhouse. However, the prime piece in the collection, a several-pound ridged molar from a Pleistocene mammoth, likely came from Alaska. Grandfather's formal education did not extend beyond the eighth grade, but his periodization schemes ranged from the glacial age, to the books of the Bible, to the grace notes in Edvard Grieg's musical compositions. The device of unfolding the history of Follinglo Farm and its people in increments of canine life cycles seemed logical enough to Grandfather and also had the advantage of holding the interest of his children.

Whether *The Follinglo Dog Book* should be read as history comes down to definitions. As a young historian I participated in a lively discussion that identified time, place, people (including their ideas), and events as the building blocks of history. In literature, one or more of these elements is imaginary. I have checked many of Grandfather's facts against census records or other historical records. They pass the test of historical authenticity. One exception involves his references to an American Indian "reservation" at Liscomb in Marshall County, Iowa. Native Americans may have clustered there in the early years of Grandfather's life (just as they did on the Skunk River not far from Follinglo Farm), but I can find no evidence of a government reservation at Liscomb. Unwittingly, Grandfather made a mistake. He apparently wrote, with few written records to aid his memory, about events that occurred years earlier. *The Follinglo Dog Book* is not exempt from the usual limitations of reminiscent accounts. In places, Grandfather employed literary license, including exaggeration, in the telling of his tales. These instances are readily apparent to discerning readers.

To understand the dynamics of the Tjernagels of Follinglo Farm and to be on the same footing as the children for whom the dog book was written, it is helpful to know something of the lives of Grandfather's parents, Ole Andreas Larson Tjernagel and Martha Karina Anderson Follinglo Tjernagel, and their children. The summary biographies that follow are indicative of how I acquired knowledge of my Tjernagel forebears and of how I now perceive them.

OLE ANDREAS LARSON TJERNAGEL, 1836–1919

As the dog book relates, the founders of Follinglo Farm, Grandfather's parents, Ole Andreas and Martha Karina, natives of Norway, came to central Iowa from Illinois in 1864 in a prairie schooner or covered wagon. Ole Andreas was born in Lien, in the parish of Sveio, 10 April 1836. When he was fifteen the family moved a short distance to Tjernagel, a village on Norway's west coast between Bergen and Stavanger.[2]

The literal meaning of Tjernagel is "tar nail," for which there are two plausible explanations. One is that boat builders at this place were known for dipping their nails in tar. The other explanation is more complex. The small deepwater cove at Tjernagel is rimmed with sheer rock. During storms, fishing boats turned into the cove for protection. Seamen drove mooring spikes into the rock and tied up their boats. They circled the nails with tar so that they could see them from a distance. Hence the name Tjernagel.[3]

A few warehouses and a small store and post office were the only commercial establishments I detected at Tjernagel during a 1983 visit. Nearby, I met a distant relative who used an ancient horse as his motive power to till the rocky soil. He found a mallet and a stone chisel and led me to a cleft in the rock above Tjernagel where I chiseled my name beside those of others of our blood who had visited the site during the past century and more.

Ole Andreas foresaw a life of poverty if he remained at Tjernagel. Therefore, he spent his twentieth birthday on a sailing vessel bound for America. A sensitive and industrious man, he arrived at his destination, Ottawa, Illinois, 4 July 1856, with the objective of becoming an independent farmer. He worked his way up the "agricultural ladder," first by hiring out, then by working land on shares, renting, and finally by purchasing his own farm. He thrived in the New World but never forgot the poverty of his family in Norway.

When he took out his citizenship "intent" papers in LaSalle County, Illinois, he apparently used the name Ole A. Larson. He did not serve in the American Civil War but waited until three years after it was over before "Ole A. Larson" renounced his allegiance to the "King of Sweden & Norway" and became a citizen of the United States. This he did at Nevada, Iowa, 21 April 1868, a month after the birth of his third child. Only then did he assume the full rights and responsibilities of citizenship.[4]

Ole Andreas and his sons had more than subsistence agriculture in mind for Follinglo Farm (as we shall see in the section on the farm in the sketch of Peder Gustav). Ole Andreas embodied the classic enigma of the Iowa farmer. Innately conservative, he nevertheless adopted the most advanced farming techniques available. That was apparent when he drove his spirited team of geldings to Follinglo Farm in May 1864. Plodding oxen were too slow for him. He neither owned oxen nor used them to break the Iowa prairie as did his brother and many of his neighbors. As mechanized equipment became available, Ole Andreas and his sons acquired the best available.

Under the leadership of Ole Andreas, Follinglo not only became an efficient farm but also a haven for "alcoholics, Arabian peddlers, beggars, and stray dogs." "Grandpa would welcome any and all dogs," my mother claims. "There seemed to be a mutual attraction that was irresistible."[5] Thus Peder Gustav came by his interest in canines honestly. *The Follinglo Dog Book* and the accounts of Ole Andreas' wife and children that follow contain many details of his long and useful life.

MARTHA KARINA ANDERSON FOLLINGLO TJERNAGEL, 1845–1907

Martha Karina's parents, Nils Anderson Follinglo and Barbru Mikkelsdottir, were engaged for a time, but they never married. Prosperity eluded Nils and Barbru on both sides of the Atlantic. He appears in some chapters of the dog book as Nils Murar, or Nils the mason, which occupation he followed. Born out of wedlock 10 July 1845 at Bomeloen, Norway, Martha Karina experienced a difficult childhood. Nils, who worked for a time at Avaldsnes near Haugesund, also on Norway's west coast, took Martha Karina away from her mother and did his best to raise her.[6]

Avaldsnes is rich in tradition. The church there, built on a pre-Christian worship site, dates from the end of the Viking era. To this day pagan symbols dominate the churchyard in the form of stone "needles" that lean toward the church. According to local tradition, the end of the world will come when one of the needles touches the church. It is rumored that the Lutheran clergyman at Avaldsnes uses a stone saw to prevent this from happening.

When Martha Karina was eleven, Nils and his wife, Margreto, brought their blended family to Illinois, close to the place where Ole Andreas worked as a hired hand. Martha Karina was only fifteen when she married Ole Andreas 11 June 1861. He once told my mother, also named Martha Karina, that he became "the happiest man in the whole world" that day.[7] Throughout life Martha Karina had respiratory problems. Nevertheless, she worked diligently, gave birth to eight children, cared for them, and dispensed hospitality for nearly four decades at the farm named Follinglo in her honor. In 1884, when Martha Karina learned that her birth mother was living in dire straits in Norway, she sent for her and cared for her until Barbru died in 1890.[8]

As I was growing up, Mother told stories about the "olden days" while rocking her youngest child to sleep. On the wall nearby was an oil painting of two Martha Karinas, one her elderly grandmother, the other herself as a robust little girl looking at a book. In 1902 Martha Karina and Ole Andreas moved from Follinglo Farm to a small house in Story City, where they lived until she died 16 April 1907. Ole Andreas then moved back to the farm, where he lived twelve more years. Thus as a child Mother absorbed more from her grandfather than from her namesake. Her father, Peder Gustav, could consult with Ole Andreas on a daily basis as he wrote *The Follinglo Dog Book*. In some ways it is Ole's book, too.

Mother imparted much family lore. However, the stories of her five paternal uncles and one aunt went back another generation. The final years of their lives overlapped the opening decades of mine. With the exception of the first-born girl who did not survive childhood, I interacted with all of them. The children of Ole Andreas and Martha Karina were: Lars Johan, Peder Gustav, Nehemias, Helge Mathias, Bertha Kjerstine, Martin Olai, the second Bertha Kjerstine, and Gustav Adolph.

Born in Illinois, Lewis claimed to remember the founding of Follinglo Farm and loved to tell stories about the role of the Tjernagels in the passing of the prairie. One morning in 1941 a bachelor uncle who was tending me at the farm loaded me into a pickup made from a Model A Ford sedan and dropped me off at Lewis' home in Story City. That uncle needed relief from my incessant questions. Lewis, an octogenarian attorney whose wife had died in 1914, had reached a time of life when transmitting family lore was a high priority. He and I spent an idyllic day together at the happy junction of the inquisitiveness of youth and the communicativeness of old age.

Lewis' stories about his uncle Store Per (Big Pete), the Norwegian American Hercules after whom my grandfather was named, rendered me speechless. My favorite Store Per story does not appear in the dog book, nor does it demonstrate Per's physical strength. To my knowledge, Lewis never recorded it, but Grandfather did.[9]

Store Per (Peder Larson) left Stavanger, Norway, in 1851 on a sailing vessel bound for Quebec, Canada. A veritable giant, he was the life of the party wherever he went — "an athlete of the highest order, a humorist, a musician, and to crown it all, a man with an even temperament." To banish the blues on the tedious voyage across the Atlantic Per would bring out his violin. His folk tunes and dances lured "sulking maidens out of their retreats" and "grouchy young men brooding over their last attack of sea sickness out of their hiding places." After ten weeks at sea, Per's party proceeded, by inland waterways, to Green Bay, Wisconsin, en route to Waupaca, where they were to meet relatives who had come earlier. As they approached the headwaters of the Winnebago River in central Wisconsin, the reality of being in an unfamiliar country settled in. The only English words they understood were yes and no. But Per could speak "a universal language with his fists if it should come to the worst."

That seemed inevitable as they proceeded up the Winnebago River. Submerged trees and drift logs impeded the progress of the vessel they had engaged, whereupon the captain unceremoniously deposited the party on the riverbank, well short of their destination. But the captain slipped away before Per could get to him. With meager food and no shelter they were in a predicament. The party devised a plan. Per would remain with the women, children, and baggage while the rest of the men would go on a foraging expedition.

The two groups separated, whereupon the huddled members of Per's party looked upriver and saw a flotilla of American Indian canoes, manned by "a goodly number" of Winnebago warriors on the warpath. The children began to bawl, "and the women started to act up in a manner peculiar to the weaker sex." Per took charge. His first impulse was to fight the whole flotilla. Then his better senses prevailed, and he thought the Winnebago might pass by without incident. But, no, they beached their canoes and came ashore. The terrified immigrants "beheld their fine athletic bodies, their bows and arrows, tomahawks and scalping knives, yes, even firearms."

Fighting would be futile, reasoned Per, but his violin could speak another universal language. "With an air of unconcern, he lifted the cover of his massive immigrant chest and drew forth his violin, clapped down the cover, sat down on it, and the concert was on." His first selection, a Lutheran hymn, gave the immigrants "an assurance that the good Lord and his protecting angels were hovering near." It also thawed the hearts of the Winnebago warriors. As the concert proceeded, the Winnebago men came closer and finally encircled the group, whereupon Per offered music of a lighter vein, "folksongs, love songs, and finally wound up with a rollicking 'Spring Dance.'"

No applause followed the concert, but the "grim visaged countenances . . . transformed into winning smiles." The Winnebago understood that Per's party needed food and shelter and generously provided both for four days and four nights. The two races could not speak to each other, except through the medium of sign language. "Of course, Per would tell them a story through his violin, whenever he deemed it expedient." This he did until "succor rolled into camp in the shape of a yoke of oxen, hitched to some wheels made out of disks, sawed from a proper sized log to make a wheel." As the foraging party followed the oxen and the crude *kubberule* into camp, the Winnebago "took their departure just as quietly as they had come."

Store Per eventually came to Illinois and settled at Norway, not far from Ottawa. Ole Andreas and Martha Karina were married at his house.

Lewis' mental storehouse brimmed with such tales, and he had a knack for telling them. His brother Peder Gustav wove several Store Per tales into *The Follinglo Dog Book* and recorded a few more elsewhere.

During that idyllic day in 1941, Lewis and I had an adventure of our own. It began when he fetched a cane my grandfather had made, and we set out on foot for Story City's ice cream parlor. The distance was only a few blocks, but the expedition took a half day. We stopped frequently to talk with people on the streets and in the shops. Lewis was then collecting biographical information on pioneer families of the area. Therefore, he did not miss opportunities to add facts to his mental files. The conversations opened with pleasantries, then transformed into stories told in Norwegian, English, or a mixture of the two languages. When my attention flagged Lewis explained that I was "Martha's boy." For those who did not remember my mother (or perhaps for my benefit) he explained that Martha Karina, "daughter of Peder Gustav and Jennie," had married the preacher in 1931 and gone off to live in Madison, Wisconsin, a few blocks from the state capitol.

Eventually, we ate ice cream, reversed direction, and completed our expedition. Little did I realize, as I returned to Follinglo Farm in the Model A, that I was storing up memories for a lifetime, learning that history has layers and that I am embedded in one of them and nudging myself toward a career as a historian.

As an adolescent I became curious about Lewis' business ventures, particularly after seeing references to the L. J. Tjernagel Livestock Commission Co. with offices in the Chicago Union Stock Yards.[10] When queried, loquacious Lewis led younger members of the tribe to believe that he had come close to *owning* the Union Stock Yards. Rife with "almosts," his business ventures also involved newspapers, publishing companies, banks, investment houses, and more. In his later years he developed Story City real estate and worked to improve that town's park system.

I remember Lewis as a surrogate grandfather, an imparter of family lore, and a storyteller par excellence. One vestige of his mischieviousness persisted into old age; he used his cane to tease, without mercy, the dogs of Follinglo Farm.

PEDER GUSTAV, 1865–1932

Ole Andreas and Martha Karina had strong nesting instincts when they came to central Iowa in 1864. He soon began hauling lumber for the construction of the central core of the house that four generations of Tjernagels would call home. He chose high ground for the building site, but not the highest of the undulating hills on his forty-acre tract. To divert an unofficial "prairie road" from both the farmstead and his property, Ole Andreas erected a few panels of rail fence. The tactic worked, but this was not the last threat to Follinglo Farm from a road.[11] Through the decades there has been no deviation from the initial plan of where the buildings should cluster.

While the house was under construction Martha Karina became pregnant with her second child. The next spring on Norway's national holiday, 17 May 1865, she gave birth to Peder Gustav in the family's new home. He and Follinglo Farm matured simultaneously. The United States and Iowa census schedules verify many facts in *The Follinglo Dog Book*. These government sources also add detail and provide perspective.

When the federal census taker came to Follinglo Farm 28 July 1870, he recorded the head of the household as Ole A. Larson, age thirty-four, with the following members: Martha C., twenty-five; Lewis J., eight; Peter G., five; and Nehemias, two. The two older boys were "at school." Peder Gustav and his siblings appear under the name Larson in all extant census schedules until 1895, when they first appeared as "Tjernagel." Ole Andreas continued with Larson until 1915, when, at age seventy-nine, the State of Iowa enumerator recorded him as "O. A. L. Tjernagel."

The 1870 census recorded a base for measuring the development of Follinglo Farm. The population schedule listed the value of the real estate at $2,000 and the personal estate at $1,100. The agriculture schedule indicated that the 120-acre farm produced 100 bushels of wheat (a cash crop), 400 of corn, 80 of oats, 20 of potatoes, and also twenty-five tons of hay. The farm supported six horses, four milk cows (that produced 200 pounds of butter), two "other cattle," and eight swine. Debts are listed at $2,200. It was a typical Scott Township farm of the period.

The population schedule of a decade later corroborates the account of the growing family portrayed in *The Follinglo Dog Book*. At age fifteen, Peder G. was "Laboring," and Lewis J., two years older, was "Teaching School." Nehemias, twelve, was "attending school." The entry for Henry M., nine, indicates that he had attended school within the year. A line is drawn through the name of Bertha C., five. Martin O., two, was then the youngest child. Two additional people rounded out the household: "Boarder teacher" R. G. Pierce, twenty-four; and "Servant" Minnie Nelson, sixteen, a native of Norway. Thus Martha Karina, mother of six, received help with the household tasks.

The 1880 agriculture schedule reported the farm forty acres smaller than in 1870, with sixty-five acres of tilled land and fifteen of meadow. The value of the land, fences, and buildings totaled $1,700; farming implements and machinery, $300; and livestock, $517. Ole Andreas paid $50 in labor and estimated the value of farm production at $500. One team of horses provided motive power, and seven cows produced 600 pounds of butter. There were also four calves, sixty-two swine, and poultry that produced 140 dozen eggs. Of the tilled acres, thirty in corn produced 1,200 bushels, twenty in oats 622 bushels, ten in wheat 120 bushels, and fourteen in flax 200 bushels. The meadow produced forty tons of hay. In summary, corn and livestock were on the rise.

Peder Gustav took more interest in farming than did any of his brothers. Machinery fascinated him; hand implements such as the scythe and cradle for harvesting grain held only historic interest. A Manny Reaper was the first machine to harvest grain at Follinglo Farm. One man drove the horses while the Manny cut a swath of grain and dropped it on a platform. A second man rode the reaper and raked off grain in bundle size. Others followed in the field to tie the bundles and shock them. Ole Andreas bought a Manny, adapted it for hay cutting, and did custom work for his neighbors. Next came the Marsh Harvester, which allowed two men to tie bundles while riding. Then came the self-rake McCormick and Manny reapers with mechanical platform rakes. These advances came rapidly for Ole Andreas, whose son Peder Gustav bought the first self-binder that replaced all former means of harvesting grain.[12]

The 1895 Iowa census reported a family in transition. "Peder G. Tjernagel, 29," now appeared as a farmer subject to military duty and entitled to vote. No longer a part of the household, Lewis had received his law degree from the University of Iowa in 1884 and gotten married in 1885. Nehemias' occupation is listed as "musician." Gustav, the youngest child of Ole Andreas and Martha Karina, was a ten-year-old. All members of the family are listed as Lutheran.

On 31 August 1895 Peder Gustav married Ingeborg Johanna Olsen, a twenty-three-year-old seamstress of Duncombe, Iowa, and a worthy match for an ambitious young farmer. After a honeymoon in Decorah, Iowa, he brought "Jennie," as she was known, home to Follinglo Farm. Her style, quiet humor, and hospitality are legendary. For the next sixty-five years, as long as strength permitted, she was the gracious hostess to all Tjernagels and others who came to the farm.

By 1900 the leadership transition from Ole Andreas and Martha Karina to Peder Gustav and Jennie was complete. The federal population schedule recorded "Tjernagle [*sic*], P., Farmer" as the head of the household and an owner of the farm. "Ole A. and Martha C. Larson" appear at the bottom of the list of those residing in the household, with no occupation given for either of them. They were slowing down.

When the federal enumerator arrived at Follinglo Farm in mid June 1900, Jennie already had three children — Otto Alfred (1896–1958), Herman Arnold (1898–1987), and Elizabeth (1899–1976). This brought the household to an even dozen, namely: Peder Gustav and his wife; their three children; Peder's parents; and five of Peder's siblings, Nehemias

("Farmer"), Henry ("Theological Student"), Martin ("Farm Laborer"), Bertha, and Gustav ("Farm Laborer"). That October Jennie gave birth to Erling Martin (1900–1958). Seven more were yet to come: Alfred Gustav (1902–1987), my mother Martha Karina (1904–), Olaf Johan (1905–1970), Bertha Margarethe (1907–1910), Peder Julius (1909–1909), Peder Julius (1910–1969), and Sigurd Lauritz (1916–1987).[13]

Grandfather wrote *The Follinglo Dog Book* in 1909. Thus it is a product of the golden age of Iowa agriculture and the heyday of Follinglo Farm. The 1915 State of Iowa census contains the body of agricultural data closest to the period of the dog book. As of the first of that year, P. G. Tjernagel, age forty-nine, reported the value of the farm and home as $40,600, with an encumbrance of $7,000. On the farm were twenty-eight shorthorn cattle valued at $1,290, including "6 Cows kept for milk." Presumably, more cows would freshen in the spring. The seventeen horses valued at $1,430, eight of them under the age of two, indicated a sizeable horse-breeding operation. Valued at $1,525 were 150 swine, 25 of them under six months. Peder Gustav reported no swine "lost by cholera in 1914." "Fowls, all kinds" numbering 160 and valued at $64 rounded out the report on the animals. The 1915 census did not report on acreage or crops. No census reported on dogs.

During the second decade of the twentieth century the "Tjernagel Brothers" 240-acre operation (owned by Peder Gustav, Nehemias, and Martin and masterminded by Grandfather) was widely regarded as a model farm of advanced design. Grandfather had no desire to earn a living in any way other than farming. Nevertheless, he and his brothers also cultivated additional interests and integrated them into their lives. The family welcomed journalists, several of whom wrote glowing accounts of what they observed at Follinglo Farm between 1914 and 1917.[14]

It impressed the journalists that dried grapevine spelled out FOLLINGLO in large letters on the south side of the cattle barn facing the road. The "permanent" concrete buildings drew superlatives. "The Tjernagels have what is probably the only corn crib in Iowa that is made entirely of concrete," reported the *Des Moines Register and Leader* 31 July 1915, "and they put up the structure themselves." Built in 1914 for $650, it measured forty-eight feet long, thirty-one feet wide, and twenty-one feet from the floor to the plates where the rafters rested. Even the shingles were concrete. The drive-through design and mechanical devices for filling and emptying the cribs fascinated the most experienced farm journalists. One explained: "The two sides of the crib hold 4,500 bushels of corn which is unloaded by a vertical elevator built into the structure and operating by means of a dump in the floor. Above the driveway is a series of bins with a total capacity of about 4,000 bushels of shelled corn or small grain."[15]

A seed house built in 1916 of concrete and wood followed the design of a Norwegian granary. "It Takes Originality to Build a Seedhouse Like This," read the caption under a picture of the structure in the 30 December 1916 *Prairie Farmer*. Peder Gustav explained, "Just because a man is a farmer is no reason why he should lose his sense of the artistic and the beautiful." He elaborated, "When we build a building, if only a chicken house, it is just as easy to make that structure attractive as it is to make it ugly." On 26 December 1914 the *Des Moines Register and Leader* concluded that the Tjernagels' buildings "are about the best of the many fine farm structures Iowa has to offer."

In 1915 Peder Gustav showed a reporter his woodworking shop on an upper floor of the cattle barn, where he had recently completed three chairs made from the wood of a native cherry tree. "They are about as beautiful pieces of furniture as one can find anywhere," the reporter concluded; "it is impossible to buy anything like them in furniture stores."[16]

Steel-reinforced concrete fence posts and more than two miles of wire surrounded and subdivided the Tjernagel's 240 acres. "How easy to sink into the ground a mammoth corner post made beautiful as you please, and everlasting as well, a joy to see, and a buttress of strength to the whole line fence," wrote Nehemias in *Wallaces' Farmer* 22 December 1916. It amused the family when visitors referred to the "college" posts on their farm. Although Peder Gustav frequently exchanged ideas at the agricultural college at Ames, the Tjernagels designed their own fencing system and manufactured the posts themselves. They bought the steel and the concrete; the sand and gravel came from their own farm. With a small mixer, Nehemias explained, the farmer can build "a veritable little forest of pretty creations in the form of buildings, fences, and the like."

When quizzed about their blooded shorthorn cattle and Poland China swine, the Tjernagels consistently responded that it was profitable to improve bloodlines constantly, even for the "100 to 125" hogs that went to market each year. The 31 July 1915 *Des Moines Register and Leader* reported keen competition at the Tjernagels' spring livestock sale; "fifty-seven sows [sold] in thirty minutes."

Peder Gustav, his brothers, and his children made quick transitions from the barnyard to the fine arts, as witnessed by a *Prairie Farmer* writer who said that he was not sure that he could "distinguish the 'Tune the Old Cow Died On' from grand opera." Yet "one of the most pleasant evenings I ever spent was a night last June when I sat in the front yard at Follinglo and listened to the orchestra." Peder Gustav played the cello and all of the children, except the youngest, "play one to three or four musical instruments," and their father "gravely assured me that the babies should learn when they are old enough." To top off the evening, Martin, Nehemias, Peder Gustav, and an unnamed visitor (probably John Dahle) formed a quartet and sang "the national songs of Norway." With a tinge of bewilderment, the Yankee journalist confessed that it was hard to know "where to begin and where to end" in writing about the Tjernagels.[17]

The mature Peder Gustav's idea of the good life at Follinglo Farm involved Christianity, family, classical music, literature, weedless fields, blooded livestock, a good dog, attractive buildings and furniture, tasty food from Jennie's kitchen, wit and humor, and a steady stream of interesting guests — all in harmony and properly orchestrated.

Friends in high and low places understood his values and the striking juxtapositions they could produce. Such was the case when the Minneapolis Symphony Orchestra came to Ames. Maestro Oberhoffer told Peder Gustav that he wanted to come out to Follinglo Farm to "get a good whiff of manure!"[18]

A unique and gentle soul, Nehemias had his moment in history. He acquired a love of music from his parents, played in bands and orchestras with his siblings and neighbors, and went on to study music at Ames and then in Norway and Germany in the 1890s. He also traveled widely on the Continent and in the Middle East.[19] Nehemias never married. During his long life, most of it spent on Follinglo Farm, he became uncle and great uncle to dozens, which earned him the sobriquet "Unko."

Early in 1910 while Unko was packing for a trip to Norway, "lille Madit" (little Margaret), the three-year-old daughter of Peder Gustav and Jennie, perched on his chest and sang "snatches of songs from operas or themes heard during rehearsals of the family orchestra." She "clung to my breast," he wrote, "imploring me not to go so far away and leave her."[20]

Unko wrote home 23 January 1910 from aboard the Cunard liner *Lusitania*: "Great ship. Screw tears up water in great shape. Terrific power." The weather, accommodations, and food were excellent, but he would have preferred to douse the woman in the next compartment, an "Italian rattle box," head first in the brine. Sometimes the ship rolled from side to side. One night a "fellow slid 40 ft. How I laughed." In a private note to his sister, Nehemias waxed philosophical. "Bertha dont you worry about lesser incidents. We are here to do good & pray for Gods will to be done & be happy & satisfied whichever way He fixes it for us." He advised, "Ask Him for what you want but dont kick if you dont always get it. He knows best. Work & be happy & then die & all is well." He explained: "The above is the philosophy of a seasick man."[21]

Nehemias had good reason to be present at Norway's Royal Castle at Christiania (now Oslo) 5 May 1910. That was the day ex-president Theodore Roosevelt received the Nobel prize for peacemaking in the conflict between Russia and Japan five years earlier. On that spring day a "skinny Iowa farmer in thread-bare coat, bowler hat, and rubbers" stood anonymous at the curb while the royal band struck up "Stars and Stripes" by John Philip Sousa followed by "The Roose-velt Overture" by "N. Tjernagel."[22] Assigned no place of prominence, Unko took in the pageantry, including his own music. Later, he explained the origins of the composition that marked the high point of his musical career. Snatches of inspiration came from his brother Martin; "also something from Pete's geist caught on the wing."[23]

While he was abroad word reached Unko that his niece little Madit had died suddenly 6 August 1910 (quite possibly because of a ruptured appendix). Grief-stricken at the loss of this "bundle of sweetness, love and affection," Nehemias composed and published a beautiful song, "Lille Madit," set in the key of D minor, in her memory. Translated into English, its closing lyrics read:

Dull pain again enfolds her, it trembles on her brow;
Then upward Madit gazes, — her eyes glint strangely now —
In rapture fond exclaiming! I see the angel fair,
So sweetly to us smiling, come let us join him there![24]

No Tjernagel gathering is complete without a vocal or instrumental rendition of this haunting piece.

In 1911 Unko organized an American concert tour for one of Norway's leading musicians, Eivind Alnaes, an organist, pianist, and composer under whom he had studied. Follinglo Farm became "home base" for the tour that lasted several months. Alnaes, one of several noted musicians and artists who enriched life at Follinglo Farm, took a special liking to my mother, one of the children for whom the dog book was written. To this day she has the gold ring that Alnaes gave her. "I was teased a lot for having a boyfriend from Norway at the age of six," she recalls. Also through Unko's contacts, a vocalist from Norway, Bergliot Tillish and her young daughter, stayed at the farm for a time. She raved at the thinly sliced dried beef "that had first been cured, then smoked and dried in our smoke house."[25]

In addition to secular and sacred music, Unko published books about his travels in Norway, Egypt, and Palestine.[26] He worked for a time at a publishing house in Minneapolis and also for his brother Lewis' L. J. Tjernagel Livestock Commission Co. in Chicago. Unko left it to others to relate his accomplishments.

By World War I Unko's interests centered on Follinglo Farm, and his international travels ceased. For the remainder of his ninety years he was known in the community as a wise and pious man who studied the Bible, read church periodicals, and kept up with theological issues within the Lutheran church.[27] He never learned to drive a car, use a milking machine, or operate any modern equipment. For him, television was not only a waste of time but also an abomination. An excellent conversationalist, Unko was a good listener, too. Many, including my parents, enjoyed his company and sought his counsel.

Unko took children on walks through lanes and along fence lines in search of native grasses and wildflowers that had once covered central Iowa. Often there was a stop at the Sheldall school, which he and his siblings had attended. In my childhood it was a community museum surrounded by a rail fence. I went there many times and was allowed to handle an ox yoke (that even Ole Andreas regarded as obsolete) and other relics of pioneer days. Unko also took the older children outdoors on clear, moonless nights to view the stars and constellations. The pitch-darkness of rural Iowa tempted wide-eyed city children to reach out to touch the heavenly bodies. With Unko behind us pointing out celestial features, we stood in awe of God's creation.

As he went about the farmyard to feed swine and to attend to other chores, Unko *pulled* his wheelbarrow. This unorthodox habit amused his grandnieces and grandnephews. Pulling required less energy than pushing, he insisted. (Secretly, we all tried it and found that he was right.) When he went into a hog pen a hammer dangled from the loop of his solid blue overalls. Swine can be ferocious animals, and this weapon constituted Unko's defense.

Everyone loved Unko, including my uncles. In contrast to him, they wore striped work overalls. The two generations differed in other ways, too. Unko did not approve the use of alcohol in any form. One hot July day toward the end of World War II Peder Julius was cultivating corn with the John Deere some distance from the farm buildings. Erling took

Prologue

compassion, cooled some beer in the concrete cow tank fed by the artesian well, and gave me precise instructions for hazardous duty. I was to put a bottle of beer in a clean grease can and carry it toward the tractor, acting all of the way as though my burden were heavy. Unko would be "as ornery as a Russian bull," I was told, if he learned what was in that container. That was hard for me to imagine, but I successfully smuggled the contraband past Unko, at work in the farmyard, and out to a puzzled but pleased uncle in the cornfield.

A classic story from earlier in the century involved "Nehemia," as the neighbors called him. (They usually dropped the final "s" of his name.) One day a neighbor with a weakness for strong drink decided to stop at Follinglo Farm rather than to proceed home, intoxicated, to a scolding wife. Repentant but still confused, and with a thick tongue, he came to the Tjernagels' barn and announced that he had come to see "Messiah."[28] The family never let "Nehemia" forget the episode.

At least in theory, the eternal "straight man" of Follinglo Farm regarded laughter as therapeutic. "Few, if any, have died from laughing," Unko once wrote, "but many have sickened unto death for want thereof."[29]

HELGE MATHIAS (HENRY), 1871–1940

A powerful man built in the proportions of Store Per, Henry graduated from Luther College, Decorah, Iowa, in 1894 and from Luther Seminary, Hamline, Minnesota, in 1902. His first pastorate was at Stanwood, Washington, where he found a wife and remained eight years. The family then moved to Teller, Alaska, where Henry served as a missionary until 1913. Henry's "unusual bodily strength and vigor," wrote his brother Nehemias, "enabled him to withstand the rigors of climate in the arctic, and his dog teams took him over the snowy wastes from one mission post to another, undaunted in spite of the hardships encountered."[30]

After serving parishes in Santa Barbara, California, and Crookston, Minnesota, Henry returned to missionary work in 1918, this time to American Indians at Gresham, Wisconsin, where the family resided until 1923. Seventy years after his uncle Store Per had calmed a band of Winnebago with his violin, Henry served that very tribe, "thus giving him the privilege of hearing them sing the very same Lutheran hymns that Per played for their grand and great grandfathers."[31] Music was important to Henry's ministry wherever he served.

Uncompromising regarding Christian doctrine, Henry refused to go along with a 1917 merger of three Norwegian Lutheran synods. He cast his lot with a small body now known as the Evangelical Lutheran Synod that remains the church home of many Tjernagels. Henry served as president of this synod from 1930 to 1934.

Henry and his wife, Anna Brue, had a dozen children, eight of whom survived to adulthood. Anna died after the stillbirth of their last child in 1924. To extend comfort, Peder Gustav came to Saude, Iowa, where his brother was then serving as a country pastor, and helped Henry build a log cabin in a Norwegian motif in Anna's memory. They called it the Strandebarm after Anna's ancestral family home in Norway. For a time it housed a Christian day school for Henry's daughters and other children of the community. It still stands on the grounds of the church and parsonage at Saude.

"If ever a ship needs a good pilot," Henry told my parents when he married them in 1931, "it is the ship that lifts anchor with a bride and groom aboard. That ship never reaches the open seas where there is no danger of reefs and rocks and shoals. . . . You are helpless to escape the dangers that threaten you on the various stages of your journey. Without a pilot, tried and true, you will be shipwrecked on Scylla if you escape Charybdis." He worked the metaphor through an eloquent homily, which he closed by quoting the hymn "Jesus, Savior, Pilot Me."[32] On 14 November 1935, the day after I was born (third of my parents' ten), Henry wrote my father: "I envy you the thrill that is yours these days; your steps are light as though your feet had no weight, the very air seems different, and there is a strange something about everything, that one can only feel. We certainly rejoice with you. God bless you all five."[33]

That was characteristic of Henry's heartiness and indicative of the value he placed upon life. I remember his visits to our home in Madison, Wisconsin, during the Great Depression. On one occasion he bought my mother a bouquet of flowers. His grateful niece never forgot the gesture.

Busy first with his education, then with his ministry and his immediate family, Henry did not spend as much time at Follinglo Farm as did his siblings. Nevertheless, he sustained a life-long love of the ancestral homestead and also transmitted it to his children.

BERTHA KJERSTINE, 1874–1879

According to family lore, the two names of the newest baby and first girl came into the family via Scotland in the 1700s. Peder Gustav recorded the story as follows.[34]

Two dairy maids who were sisters, Kjerstine and Bertha, lived on the coast of Scotland in a little cottage. Their family pastured cows on a small island a short distance from the mainland. Morning and evening, they would get into a skiff and row out to the island to milk the cows and feed the calves.

One evening while they were about their chores, a thick fog rolled in. "The girls took alarm and made for their boat, knowing from past experiences that such conditions were usually the forerunner of a storm. In their excitement they became confused and lost their sense of direction." By the time the fog cleared, "the poor girls found themselves in the throes of a fierce storm, drifting lustily away from the shores of Scotland."

Fortunately, they had finished milking "and had the milk in the boat, in light wooden containers." Otherwise they would have starved during the several days and nights they were destined to spend at sea. As Grandfather learned from a "very, very old grand aunt," the girls drifted across the vast expanse of the North Sea. As the inhabitants of Tjernagel saw them approach their craggy shores, they could not believe that mere mortals, particularly young girls, could navigate the North Sea in such weather in an open boat. They mistook Kjerstine and Bertha for dangerous spirits and approached them with clubs and boat hooks. Being the older and more resourceful of the two, Kjerstine stood up in the boat and made the sign of the cross. "This was all the password needed. They were welcomed ashore."

The two Scottish girls vowed never to cross the North Sea again. They remained in Norway, mastered the Norwegian language, and captivated the hearts of some Vikings, "of which a young man from Tjernagel was one of the lucky ones. He married Kjerstine." This couple became one set of Ole Andreas' great-grandparents. Upon checking the records of an early-twentieth-century family reunion, Peder Gustav estimated that they had 600 descendants living in the United States, most of them in Iowa.

According to *The Follinglo Dog Book*, Dr. B. F. Allen "happened to be sober" the day Ole Andreas summoned him to Follinglo Farm to see little Bertha Kjerstine who was gravely ill. The kindly doctor promptly diagnosed a case of diphtheria, "the most dreaded of all diseases," and said he could do nothing. The mortality schedule of the 1880 federal census for Scott Township lists Dr. Allen as Bertha's attending physician and verifies her death at age five from diphtheria during the month of November 1879. Her name heads a list of fifteen children, age eleven and younger, who died of diphtheria in the township between November 1879 and April 1880. Only one adult died in the township during those months, a sixty-year-old farmer mortally wounded by a bull. Peder Gustav's boyhood fear of bulls on the lonely prairie was well founded. A lamb marks Bertha's grave in Mamrelund Cemetery near Follinglo Farm.

MARTIN OLAI, 1877–1959

Martin often told his family that he and his siblings "went to sleep at night hearing their parents singing hymns."[35] Following the human voice, the next musical instrument to come to Follinglo Farm was Ole Andreas' accordion, which he learned to play quite well. Then came an Esty pump organ. By the time Martin was ready to learn an instrument his older brothers and some neighbor boys had already formed a band and had purchased the obsolete Sheldall schoolhouse as a place to practice.

By "virtue of being a nuisance" around the practice room, young Martin became an early recruit for the band.[36] He walked to Jewell, a town six miles from Follinglo Farm, for his first music lessons. Professor Anton Pederson, a professional musician from Norway, lived there and did much to raise the level of musicality in the community. Eventually, he joined John Philip Sousa's band. Under Pederson's discipline, the Riverside Band earned a statewide reputation. With natural talent and good instruction, Martin became an outstanding trumpet soloist and the star musical performer of the Tjernagel family. Following his mastery of the trumpet he went on to play many band and orchestra instruments.

In 1887 the Riverside Band entered a tournament in Storm Lake, Iowa. Self-conscious and apprehensive, the farm boys boarded the train in their new uniforms while the passengers looked on with amusement "for the likes of this red-necked, gaily caparisoned crew." One day the organizers loaded the Riverside Band on the lower deck of a two-decked steamer. They began playing the "Montrose Quickstep," whereupon a band on the upper deck answered with a march. "We challenged them with 'Kutsche Polka' to which they retaliated in kind; and so it went in alternate musical shifts back and forth till we returned to shore." As the competition progressed, the boys from central Iowa gained confidence. Their classical repertoire, good ensemble playing, and Pederson's flute commanded respect. When the tournament manager sought accompaniment for some vocalists, director Pederson stepped forward and arranged parts on the spot, and he and his boys provided the required support. The Riverside Band "did itself credit" and ranked high among the bands present. "Covered with glory, but empty of purse," the "Cornfield Canaries," as Peder Gustav termed the band members, headed back to their farms in the Skunk River valley.[37]

On other occasions the Riverside Band played at community festivals, political gatherings, and the State Fair in Des Moines for a dollar a number. They were present at nearby Ellsworth when Iowa's most promising politician, Jonathan P. Dolliver, debated the free silver issue. Legendary in his repartee, Dolliver climaxed "a stirring arraignment of his opponent with the words, 'And this is what he said.' Just then a donkey brayed dolefully and Dolliver instantly retorted, 'I did not know this was to be a joint discussion.'"[38] At such venues bands played while the politicians mingled with the crowds or prepared for their next salvos.

Martin grew up with such experiences. At first he tagged along with his brothers, then played in the band, developed into a crowd-pleasing soloist, and eventually provided leadership for several musical organizations in the area. For two decades he directed the Story City Band. In 1916 he took the band on tour to Illinois. Ole Andreas, by then a widower, came along. Between engagements, the father showed his son where he had lived upon his arrival from Norway, where he had met Martha Karina, and where Lewis was born. On the same trip the Story City Band played before 40,000 White Sox fans in Chicago. Charles A. Comiskey took Martin to and from the park in his limousine. "The whole trip seems a pleasant dream," Martin wrote his brother Henry.[39]

In addition to directing the Story City Band, Martin led bands at Gilbert and Roland, Iowa, and directed the choir at North St. Petri Lutheran Church where the Tjernagels were members (until a doctrinal compromise of 1917 caused them to withdraw). He also taught music at Jewell Lutheran College.

"We do not know who had the inspiration for forming a family orchestra," wrote a member of Martin's family, "but whoever it was, it became a well known group in the area."[40] Follinglo Farm prospered during the World War I era. It was then that Peder Gustav purchased a set of stringed instruments from Knut Reindahl, an eminent violin maker in Madison, Wisconsin.[41] The instruments still exist and have been passed down to musicians in the family. In a 1916 letter to his brother Henry, Martin told about the orchestra's first public performance. It was in Roland during Farmer's Institute Week. Their second was at Ames during an agricultural short course; all their expenses were paid. Then came an eight-concert tour in Iowa and Minnesota. By the end of the year earnings totaled $135. After paying train fares and other expenses they had enough profit to purchase a flute.[42]

Martin married Louise Lillegard in 1919. They lived on a wooded acreage on the Skunk River a short distance from

Follinglo Farm. Here they raised poultry and sheep. Martin also continued his partnership in Follinglo Farm, where he took a special interest in the selection, processing, and selling of cross-pollinated seed corn. Four musical daughters joined the Martin Tjernagel household. I took piano lessons from Margaret, the oldest, during summers spent on the farm in the 1940s but did not make the most of the excellent instruction I received. My interests then ran more toward the Norwegian elkhounds Martin was breeding from prizewinning bloodlines. If my favorite, Paulette, was in the yard with a litter of pups, it was hard to concentrate on the bass clef notes of "The Merry Farmer."

When my parents moved to rural Minnesota in 1946 with nine children (the tenth was yet to come), word reached Martin that our family needed a dog. In due course he shipped a beautiful puppy, Chum, whose devilish instincts motivated him to howl whenever the church bell rang. This he never outgrew. Therefore, it became my duty to put Chum in the barn on Sunday mornings so that he would not offend the sensitivities of Father's parishioners.

On into old age Martin kept a twinkle in his eye and an ocarina in his pocket, which he played upon request. The last time I saw Martin was at my own wedding in Albert Lea, Minnesota, 10 August 1957. In the receiving line following the ceremony Martin, grieving over the death of his wife 17 July, demonstrated the staying power of family bonds among Tjernagels. He shared with my bride and me a letter of marital advice his brother Henry had given him and his bride thirty-eight years earlier. Thus Grandfather's generation had a presence on that important day of my life.

BERTHA KJERSTINE (TANTE), 1881–1969

Named after the two Scottish girls and her predeceased sister, Bertha attended local schools and then went off to the Lutheran Ladies Seminary in Red Wing, Minnesota, to become a nurse. Hers was a life of service. She practiced in Chicago as a home nurse early in the century and until 1924, when her brother Henry's wife died. She then moved to the Lutheran parsonage at Saude, Iowa, and took charge of that lively household. After Henry died in 1940, Bertha returned to Follinglo Farm and shared household responsibilities with Peder Gustav's widow, Jennie, my grandmother.

People of my mother's generation and mine did not call Bertha by her name. We called her "Tante." Although she never married, babies were her specialty. Tante's gentle touch and mint potions calmed many a colicky infant in and beyond the Tjernagel clan. Wherever they resided, the Tjernagel women (including Tante and Mother) sang a soporific cradle song that put many a wee one to sleep on the prairies of central Iowa and, before that, on the farms and in the fishing villages of Norway's west coast. "Bye-ya/, bye-ya/, ba/-by," four notes, over and over again in decrescendo, like the sweet whispers of a fading breeze, until small blue eyes closed in slumber.

Tante came to our house at birthing times, which meant that she came often. She was present, for example, for the birth of my fifth sister, Lydia Louise, 16 March 1941. To thin the ranks in preparation for the event, I had been sent to Follinglo Farm under the care of Grandmother and Uncle Olaf. The day of the baptism Father wrote me that Tante had taken complete charge of little Lydia Louise. "Everybody stayed through the whole service too," he reported with satisfaction. Tante understood both family dynamics and sibling rivalry. Prior to that Sunday she had knit a new skirt for two-and-a-half-year-old Elizabeth. "She was a happy girl in her new outfit too," Father reported.[43]

Always enthusiastic, Tante found the right project for each of her charges. It might be needlework for a ten-year-old or a scrapbook for a younger child. According to Father, my five sisters were thriving under Tante's care. "But I bet you have a lot more fun on the farm than they have here at home," he added. "I hope you are good to Harpo. Do you have much fun with him?"[44]

Actually, the then-presiding canine of Follinglo Farm terrified me. Harpo, a medium-sized black mutt with a few white markings, chased all moving objects and growled and barked at any affront, whether real, anticipated, or imagined. Shortly after my March 1941 arrival at the farm, I had made the mistake of approaching Harpo just after Grandmother served him a bowl of warm eggs, mush, and milk. In no uncertain terms Harpo let me know that he would brook no competition for such fare. After a traumatic experience for Harpo we reached an accord. Harpo's overgrown claws needed clipping, but he flatly refused to volunteer for the procedure. Therefore, my uncles wrapped his head in a feed sack and put him, head first, into a keg of just the right size. Even then it took three strong men to extract one leg at a time and safely clip his claws. Although I was an innocent bystander, Harpo assumed that I had been responsible for this ordeal and accorded me a respect I had not earned. A few days later word reached Tante and my parents that Harpo and Peter "lie in the hay in front of the cows and listen to the radio." [45]

Tante recorded the details of life at Follinglo Farm in her diary and in a steady stream of letters and postcards to relatives and friends. When she was absent on birthing missions she expected others to keep her abreast of Follinglo news. Therefore, in March 1941, Uncle Olaf, simulating my boyish perspective, reported the sale of a five-year-old shorthorn bull. "He is a lot bigger than me," the letter reads. Laboratory tests were necessary to consummate the sale and to facilitate shipping across state lines. "We took some blood out of the big bull's throat," reads the report. "We tied him with rope. He went far away on the train to a nice farm in Utah." [46]

The next letter opens with an account, again penned by Olaf but allegedly from me, of a sow who became so sick that she could not nurse her litter. "Unko took the baby pigs from the mother and . . . gave two [each] to other mother sows until they were all gone. . . . She can't stand and she can't walk or run. She lies down when she eats." Then, invoking high authority, I explained: "Unko thinks the mother sow will get well. She won't get her babys back after she gets well. Unko said so." [47]

Tante hungered for such detail and disseminated it widely. After her nephew Olaf was inducted into the Army Air Corps 13 June 1942, Tante kept him informed of myriad details of farm and family, including: Harpo's antics, the size and health of the leghorn flock, egg and milk production, commodity prices, the details of the grain harvest, the comings and goings of family members, the weather, his mother's declining health, and much more. Olaf responded as he moved from base to base in the United States, then was transferred to England and finally to the Continent. A propeller mechanic for the 379th Fighter Squadron, he was severely limited in what he could communicate. Both Tante and Olaf employed a mixture of English and Norwegian in their letters until the censors apparently ordered Olaf to stop using the latter. Both kept the letters they received during World War II, dozens of which are microfilmed and are on deposit at the State Historical Society of Iowa in Iowa City.

As Grandmother Jennie's health declined, Tante assumed her workload. When a stroke required Grandmother to use a wheelchair, Tante became her primary caregiver. It became progressively harder for Tante to leave the farm to help her nieces as their families grew. Through the war years she continued to come to our house in Madison, Wisconsin, where she was a godsend. Tante took charge unobtrusively, worked tirelessly, and maintained special relationships with each person in the household. She also managed to progress with her knitting, crocheting, and needle projects and was in full glory when a youngster sought handicraft instruction from her.

Tante's nimble fingers wrought beautiful work. However, she began one project with Mother which, for political reasons, they never completed. From time immemorial, Nordic people used a swastika pattern as a design in their handicrafts. Tante, among the gentlest of God's people, learned to crochet it along with many other designs. At one point she and Mother started to make a table runner featuring the swastika pattern. Precisely what action of the Third Reich motivated them to halt the project cannot now be determined. However, Mother still has remnants of the project tucked away in a drawer.

When one was near Tante stories abounded, many of them about commonplace things in the lives of the people in her circle of relatives and friends. She recorded, thoroughly enjoyed, and shared the sayings of children. She saw wisdom, humor, and pattern in unexpected places. On one of my visits to Follinglo Farm as a teenager I helped her clean up after a mid-morning snack of *kringla* (a delicious Norwegian cookie that she made) and coffee. She stopped cold in her tracks when she spotted a coffee stain in a dirty cup in the nearly perfect form of a camel. That cup went unwashed for days.

On only one occasion did I see Tante lose her composure. It occurred in the sun parlor of our home when I was about eight years old. In that room our family had a piece of furniture designed to seat three adults. Mounted on two hanging leaf springs, the "glider," as we called it, often accommodated twice that number of rambunctious children who pushed it to its physical limits. In the evening, however, we relinquished the glider to diminutive Tante so that she could rock our youngest brother to sleep. One evening while Tante gently rocked the baby, a spring broke and the glider crashed to the floor to the astonishment of both Tante and the baby. Father got the spring welded. Tante resumed her routine, whereupon the other spring broke, with only Tante and the baby aboard. This was more than she could bear. Tante held herself personally responsible for the breakage and cried until my parents persuaded her to see the humor of the situation. During the half century that has since transpired, the twice-welded glider has borne countless adults and three generations of children with no further repairs.

Through the decades, family artifacts gravitated to Tante. She had a hut erected near the house at Follinglo Farm where she cared for her treasures. When she reached her eighties she began distributing items to younger members of the family, along with explanations of their provenance and use. In an undated letter from the mid 1960s she explained that my "piece" was to be "a little catch all writing box," called a *skrin* in Norwegian, "pronounced same as screen for window." A male cousin of Martha Karina brought it from Norway and gave it to my grandfather, Peder Gustav, she explained. "Perhaps it's crude but I think it is quite a keep sake." [48]

Upon inquiry I learned that Norwegian emigrants used these lap desks for their most intimate possessions and that it was an invasion of privacy to look into another person's *skrin*. Inside my box were three items — a key, a remnant of some beadwork, and a small wad of paper in a back corner. I carefully unfolded a four-and-a-half-by-six-inch advertisement dating from the turn of the century, for "French

Art Photos," available through the Art Photograph Company of Augusta, Maine. It promised, "WE CAN SUPPLY YOU WITH ANYTHING YOU DESIRE IN THE ART PHOTO LINE." I did not share this find with Tante when I thanked her for the *skrin*.

Like her mother, Tante developed respiratory problems. By middle age Tante's vocal chords were severely damaged, and she spoke in a raspy whisper. At some point in her nursing career she had picked up the tuberculosis bacillus, and the disease flared up from time to time. Even with the best medical care available, she could not gain the upper hand over it. This was a cruel blow because Tante could no longer cuddle the Tjernagel infants she loved so much and cared for so ably. Always cheerful, she spent her last years in the Oakdale State Sanitarium near Iowa City, where she died in 1969.

GUSTAV ADOLPH (GUS), 1884–1954

Gus, as his siblings called him, was often sickly and did not take to the hard physical work of farming. The Tjernagel family doctor of the pioneer period, B. F. Allen, had no trouble diagnosing the first Bertha Kjerstine's diphtheria, but he had no treatment for her. Nor did modern medicine do anything for the acute abdominal pain of Gus' niece, "little Margaret," in 1910. The best of the "regular" physicians could then diagnose accurately, and they knew anatomy and physiology. They were also quick to learn about the pathogens European scientists discovered in their laboratories. Nevertheless, all they could do for their patients was to lend assistance during childbirth, inoculate against smallpox, set broken bones, perform amputations and some minor surgery, treat a very few diseases, kill pain with morphine, and advise their patients to avoid "germs."

In Gus' case, no local practitioner could diagnose, much less treat, a specific medical problem. Following false starts with his higher education at Albert Lea Academy in Minnesota and at Luther College in Decorah, Iowa, Gus looked beyond traditional medicine for relief from his chronic disorders. In due course he learned about an alternative health care system based in Davenport, Iowa, for taking the initiative against human ailments through manual manipulation of the spine. In fact, Gus devoted his life to this cause. He went off to Davenport to study modern chiropractic in the school Daniel David Palmer founded and also continued his studies and treatments in Chicago. Some chiropractors confined their practice to the manipulation of their patients' spines to deal with structural disorders of the joints and muscles. Others, including Gus, believed that much more was possible. They contended that improperly aligned vertebrae lowered the body's resistance to diseases and, in many instances, actually caused diseases. "Broad constructionists" of Dr. Palmer's principles, Gus among them, believed that they were in the vanguard of medical science.

Gus returned to Follinglo Farm and began practicing out of the family home. He is listed in the 1910 federal census as a farmer working on his "own account." Many people respected the Tjernagels, whose farm was then among the most progressive in Iowa. Such associations helped Gus expand his business. He practiced, successively, in nearby Ellsworth and Roland and found a wife, Martha Durby, in the latter town in 1921. In the early 1930s he practiced in Sumner, Iowa.

As a child I heard undercurrents along the lines that if Peder Gustav (whose final illness began with what seemed to be an earache) and Henry (who died of uremia) had eschewed the chiropractic of their youngest brother and sought mainstream medical care sooner, they might have added years to their lives.

Gus and Martha were kindly and concerned people. Having learned of Peder Gustav's persistent earache in the wake of a prolonged bout with the flu, Gus came to Follinglo Farm from Sumner 27 March 1932 and treated his brother. He also brought his patient back to Sumner to continue a chiropractic regimen. Peder Gustav referred to the accommodations provided by his brother and sister-in-law as "his Pullman." Nevertheless, he took a turn for the worse on 5 April and "seemed to have a light stroke." Jennie arrived. The family brought in an orthodox specialist from Minneapolis who advised immediate hospitalization and an operation "to remove the gathering that had formed in his head." The family brought Peder

Gustav to the hospital at New Hampton, but it was "too late" to operate. He died 9 April.[49]

When the *Story City Herald* reported the cause of death as cerebral meningitis "following an illness of two weeks," Gus was upset. "This report conveys a false impression and puts us in a nasty position as most everyone knew where he was," he protested in a letter to Unko. Peder "improved while here as you know," Gus insisted. "It must be made plain that he was sick most of the winter and then the head abscess bursting was the cause [of death]."[50] Unko, the family peacemaker, obliged. A lengthy article appeared in the *Herald* explaining that Peder Gustav had "enjoyed" his visit to Sumner "very much" and was "improving wonderfully." Then came what seemed to be a stroke. "The body was saturated with poison from the gathering and they gave no encouragement for his recovery." Following the revised medical report came a biography of the deceased, emphasizing his musical accomplishments, and details of the funeral. Two sons-in-law furnished music for the 13 April funeral: Christian Olsen sang "Lille Madit" and Rev. Adolph M. Harstad played the organ.[51]

As the Great Depression of the 1930s wore on, Gus and Martha returned to central Iowa. I remember their house on a hill above the Skunk River between Follinglo Farm and Story City. It impressed me that they remodeled their home to accommodate Gus' practice of chiropractic. Tjernagel cousins and second cousins a few years older than I remember Gus' good humor and the chiropractic treatments he gave when they came to visit. In 1942 Gus and Martha moved to California and settled in Pasadena with the younger of their two boys. Their older son was already in the Army Air Corps.

Despite valiant efforts in the mild climate of southern California, Gus could not get his body into proper alignment. His letters are filled with vague symptoms. On 20 October 1943 he wrote from Pasadena that his Oldsmobile had to "plow through" heavy traffic and 102 stop signs between his home and the office in South Los Angeles where he took his treatments. On 8 March 1944 Gus reported: "I took a treatment to rid the body of all filth accumulations. This treatment is a painful ordeal but one of the greatest I have yet found."[52]

Poor health prevented Gus from pursuing his profession in California. At one point his weight fell to 126 pounds. He did the cooking and housework while Martha, a trained nurse, took a defense-related job rather than work within the traditional medical system. "The boss says I rate low outside of the kitchen," Gus wrote, "but since the advent of a vacuum cleaner I am doing better." On 30 September 1943 Martha related that she was "about ready to don my slacks and badge. Wish you could see us marching in and getting our tools. . . . I am getting 81 cents an hr. with time & a half for Sat."

Their son's progress in the Army Air Corps prompted correspondence with Olaf, their nephew in the same branch of the service. But Gus and Martha's letters never strayed far from the subject of chiropractic. Martha, in fact, attempted to invoke the authority of Olaf's father in an endorsement for that controversial system. Martha said that Peder Gustav felt safe with them "as he was so afraid of being Xrayed etc and pushed to a hosp. this he dident want. . . . his loyalty to drug-less healing binds him to us in a different way than the rest."[53] Gus and Martha yearned for an ally for chiropractic in Peder Gustav's family and tried to recruit Olaf for this role. After high praise for Peder and his sons, Martha concluded, "Forgive me Ole, I am living in the past today and its not a bad idea sometimes."

Olaf's mind, too, turned to the past. While he crossed the Atlantic on a troop transport he wrote Gus about things he had learned from Ole Andreas. "Gustav was thrilled by the mention of Grandpa Tjernagel," Martha replied 8 March 1944, "and that you remembered the stories he told about his ocean voyages!" Between acknowledging such points and launching into a description of Gus' most recent "fight for his life," Martha reported that "a continuous prayer for our boys safety and return is going up all the time." Olaf appreciated that, but there is no evidence that he sent the endorsement for chiropractic that Gus and Martha wanted from him.

The "continuous prayer" was answered. Gus and Martha's son and Uncle Olaf returned home safely from World War II. Gus' health problems persisted until he died in Pasadena in 1954. Martha lived for another twenty years.

Anderson, Lewis
husband of Martha (Follinglo) Anderson

Christenson, Anders
aka Uncle Anders, husband of Helga (Larson) Christenson

Christenson, Christen Johan (1855–1911)
*son of Anders and Helga (Larson) Christenson and first cousin of
Peder Gustav Tjernagel*

Christenson, Helga (Larson) (1830–1897)
aka stora fastero *(Father's big sister), paternal aunt of
Peder Gustav Tjernagel*

Christenson, Lars (1857–1865)
*son of Anders and Helga (Larson) Christenson and first cousin of
Peder Gustav Tjernagel*

Follinglo, Anders (1856–?)
*aka Uncle Anders, son of Nils Anderson and Margreto (Tonge)
Follinglo and half uncle of Peder Gustav Tjernagel*

Follinglo, Gurrina (1862–1929)
*aka Julia and Aunt Julia, daughter of Nils Anderson and Margreto
(Tonge) Follinglo and half aunt of Peder Gustav Tjernagel*

Follinglo, Hans (1861–?)
*son of Nils Anderson and Margreto (Tonge) Follinglo and half uncle of
Peder Gustav Tjernagel*

Follinglo, Margreto (Tonge) (1821–1913)
*wife of Nils Anderson Follinglo and step-grandmother of
Peder Gustav Tjernagel*

Follinglo, Martha
*aka Aunt Martha, daughter of Nils Anderson and Margreto (Tonge)
Follinglo and half aunt of Peder Gustav Tjernagel*

Follinglo, Nils Anderson (1822–1901)
*aka Nils Murar (mason), maternal grandfather of
Peder Gustav Tjernagel*

Harstad, Adolph M. (1902–1988)
*husband of Martha Karina (Tjernagel) Harstad and son-in-law of
Peder Gustav Tjernagel*

Harstad, Elizabeth (1939–)
daughter of Adolph M. and Martha Karina (Tjernagel) Harstad and granddaughter of Peder Gustav Tjernagel

Harstad, Lydia Louise (1941–)
youngest daughter of Adolph M. and Martha Karina (Tjernagel) Harstad and granddaughter of Peder Gustav Tjernagel

Harstad, Martha Karina (Tjernagel) (1904–)
daughter of Peder Gustav Tjernagel

Harstad, Peter Tjernagel (1935–)
oldest son of Adolph M. and Martha Karina (Tjernagel) Harstad and grandson of Peder Gustav Tjernagel

Larson, Ole Andreas
See Tjernagel, Ole Andreas Larson

Larson, Peder (1826–1863)
aka Per (Pete) and Store Per (Big Pete), older brother of Ole Andreas Larson Tjernagel and paternal uncle of Peder Gustav Tjernagel

Mikkelsdottir, Barbru (?–1890)
mother of Martha Karina (Anderson Follinglo) Tjernagel and maternal grandmother of Peder Gustav Tjernagel

Murar, Nils
See Follinglo, Nils Anderson (in Norwegian, Murar means mason)

Olsen, Christian (1899–1978)
husband of Elizabeth (Tjernagel) Olsen and son-in-law of Peder Gustav Tjernagel

Peterson, Larsina (Larson) (1842–1925)
aka "litla fastero" (Father's little sister), paternal aunt of Peder Gustav Tjernagel

Peterson, Lewis (1866–1929)
aka cousin Lewis, son of Nils and Larsina (Larson) Peterson and first cousin of Peder Gustav Tjernagel

Peterson, Nils (?–1913)
aka Uncle Nils, husband of Larsina (Larson) Peterson

Phillops, Martin
distant paternal relative of Peder Gustav Tjernagel

Tjernagel, Alfred Gustav (1902–1987)
son of Peder Gustav Tjernagel

Tjernagel, Anna (Brue) (1882–1924)
wife of Helge Mathias Tjernagel and sister-in-law of
Peder Gustav Tjernagel

Tjernagel, Anna Brue (1937–   )
granddaughter of Helge Mathias and Anna (Brue) Tjernagel, daughter
of Neelak Serawlook and Ada (Studholme) Tjernagel, and niece, once
removed, of Peder Gustav Tjernagel

Tjernagel, Bertha Kjerstine (1874–1879)
sister of Peder Gustav Tjernagel

Tjernagel, Bertha Kjerstine (1881–1969)
aka Tante, sister of Peder Gustav Tjernagel

Tjernagel, Bertha Margarethe (1907–1910)
aka lille Madit (little Margaret), youngest daughter of
Peder Gustav Tjernagel

Tjernagel, Clarence
son of Lars Johan and Sarah (Solberg) Tjernagel and nephew of
Peder Gustav Tjernagel

Tjernagel, Elizabeth (1899–1976)
oldest daughter of Peder Gustav Tjernagel

Tjernagel, Erling Martin (1900–1958)
son of Peder Gustav Tjernagel

Tjernagel, Gustav Adolph (1884–1954)
youngest brother of Peder Gustav Tjernagel

Tjernagel, Helge Mathias (1871–1940)
aka Henry, younger brother of Peder Gustav Tjernagel

Tjernagel, Herman Arnold (1898–1987)
son of Peder Gustav Tjernagel

Tjernagel, Indre
first cousin once removed of Peder Gustav Tjernagel

Tjernagel, Ingeborg Johanna (Olson) (1872–1960)
aka Jennie, wife of Peder Gustav Tjernagel

Tjernagel, Ingeborg Marie (1956–   )
youngest daughter of Peder Julius and Marie (Andreson) Tjernagel and
granddaughter of Peder Gustav Tjernagel

Tjernagel, Lars Johan (1862–1950)
aka Lewis, older brother of Peder Gustav Tjernagel

Tjernagel, Lewis
See Tjernagel, Lars Johan

Tjernagel, Louise M. (Lillegard) (1886–1957)
*wife of Martin Olai Tjernagel and sister-in-law of
Peder Gustav Tjernagel*

Tjernagel, Margaret (1921–   )
*daughter of Martin Olai and Louise M. (Lillegard) Tjernagel and
niece of Peder Gustav Tjernagel*

Tjernagel, Marie (Andreson) (1917–   )
*wife of Peder Julius Tjernagel and daughter-in-law of
Peder Gustav Tjernagel*

Tjernagel, Martha (Durby)
*wife of Gustav Adolph Tjernagel and sister-in-law of
Peder Gustav Tjernagel*

Tjernagel, Martha Karina (Anderson Follinglo) (1845–1907)
*daughter of Nils Anderson Follinglo and Barbru Mikkelsdottir who
never married and mother of Peder Gustav Tjernagel*

Tjernagel, Martin Erling (1950–   )
*youngest son of Peder Julius and Marie (Andreson) Tjernagel and
grandson of Peder Gustav Tjernagel*

Tjernagel, Martin Olai (1877–1959)
younger brother of Peder Gustav Tjernagel

Tjernagel, Michael Peter (1948–   )
*oldest son of Peder Julius and Marie (Andreson) Tjernagel and
grandson of Peder Gustav Tjernagel*

Tjernagel, Mildrid Genevieve (1925–   )
*daughter of Otto Alfred and Amanda (Huso) Tjernagel and
granddaughter of Peder Gustav Tjernagel*

Tjernagel, Neelak Serawlook (1906–1994)
*oldest son of Helge Mathias and Anna (Brue) Tjernagel and nephew of
Peder Gustav Tjernagel*

Tjernagel, Nehemias (1868–1958)
aka Unko, younger brother of Peder Gustav Tjernagel

Tjernagel, Olaf Johan (1905–1970)
son of Peder Gustav Tjernagel

Tjernagel, Ole Andreas Larson (1836–1919)
aka Ole Andreas Larson, father of Peder Gustav Tjernagel

Tjernagel, Otto Alfred (1896–1958)
oldest son of Peder Gustav Tjernagel

Tjernagel, Peder Gustav (1865–1932)
author of The Follinglo Dog Book

Tjernagel, Peder Julius (1909–1909)
son of Peder Gustav Tjernagel

Tjernagel, Peder Julius (1910–1969)
son of Peder Gustav Tjernagel

Tjernagel, Sigrid Joanne (1953–   )
*oldest daughter of Peder Julius and Marie (Andreson) Tjernagel
and granddaughter of Peder Gustav Tjernagel*

Tjernagel, Sigurd Lauritz (1916–1987)
youngest son of Peder Gustav Tjernagel

THE TEXT

As a professional historian, I have long had a passion for original sources. First and foremost comes the matter of authenticity. Does the text in question, whether holographic, typed, or electronic, truly come from the mind and hand of the purported author? For what readership was the text prepared? Is it a first draft? Is it the author's best and most polished draft? Did others assist in the making of the document? If so, when, in what capacity, and to what extent?

Original documents often contain clues and convey subtleties. The truly curious of each generation deserve the opportunity to consult them rather than to rely upon transcriptions or published versions. I have searched diligently to find the text Grandfather alluded to in his preface and in the last paragraph of the book, written in pencil in a tablet given to him by his son Alfred. I have been unable to locate such a text (referred to hereafter as Text A).

Grandfather's preface proves that he chose to communicate his dog stories both orally and through the written word. My mother is the only person left in this world who heard Peder Gustav tell the dog stories to his children at bedtime. Under the best of circumstances documents have the potential of lasting longer than oral traditions. To do so, however, documents need both caretakers and good luck. The text of *The Follinglo Dog Book* received the former but not the latter.

Thomas Jefferson advanced the idea that publishing historical documents is a legitimate means of preserving them, or at least their content. The fate of the dog book affirms Jefferson's wisdom. Posterity is deeply indebted to the late Dr. Neelak S. Tjernagel, son of Peder Gustav's brother Henry, and the people Neelak mentions in the following preface to his 1966 edition of *The Follinglo Dog Book*, a work prepared primarily for members of the Tjernagel family:

> This is the tale of the Follinglo dogs. It begins in the year 1864 when Grandpa Tjernagel brought home a yellow pup named Milla. It ends with the death of Noble in 1908.
>
> It is the story of a son of the Iowa prairie told in words of warm compassion, sincere affection, and an enchanting sense of humor. The manuscript was written in pencil on a school pad by Peter Gustav Tjernagel in the year 1909.
>
> The book is published by Herman Tjernagel, a son of the author, as a tribute to his parents and as a memorial to the sturdy men and women (and the dogs) that made the Iowa prairie an agricultural paradise.
>
> The manuscript has been edited by Neelak S. Tjernagel. Proof and copy reading have been done by Ada S. Tjernagel and typing by Anna Brue Tjernagel.
>
> Follinglo Farm
> Story City, Iowa
> July 26, 1966

Were it not for Neelak's edition, financed and distributed by Herman, posterity would now have the preface and most of the first chapter of *The Follinglo Dog Book*, but no more. That was Neelak's title for the 1966 book; Grandfather's title for the manuscript was "From Milla to Chip the Third."

Whether Neelak and his family worked from Text A, "written in pencil on a school pad," is problematical. No evidence in Neelak's 1966 book addresses the issue more specifically than those words. Both Neelak and his wife, Ada, are deceased. When queried, their daughter Anna Brue Tjernagel had no recollection of working with Text A, nor did Anna's siblings find it (or any) working papers for the dog book among their father's effects.

Neelak worked on historical projects in an orderly manner. An ordained Lutheran clergyman who held a Ph.D. in history from the University of Iowa, he published widely on the subject of the Protestant reformation. When he completed and published for the family *Nehemias Tjernagel: An Affectionate Biography* in 1976, he returned some of his sources to Follinglo Farm in the custody of Michael Tjernagel, son of Peder Julius and Marie, and deposited others in the State Historical Society of Iowa in Iowa City.

Upon completion of the dog book project in 1966, Neelak likely returned his sources to Follinglo Farm, where his Aunt Bertha (Tante) stored her collection. If so, it is highly probable that they were consumed by flames 9 December 1968 under circumstances explained in the epilogue. Tante was then at Oakdale.

What text did Neelak work from in 1966? It is possible that he had Text A, but doubtful given Anna's testimony and additional evidence that follows. It is nearly certain that he had Text B, a version of the manuscript typed by Tante and Peder Gustav's daughter Elizabeth at Follinglo Farm during the 1920s. Given Peder's craftsmanship in all things, it is hard to imagine that Text B was a literal transcription of a static Text A. Peder Gustav likely had his daughter and his sister type the best version of the manuscript he was then capable of producing. My mother has a clear memory of Tante and Elizabeth preparing Text B, "using the hunt and peck" method of typing. Neither Tante nor Elizabeth was an expert typist; Peder Gustav did not type at all.

Many Tjernagels knew of the existence of Text B and read it while visiting Follinglo Farm. Upon completion of Text B, Text A may have been regarded as obsolete. It would not have been characteristic of Tante or Jennie, Peder Gustav's widow, to destroy it. There is incontrovertible evidence that both Tante and Jennie were good caretakers of Text B.

In 1946, prior to the universal availability of electrostatic copy machines, Mildrid Tjernagel, daughter of Peder Gustav's oldest son, Otto, borrowed Text B for the purpose of typing a copy of it for herself. With the permission of her grandmother and Tante, Mildrid took it from Follinglo Farm for that purpose. She got as far as page fourteen, fell in love with her future husband, and returned the manuscript to Follinglo Farm at Grandmother's request. But she kept the fourteen pages that she so neatly typed and shared them with me during the summer of 1998. It is reasonable to assume that Mildrid's copy is a *verbatim ac litteratim* transcription of Text B. I made a machine copy of Mildrid's 14 pages, placed that copy in the Tjernagel Collection at the State Historical Society of Iowa in Iowa City, and returned to Mildrid the pages she typed in 1946.

By comparing Mildrid's copy with the opening pages of Neelak's 1966 edition (Text C), it is possible to determine how Neelak worked. His version is not a *verbatim ac litteratim* transcription of Text B. The most significant difference between Neelak's text and Mildrid's copy is that Neelak cut Peder Gustav's preface in half. The version of the preface in this book follows Mildrid's copy with minor editing.

Mildrid's copy ends abruptly with the birth of Peder Gustav, three paragraphs from the end of the chapter entitled Milla. This nearly complete version of the chapter can be compared with the corresponding portion of Neelak's Text C. In the first sentence Neelak added that the Fox River settlement was located "near Ottawa, Illinois." He eliminated wordiness but cut nothing significant in the chapter. Neelak broke up long paragraphs and sentences and improved the punctuation. He added translations of Norwegian terms and placed them in parentheses. In a very few instances he selected an alternate word. For example, Mildrid's copy records Martha Karina as Ole Andreas' "juvenile" bride; Neelak substituted the adjective "youthful." A few lines below, Neelak dropped the name of the peddler, "Kjyten." (Peder Gustav wrote of this man elsewhere.) [54] Neelak also dropped the adjective "beautiful" in one reference to Martha Karina.

He changed a few incorrect usages and nipped some cliches. Upon comparing the two versions of the Milla chapter, it is clear that Neelak's role was that of a thoughtful person transforming a manuscript into a book for a respected uncle.

It is highly probable that Neelak worked from Text B to produce his text and that A and B no longer exist. It was a labor of love for Neelak and his family to bring out the 1966 edition and an act of love for Herman to finance the venture.

When I received my copy of the 1966 edition I was a thirty-year-old history professor with a wife and three children. At last I could place my maternal grandfather within the context of what I knew about his extended family, about Follinglo Farm, about parenting, and about life. All of the sources available to me led to the conclusion that the elements of Peder Gustav's personality were in fine balance. He was so gentle, his pastor said, "that when he spanked his children he did so with his sox." [55] During the tumultuous and violent years of the late 1960s, here was a man to emulate.

I shared the dog stories with my own children, first by paraphrasing them when the children were small and later by reading them aloud at bedtime. The Store Per tales still carried messages to young males about the use of physical strength. Milla's canine sexuality still caused trouble, her early demise, and bewilderment on the part of readers and listeners. During sessions with the children I often sat, with our youngest in my lap, in a sturdy rocking chair Grandfather made of native cherry. Although Grandfather had been dead since 1932, he was again communicating with his descendants. My children raised questions, which led to opportunities for me to slip in a few Follinglo Farm stories of my own. Since the mid 1980s, my offspring have had children of their own, adding yet another generation of Tjernagel progeny and more lovers of the dog stories.

Nehemias Tjernagel (Unko) once wrote that all of the children of Ole Andreas and Martha Karina liked to talk — even his brother Peder Gustav "when he had a chance." Peder Gustav, however, "had a way of being entertaining. Did not weary his listeners." [56]

His grandson and namesake hopes that these pages devoted to the Tjernagels of Follinglo Farm and their dogs do not weary our readers. With the present edition of *The Follinglo Dog Book*, we share our heritage with a wider readership.

ACKNOWLEDGMENTS

The Tjernagels are grateful to Linzee Kull McCray for bringing the 1966 edition of *The Follinglo Dog Book* to the attention of Holly Carver, editor at the University of Iowa Press, and to Mary Bennett of the State Historical Society of Iowa in Iowa City for putting Holly into communication with our family. Holly shared the dog book with Wayne Franklin, which led to the decision to publish it as a volume in the American Land and Life Series, which he edits. My communications with Holly and Wayne have been both pleasant and stimulating. Acting as envoy between the University of Iowa Press and the Tjernagel family and delving into family history to prepare material to accompany the text of *The Follinglo Dog Book* brought me much satisfaction during 1998. Robert Burchfield of the press deftly handled many details which could have overwhelmed me, given my duties as executive director of the Indiana Historical Society. My administrative assistant, Emily Featherstone, cheerfully provided clerical assistance.

The following people provided photographs: Sigrid (Tjernagel) Hanson, John I. Harstad, Martha Karina (Tjernagel) Harstad, Peter Tjernagel Harstad, Margaret (Harstad) Matzke, Mildrid (Tjernagel) Nickson, Lucile Tjernagel, Ingeborg (Tjernagel) Schey, Marie (Andreson) Tjernagel, Sven Tjernagel, and Lois (Tjernagel) Van Rooy. Photographer Kim Charles Ferrill of Indianapolis worked wonders in his lab with faded images.

While engaged in this project I received insights, information, and inspiration from: my mother, Martha Karina (Tjernagel) Harstad; my siblings Mary, Margaret, Grace, Elizabeth, Lydia, John, Herman, Adolph, and Mark; my wife, Carolyn A. Harstad; my children Linda, Karen, Mark, Kristen, and David; my first cousins Amanda (Tjernagel) Madson and Mildrid (Tjernagel) Nickson, whose helpfulness knew no bounds; my aunt Marie (Andreson) Tjernagel and her children Michael,

Martin (who lives at Follinglo Farm with his family), Sigrid, and Ingeborg; the children of Neelak S. Tjernagel, Lois, Anna, and Allan; and Bernard Schey.

I alone am responsible for the accuracy of the facts and the validity of the interpretations presented in the prologue and epilogue.

NOTES

1. In the preparation of the prologue and the epilogue I have relied heavily upon my memory, prompted and corroborated by documents and interviews; Nehemias Tjernagel Papers at the State Historical Society of Iowa in Iowa City (cited hereafter as Tjernagel Papers); federal and state census records; and Inez Waltman Bergquist, ed., *Tjernagel Family: 140 Years in the New World 1836–1996* (Eagan, Minn., 1996).

2. Obit. of Ole Andreas Larson Tjernagel in 22 May 1919 issue of *Visergutten*, translated by Adolph M. Harstad (AMH) in 1976; *Across the Prairie from Illinois to Iowa, 1864: The Story Told by Ole Andreas Larson Tjernagel, Translated by His Son Nehemias Tjernagel*, mimeograph copy by AMH, 1976.

3. Neelak S. Tjernagel to Peter Tjernagel Harstad (PTH), 17 March 1989.

4. Copy in possession of PTH.

5. Quoted in PTH, ed., *Fifty Years a Family* (Iowa City, 1981), p. 5.

6. Obit. of Mrs. O. A. L. Tjernagel in *Visergutten*, undated copy (1907?) in Tjernagel Papers, translated by AMH, 1976.

7. Quoted in *Fifty Years a Family*, p. 3.

8. Obit. of Mrs. O. A. L. Tjernagel.

9. Peder Gustav Tjernagel, "The Three Kjersteens," n.d., pp. 2–5. Mimeograph copy in possession of PTH.

10. Letterhead in Box 1, Scrapbook, Tjernagel Collection; advertisement inside back cover of *Norsk Amerikansk Musik Tidende* (November 1890).

11. *Across the Prairie*, p. 9.

12. Ibid., pp. 14–16. See also Nehemias Tjernagel's long unpublished manuscript in the Tjernagel Papers, "The Passing of the Prairie," by A Fossil. Multiple versions of this document exist in

the Tjernagel Papers and among members of the family, making citation difficult.

13. *Tjernagel Family*, Name Index.

14. The following paragraphs are based on: "Cement Farm Buildings Are Contribution of the Tjernagel Brothers of Near Story City to the Greater Iowa Movement," in *Des Moines Register and Leader*, 26 December 1914; "Concrete Buildings a Specialty on Follinglo Farm Near Story City," in *Des Moines Register and Leader*, 31 July 1915; "The Story of Follinglo: How the Tjernagels Have Set Farm Life to Music," in *Prairie Farmer*, 30 October 1916; N. Tjernagel, "Farm Architecture," in *Wallaces' Farmer*, 22 December 1916; "Concrete for the Corn Crib," clipping from Universal Portland Cement Co., n.d. Copies in Tjernagel Papers, Box 4, Folder 1.

15. "The Story of Follinglo."

16. *Des Moines Register and Leader*, 31 July 1915.

17. "The Story of Follinglo."

18. Quoted in *Fifty Years a Family*, pp. 4–5.

19. Neelak S. Tjernagel, *Nehemias Tjernagel: An Affectionate Biography* (Honeoyo, N.Y., 1976), is an excellent account of Nehemias' education and travels.

20. Nehemias Tjernagel, "Madit," Tjernagel Papers.

21. Letter in possession of Martha Karina (Tjernagel) Harstad.

22. *Nehemias Tjernagel*, p. 13.

23. Fragment in Tjernagel Papers.

24. "Madit."

25. Quoted in *Fifty Years a Family*, p. 4.

26. N. Tjernagel, *Paragraphs of a Pedestrian* (Northfield, Minn., 1913); *Walking Trips In Norway* (Columbus, Ohio, 1917); *Fotturer i Aegypten og Palaestina* (Minneapolis, 1919).

27. He published an anthology, *Contributions to Church Periodicals* (Story City, Iowa, 1955).

28. Related to PTH by Martha Karina (Tjernagel) Harstad.

29. "The Passing of the Prairie," p. 69.

30. Obit. by Nehemias Tjernagel in Neelak S. Tjernagel, ed., *Breezes from Alaska: H. M. Tjernagel, Pastor and Missionary* (Rochester, N.Y., 1972), pp. 44–48.

31. "The Three Kjersteens," p. 5.

32. Reprinted in *Fifty Years a Family*, pp. 5–7.

33. H. M. Tjernagel to AMH. In possession of PTH.

34. "The Three Kjersteens," pp. 1–2.

35. Margaret Annexstad and Sarah Hassold, "Memories of Martin Tjernagel," in *Kringla Khronicle: Tjernagel Family News*, Vol. 1, No. 2, 1 July 1997, p. 1.

36. Nehemias Tjernagel, "The Riverside Band," unpublished essay in the Tjernagel Collection, pp. 4–5, 10.

37. Ibid., pp. 5–6; also a second article of the same title, prepared at least in part by Peder Gustav Tjernagel, p. 295.

38. "The Riverside Band," p. 8.

39. Quoted in "Memories of Martin Tjernagel."

40. "Memories of Martin Tjernagel."

41. Erling Ylvisaker, "A Wood-Carver's Masterpiece," in *Eminent Pioneers: Norwegian-American Pioneer Sketches* (Minneapolis, 1934), pp. 129–142.

42. "Memories of Martin Tjernagel."

43. AMH to PTH, 30 March 1941. In possession of PTH.

44. Ibid.

45. PTH to "Dear Folks" "Monday 8:30 A.M.," actually written by Olaf Tjernagel. In possession of PTH.

46. Ibid.

47. PTH to AMH "Thursday 10:30 A.M." In possession of PTH.

48. Tante to PTH, "Oakdale. Sep. 15." In possession of PTH.

49. *Story City Herald*, 21 April 1932.

50. Gus to Unko, "Saturday" [likely 16 April 1932]. In possession of Martha Karina (Tjernagel) Harstad.

51. *Story City Herald*, 21 April 1932.

52. Gustav Tjernagel to Olaf Tjernagel, 20 October 1943. In possession of PTH.

53. Martha Tjernagel to Olaf Tjernagel, "Thurs. P.M." [likely October 1943]. In possession of PTH.

54. Peder Gustav Tjernagel, "A Pioneer Story: Erik Kjyten," in *Story City Herald*, 13 February 1930.

55. "Reunion of Descendants of Peter and Jennie Tjernagel Held at Follinglo Farm, Story City, Iowa June 22, 1980," p. 2, a typewritten account by AMH and PTH. In possession of PTH.

56. Nehemias Tjernagel to Olaf Tjernagel, 18 February 1943. In possession of PTH.

Preface

It has been said that a true historian ought not to have a fatherland, but being that this will be a tale of the Follinglo dogs, I be dogged if I am willing to forsake my dear country and noble state just for the purpose of satisfying a whim of the author of the above statement. I think I can read between the lines the good man's intentions, namely this to keep the miserable historian from straying away from the unprejudiced truth. Now that is just exactly what I protest against. My brothers, nay even my dear sister, all seemed to be laboring under the false impression that they would have to take everything that I told them in the shape of a story with a grain or two of salt. Now how they could have been led astray in this manner has always been, and must necessarily be and remain, a mystery to a truth-loving fellow like myself.

Another thing that remains to be solved is why they should select me out of the whole brace of boys to give a write-up on the Follinglo dogs. But allow me to tell you all that it is with some misgiving that I undertake this work, and furthermore I wish to emphasize in stentorian tones the fact that no amount of pressure from their part would have availed them a mite on getting me started. No, the pressure had to come from another source. I have eight children ranging from two and one half years and up to thirteen. They got after me and talked dogs till I thought I could see fur of all colors and descriptions. Who could stem a tide like that? Not I. Unlike my brothers and only sister they believe every word I say. They think that I am the greatest man that ever lived. Washington Irving, Scott, and Oliver Goldsmith himself thrown into the bargain would have to take the backseat for their papa. My little son, Alfred, even went so far as to spend all his money in purchasing a tablet and a lead pencil for the coming event. The camel's back could stand no more, it snapped in twain.

It has been a part of my business (and permit me to say that I love the work) to take the children to bed and to see that they are snugly tucked into their respective beds, couches and trundle beds. Then it is a clamor for a story. When that is complied with, they say their prayers. And then they order me to take my pencil and get after the dogs. It is amid such scenes, on the dear old Follinglo Farm, that I venture to sally forth on my little story entitled *From Milla to Chip the Third*.

Now being that my sister, Bertha, was the first cause for action in this brain-racking affair, I dedicate The Dog On Tale to her.

Preface

The Follinglo Dog Book

Milla

Way back in the fifties, before the Civil War had yet cast its cruel gloom over our country, if we could have visited the Fox River settlement near Ottawa, Illinois, and found our way to the home of Anfin Krabbatvedt, one of the good old pioneers, we should there have fallen in with a young man whose nationality was plainly visible. His action and general bearing would indicate health and strength that would be ready to cope with any kind of honest labor at a moment's notice. In his eye you could read that he was in dead earnest when he undertook to do anything and that he was as honest as the dark loam that was being unmercifully whirled over by his plow. He was a Norseman pure and simple, coming from a community where liberty or death was the slogan. If Mr. Krabbatvedt had gone through the formalities of an introduction, it would have been to present him as "Mr. Ole Andreas Tjernagel, my true and trusted hired man."

Now if the good Mr. Krabbatvedt had dared to invite us into his house we might have caught a glimpse of a young girl aged about fifteen years, clad in a denim suit, continually on the go, striving hard to perform the drudgery that was being heaped upon her by an unscrupulous, worldly woman, a veritable snapping turtle, whose only ambition was to make money, even if it had to be wrenched out of the very vitals of a poor girl at her most tender age. The girl, however, had an even temperament and lots of common sense and would do nothing that would provoke a hiss and a snap from the domineering, ruling spirit of the house. No, she was striving to do her duty and let the results be what they might.

It was not out of choice that she was staying at this place. Her father, Nils Anderson Follinglo, being then as ever afterwards in poor circumstances as far as worldly possessions were concerned, had to find a place for her where she could work for her board and clothing the year that she read for the minister. Now since the meetinghouse was on the opposite side of the Fox River from where he lived, and the river would have to be forded because in those days there were no bridges, the only alternative was to apply for the position described above, where late hours and hard labor were her daily routine. No time to study her lessons was given her. That would have to be done after the family retired by the light of a dull, shaking grease lamp.

Her sweet and winning ways did not pass unnoticed by our friend, Ole Andreas. In her gentle manner he saw the qualities which he so much admired. Some bright mind has been known to say that first we pity, then we tolerate, and then we fall in love. This case was an exception to the rule. It was pity and then a quick stride over the tolerating period, ignoring it entirely, and then pure love. This, of course, resulted in a wedding shortly after Martha (for such was her name) was confirmed. A little wedding party gathered at Per Tjernagel's home to celebrate the happy union on the 11th day of June 1861. After having so successfully wrested this young girl out of the clutches of Anfin's Karen, the next problem that confronted our Ole was where to take his youthful bride. After casting about in quest of a farm to rent on shares, Ole was successful in his negotiations, and shortly afterwards the young couple was snugly installed in Quamma huse (the Quam house).

There might be many things worth recording in connection with this couple's struggle through that stormy period in which the great Civil War was raging. But space, time, and ability will not allow me to make the attempt. And, besides, I promised to chronicle the Follinglo dogs. But dogs, if they are any dogs at all, must have a master, hence this flight back to the Fox River settlement, and I will not promise even now that the rest of this narrative shall be pure dog.

No well-regulated household could be without a dog in the early days. Even if he could not do anything else, he could report when the tin peddler turned into the yard. Or, who knows, he might sometimes make it pretty hot for petty pilferers. Oh well, there are many things he could do if he wanted to, but the main thing was the idea of having a dog. Each respectable farm place was supposed to furnish its reasonable amount of barking, so as to break the monotony, especially during the long winter evenings. But be that as it may, Ole Andreas brought home a pup, and a yellow one at that. And after she got to be old enough, if she did not bark as much as reasonably could be expected of her, there were others that did.

Well, Milla and the rest of the household lived on, without any stirring events, as far as they were personally concerned, but when Lars Johan made his advent into the world, Ole Andreas got down to serious thinking, and he caught himself soliloquizing in the following manner. "I wish we had a home of our own. I wonder if Martha and the baby, in about a year and a half from now, could stand the journey out to central Iowa in a prairie schooner? There the land is cheap. 'Tis true it's quite a distance to the nearest marketplace — about fifty miles they say, but — " Thus he pondered and figured quite a while, till at length he put the question to his wife. "Do you think by next summer that you and the baby would be good for a trip out to Iowa? I've been thinking it over, and I am of the opinion that we ought to go." She answered in the following manner, which was to be characteristic of her all through life: "I think we can. The Lord will be with us there, to protect us, as well as here." After that it became a settled affair. The next move was to make the plan known to her father, Nils Anderson Follinglo (known by the name of Nils Murar). He and his family might want to join them and strike out for the woolly West. The plan was no sooner mentioned than it was accepted with enthusiasm by the Follinglos.

The only thing now was to get ready. Hickory saplings were found and bent into shape for covers on the wagons. The muslin was then tacked on, and a feed box was attached to the hind end of the wagon box on which was painted the name of the state they were going to, Iowa. Ole has always been in the habit of having things ready (*paa pinadne*), and in this never-failing condition we might have found him now, ready. About one week before the time set to start west, he hitched up Frank and Charley, a beautiful span of blacks, bundled Martha and the baby into the wagon together with such necessaries as were needed on the long journey, bade farewell to Quamma huse, forded the Fox River, and drove on up where he was to join the Follinglos and where they were to stay one week before starting out on the final journey.

Imagine their consternation when they came to look around and found that they had left Milla over at Quamma huse. Would they go off and leave her? No! There was nothing else for Ole Andreas to do but to unload what they had in the wagon and drive back for her. This was not as easy as you might think, because the treacherous Fox River was rising fast. This trip came pretty nearly losing him his team. He hurried as much as he could, drove up to the house he had but recently left, found poor Milla, who was only too glad to see him, flung her into the wagon, and was off at a break-neck speed to cope with the mad current that was gradually rising. It looked fierce, but he trusted in the strength of his noble blacks and plunged in. As far as he himself and the little dog were concerned, he had no misgivings, because if it came to the worst they could swim ashore, as they were both expert swimmers, but Frank and Charley — it would break him up and frustrate all his plans if he should lose them. He had manned the helm on many a craft on the briny deep where the odds seemed to be against him, but take it all in all that was nothing but child's play compared to this. And all for the sake of a little yellow bitch!

"Why did I bring that miserable little whelp home anyhow? How much good has she done me so far? What will be the outcome of this?" Such thoughts and comments of self-reproach were tacking through his mind while he was floundering through that stream. Meanwhile the stream was carrying team, wagon, dog, and all away from the fording place. The splendid blacks worked for their lives and finally brought the wagon up to the bank and pulled it up with great difficulty. Another rod farther downstream and they would have been up against a steep bank, when horse strength would have availed them nothing. Now that he was on terra firma again, he felt thankful that he had gotten out of this catastrophe, which looked to him very much as though it might as well have turned into something tragic. This thankful feeling had a tendency of softening him a little towards the poor cur, and, bending down, he patted her head and was just going to say: "Poor Milla, it is never so bad but it could have been worse," when out of pure glee she shook herself and sent a deluge of water right into his face, causing him to change the chain of thought into: "Den forargeliga bitjo" (That aggravating bitch), and she lit on the ground where she had to walk the rest of the way to the Nils Murar home.

I shall not attempt to picture the scenes which the preparations for the long journey to Iowa necessitated. Neither will I try to describe the unique character of the venerable old Viking, Nils Anderson Follinglo. I will not even follow the travelers across the untrodden prairie, through wooded tracts, over placid streams and swift-flowing rivers. It will be an ordinary leave-taking, bidding them good-bye and Godspeed on their long tedious journey. But I am determined to be on hand to welcome them when they make their final halt in front of Halla huse (the Hall house), after having reached the El Dorado of the West, the Hawkeye State, the "here is the place to dwell state," the state of Iowa.

When I was a little boy I imagined how they looked when they pulled out of the Fox River settlement and disappeared in a kind of mist, headed towards the setting sun. It was always like this. The restless blacks were hitched to a wagon shrouded in white, inside of which sat a young mother, cooing softly to a sleeping baby. In front sat the proud father with the reins gripped firmly in his rigid hands, while Milla, not understanding the nature of the excitement, sat placidly underneath the prairie schooner licking her chops. Everything was now in readiness awaiting the word go from Nils Murar, who was to lead the van. The last glimpse I had of them as they were swallowed up by the mist was a little yellow spot, stuck on the firmament, beneath a white canvas.

Well, as I have said, I wanted to be on hand when they arrived at Halla huse. After a journey of about twenty days, they drew up in front of this house, the Follinglos having stopped at *litla grovo* (little grove) where at the time lived Uncle Anders and *stora fastero* (Father's big sister) and their two children, Christen and Lars. This was to be their home until they could build a house of their own on a forty-acre tract, one half mile farther north. Ole Andreas had been out here five years previous to the time treated in our narrative and had secured the land, the foundation for Follinglo Farm.

But back to our story. Our little party, as you might know, was travel-worn and tired when they reached their destination. Milla made haste to get acquainted with the great big Newfoundland dog, who did not stand on ceremony but accepted in princely style the advances proffered him. She was in her seventh heaven at once, being in such congenial company as that of Skate rompo. It was not every yellow dog he would take up with like he did with our Milla. His deep bass voice and her soprano blended so nicely. Nor was it long before they had occasion to sing a duet for a ravaging band of horse thieves that pounced down upon the community and got away with most of the horses belonging to the pioneers. But the much coveted blacks remained in their stalls and, who knows, probably that duet rendered by Milla and Skate rompo might have had its effects. Halla huse was a small, rude structure, the dimensions being sixteen by twenty feet and about ten feet high. This house, together with 160 acres of land, was rented by Uncle Anders on the following conditions: George Hall, the owner of same, had enlisted in an Iowa regiment where he filled a position as fifer. Uncle Anders of the second part was to furnish Mrs. Hall with enough flour for her own personal need and sufficient corn to feed one hog. Signed, George Hall of the first part and Anders Christenson of the second part. Date, March 1861.

Into this little house then, our travelers were ushered. The floor space was very limited, but still they felt as though there was plenty of room, yes, even some to spare. This was something which would soon come in very handy, for just at that time Uncle Nils and *litla fastero* (Father's little sister) were bobbing up and down on the broad Atlantic, on a small sailing vessel, headed right for this very same house. Uncle Nils gave a graphic description some years ago of how they lived, or rather slept, the winter they stayed at Halla huse. I think it is worthwhile recording, but it will be very tame compared to the way that this master hand gave it. He said: "That winter was the coldest that I or anybody else was called upon to live through. I do not know what the thermometer would have registered. I do not believe there was one in the whole Hawkeye State. Larsina and I had our bed upstairs, where we had it placed in the middle of the floor because, you see, at the very highest point where the rafters came together it did not measure over five and one half feet. I will tell you right now that we would have to be pretty tired before we tackled the hazardous job of going to bed on our hands and knees, groping around in the dark to find our bed. We had to keep our heads pretty well down and away from the rafters. Lamps were things unknown and of candles we had none. And then, mind you, there was an inch or more of pulverized snow on the floor which had sifted through the siding. After a night's sleep we had the same terrible ordeal to go through again, with the exception of the darkness, because we stayed in bed until it got to be as light as the Lord could make it through that one little window.

"Now let me tell you how we had to fix up our bed so as to guard against freezing to death. I found some hickory saplings which I bent over the bed just like fixing up a prairie schooner. Larsina found some *norske aakle* (woven bedspreads) with which she enveloped the whole business. Now the *aakle* were made of pure wool, which was kind of shaggy and had an occasional long hair sticking out here and there. You know Jack Frost is a master hand at fashioning all kinds of fantastic figures, and there is no end to shapes and forms that he will conjure together when he has the proper elements to work on. The shaggy cover furnished just the foundation he desired. Our breath furnished the moisture, and of all things that I ever saw this capped the climax. There was Larsina, her hair just as white as snow, her eyebrows and eyelashes covered with frost about the size of a snowball giving her the appearance of a submarine diver with his goggles on. And then the frightening figures overhead suspended from this *aakle*. I assure you that some of those tiny hairs were swelled to the size of an anchor chain. Others were about the shape of a rattlesnake. I thought I could see formations that had assumed the shapes of lizards, *steinbit* (sable fish), and toads. Aa der va tau verk nork for ein ful riggar (And there was enough rope for a full rigging). Well we lived through it, and the funniest part of it was that we even enjoyed it."

Hardly had Ole Andreas and the blacks taken the necessary

rest after their fatiguing journey from the Fox River settlement before he set about making preparations for his own house. The grass was never allowed to germinate, much less grow, under this man's feet. The lumber would have to be hauled from a station called Marshalltown, a distance of about fifty miles, and he reasoned in this way — that the sooner he could get started at it the better. In an incredibly short time the lumber was on the place. Lars Ostebo was forthwith engaged as carpenter, and it was not very long before the first frame house of this section loomed up on the prairie.

It was while on one of these Marshalltown trips that he was scared nearly out of his wits by a band of Indians who espied him just as he emerged out of Clemens grove. They started to yell and run in single file, with the evident purpose of heading him off. He thought at first of urging his horses into a run, but on second thought he knew that the horses hitched to a heavy load would be no match at all to the fleet-footed Indians. He therefore suffered the team to amble along in their usual gait and trusted Providence and his wits to get him out of this predicament.

It was only a matter of a few minutes for the Indians to catch up with the wagon. They then promptly caused the team to come to a standstill, formed a circle around the whole rigging, and commenced forthwith to clamor for tobacco. I am of the opinion that Ole had a generous chunk stowed away somewhere in that load, but since he thought that his supply would hardly reach around and because he had purchased it for his own individual use, he said he had no tobacco, nor did he have any use for it. He must have borne the index of an honest character, because they questioned him no more but skulked away. He found out later that they belonged to an Indian Reservation at Liscomb, composed principally of Sacs and Foxes.

After the house was enclosed, the proud owners promptly moved in. It was a sore trial for Skate rompo when Milla had to leave him, but there was no reason in the world why he could not come and see her. Distance lends enchantment you know. He certainly did come, and others with him. But more about this later.

The following spring found the little family in the best of cheer. And indeed why should they not be happy? They had a house of their own, enjoyed good health, had enough to eat for themselves, team and cow, and what was more, they even had a pig that Uncle Anders had given to them as a present. It just made their mouths water to think of the future bacon, hams, yes even fried cakes that this thrifty little grunter would result in.

The awakening of spring on an Iowa prairie was very enchanting indeed. The first sign was usually the singing and croaking of the frogs. Then the prairie chickens in countless numbers would toot and cackle on an early spring morning. Next we had myriads of mallards (green heads we used to call them) and geese, which would blend their voices with the earlier comers. Then the crowning effect, the cranes blowing their trumpets, yes, and the wonderful aerial feats they would perform, the way they would circle around in the air and all the time winding themselves upwards, until we could barely see them, a tiny speck against the clear blue sky. A thrill goes through my whole system when I recall how we used to sit on the sunny side of a haystack watching those experts of the air.

But we must get back to the events that were crowding in upon the Ole Andreas family. The spring work, such as the seeding of wheat and oats, was finished and the corn planting pretty well under way when a fresh recruit applied for admittance into the family and was unanimously admitted. He was a big lazy-looking fellow, weighed thirteen pounds strong, and was forthwith given the name of Peder Gustav. His size more than anything else was the cause of the name, because Ole Andreas had a brother of Herculean strength bearing the name of Peder. (He was usually called Store Per [Big Pete].) This all took place on the 17th day of May 1865. All the pioneer women came and took turns looking at him. Most of them went away shaking their heads saying, "That baby is too big and good looking. He cannot live. He will not stay very long in this world." But they were disappointed, and little wonder, for if you should happen to see him now, you would all involuntarily exclaim, "I have seen lots of people a heap better looking than he that have been permitted to live." Now since this was yours truly, I myself, that so sorely shocked this peaceable community, we shall hereafter designate Ole Andreas and Martha as Father and Mother.

After this excitement was over they met with no more adversities until their pig died. The bacon, hams, and doughnuts all vanished in a single breath of that hog. Father said: "Ja naa faar me sjaa ka me ae (Yes, now we may see what we are).

Mother said: "Ja, ja."

Meanwhile what was Milla doing? We shall presently see. As has heretofore been intimated, Skate rompo and other dogs came to view the new house that had sprung up so suddenly on the prairie, and since they were there, they could not help but notice our little Milla. The news spread to the remotest edges of this and other settlements. If we had taken the number of dogs as a means of measuring the human population of this and the surrounding country, allowing one to each family, this prairie must have been densely populated. You see the pioneer dogs like their masters did not stop at fifty or seventy-five miles. Hence, this would give us the benefit of the dogs at Ft. Des Moines, Ft. Dodge, Alden, and Marshalltown, and dogs from the Boone and Des Moines squatters. According to Father's statements they must all have been here. It got to be so intolerable that the serious question at last arose, "Shall we, or shall we not, part with Milla?" (For some reason or other they laid the blame on her.)

After a while, however, there was a lull. It came in waves; they usually had a rest of about three or four months. But when the next wave was on, the fate of Milla was sealed. Eg staar kje ditta lenger!! (I can't stand this any longer!!) was an expression made by Father at midnight after a vain attempt at sleep. Poor Milla was taken into the house, but the dogs were bent on following her. The way they would bark, howl, fight, and thump up against the wall in their scramble. All sounds were magnified in the still night air. The house acted as a sound box in a piano which magnified many-fold the thumps that were being hurled against it.

The way of the world is that the innocent must sometimes suffer in place of the guilty. Poor Milla was another example added to this list of unfortunates. Rasmus Sheldall had an

Milla

old army musket brought home from the South by his brother Erick. This then was brought to bear on Milla, Rasmus being the man behind the gun. Lars (Lewis) sitting in the window looking on, not understanding what this meant at all, exclaimed, after the terrible explosion had died away: "Naa kvak Milla" (Now Milla died).

Fido

The first settlers did not venture out on the prairies but could usually be found hugging the Skunk River timber. They reasoned this way: here we can find the logs from which to build our houses, firewood for our stoves, and rails for our crook-fences. And besides it is mighty nice to be close to the river during the fishing season. Let me also add that in those days the Skunk River was liberally stocked with such formidable creatures as pike and pickerel, which were not allowed to pass by our hard-working and hungry pioneers unmolested. If they could not be lured by the hook and the innocent frog, they would be taken in a more forcible manner by seine or trap, for come they must. And who is it, may I ask, that ever tasted those excellent fellows rolled in flour and fried in butter that could so far forget themselves as to blame them? But we must leave the fish to make their regular rounds to Mud Lake, the marshes and swamps forming the course of the noble Skunk, until, let us say, Lewis and I are old enough to cope with them. But then —!

And another reason why the first settlers did not venture out from the timber was the danger of the prairie fire. If you could have seen those fires, how they swept over those boundless Iowa prairies, you would not have wondered at the settlers for trying to keep out of their reach. It was a great sight indeed (when you were in a safe place) to watch the progress of the grand old prairie fires. The first sign of them would be a red glow in the east that could be seen after dark, and by the next evening they had usually come close enough so that we could see the tongues of flame shooting up here and there while passing over the ridges. Then on the following evening we would see the fire in all its glory, a long serpent of fire, stretching itself as far north and south as the eye could reach and gradually coming towards the Skunk River valley. If the wind happened to be unfavorable, Long Dick Creek would, as a rule, check its progressing any farther. But if the wind was in its favor it would leap right over the creek and continue on its course toward the heavy timber along the Skunk. I can remember some old patriarchs of the forest (some old oak trees) right on the edge of the timber, burned just as sharp as toothpicks, but there they stood like so many sentinels thwarting the onslaught of the flames, as if they would say: "So far, not any farther."

One Hover Thompson built his log cabin and cattle sheds about three miles east of the Skunk River, took every precaution to prevent disasters from the fires, plowed three circles around his place, leaving a space of about ten rods between each circle. He thought he had everything in shape for any emergency that might arise in the form of prairie fires, but the first fire that swept the prairie jumped over his circles and made a clean sweep of everything combustible he had. Nothing remained for him to do but to pull for the woods where he built himself a log house on the west side of the river. This time he selected a spot that baffled the prairie fires. The river at this place made a bend. Right at this bend the bank rose on the side nearest to the much dreaded prairie fires.

Little wonder, then, that when the good people heard that Father was about to build his house about half a mile east of the timber on the little knoll, they tried everything that was in their power to dissuade him from the rash undertaking. Old man Johannes Mathre came to him one day and begged and implored him not to build so far east but to move at least eighty rods farther west. It was not only the fires that might ruin him, but he must bear in mind that in the wintertime he would be at the mercy of the blizzards. Father listened to the advice given by his good neighbors, but nothing could change him from his original plans. He immediately set about planting cottonwood trees and Lombardy poplars, which in turn grew like weeds. It is true, he felt a little uneasy at first whenever he saw the red glow in the far east, but I am happy to report that no bad results ever came of it.

After the house was finished, a log stable was built to accommodate the horses. After the horse-thief raid, the settlers never felt easy about their horses. Hence every precaution had to be taken. With this end in view, Father constructed a stable out of heavy logs. The roof was made out of saplings and coarse slough hay. A very substantial door made out of hardwood boards and hung on massive iron hinges was the only entrance into the stable. This door was securely locked and padlocked every evening as long as the horse-thief scare lasted. A corncrib was also built out of logs.

Soon after the completion of the above-named buildings, Father brought home another dog. This time he made sure that it was not the kind of dog that would cause a repetition of the heretofore mentioned dog carnivals. This dog developed into a noble animal of his species, a mongrel, of course, but he was able to put to shame most of the dogs I ever had occasion to get acquainted with. He was of an even temperament, always on his post, ready to take hold wherever he was needed. In size we can compare him with a large collie but of entirely a different type and a more powerful build. His color was a light brindle. What kind of a conglomeration of breeds it takes to make this kind of dog is impossible to tell, but suffice to say that whenever I desire to picture in my mind a perfect dog, a dog who was a friend to everything that was honest and just and a sworn enemy to skunks, vagabonds, and thieves, Fido, for such was his name, with his honest and true countenance, is always found painted on the imaginary canvas confronting me.

He was my babyhood, childhood, and boyhood friend. He assisted Mother in watching over me so that I did not stray away and get lost amid the tall prairie grass, which surrounded the premises. And who could tell that those tufts of grass did not hide a lurking rattlesnake, a pest that the early settlers on the Iowa prairies had to guard against? Who else could tell as well as Fido where one of those dangerous reptiles might be lodged? In those days whiskey was considered the best antidote against rattlesnake poison. Hence, under pretext of being prepared to meet any or all emergencies that might arise from coming in contact with the much dreaded rattlers a very generous amount of this antidote was always kept on hand by some of the pioneer families. They sometimes reasoned that it might be well to use it as a preventive.

The harvest season was always considered the most dangerous rattlesnake period and for the following good reason: the grain was cut and left in loose bundles on the ground,

Fido

probably for a day or two, awaiting the coming of the hands to bind it. These loose bundles offered an ideal lurking place for the lazy serpents, and it was while handling the bundles that the sturdy pioneers would sometimes encounter them, but the trusted whiskey jug was always on hand ready to wreak vengeance on the venom administered by the rattler. The trouble was that the little brown jug would be tilted and humored until it emitted its chuckling sound whether the rattler was seen or not. Father always said that out of the two poisons he did not know which one to consider the most dangerous. Therefore, there was no antidote against rattlesnakes at our house. Fido would always make his rounds, and if he found anything suspicious he would always report. Mother has told me that after I got to be old enough to toddle around, she trusted Fido to pilot me from place to place. If she lost sight of me, she would call Fido, and wherever he was she was sure to find me.

This faithful dog saved the life of one of our horses in the following manner: it was a snow white mare by the name of Nellie. She was feeding by a straw pile and must have laid down to roll, but, be that as it may, she got into a position where it was impossible for her to get up. Now this straw pile was about eighty rods away from the house, but Fido on making his rounds had noticed her and hurried home in a terribly excited manner to give the alarm. Father followed him somewhat against his best judgment, and there sure enough was Nellie on her back. She had given up all claim on the world. Father called in the assistance of our good neighbor, Andreas Meltvedt, and Nellie was speedily rescued, thanks to our Fido. Another stunt that this excellent dog would perform every evening during the summertime would be to station himself on the cattle trail leading to and from the prairie, and when the cattle belonging to the settlers came home, usually in a body, urged on by the pioneer boys and girls, Fido would select our cows out of the bunch and drive them one by one into our yard in such a quiet manner that he did not disturb the rest of the herd.

One morning just after we had finished our breakfast, Fido got himself into a scrape that caused him to feel bad for a long time. He walked around performing his duties, but he was downcast and acted as though he was all the time asking forgiveness. Poor dog! He was tempted beyond his power of self control. The door was ajar, and he saw a dainty morsel that just suited his taste and, somehow, he must secure it. He came in, raised himself upon his hind legs, placed his fore-paws on one of the leaves of the little table which rested on four legs, none too steady, and the result was that the table tipped over and dishes, molasses, milk, and butter hit the floor with a terrible crash, and Fido hit the trail and struck for the door. After that episode Father wanted us to distinctly understand that when we went through the door we should consider it our business and bounden duty to shut it. When we went through the door and he could not distinctly hear that the mechanism in the door lock struck home, he would immediately (and the pitch would generally be above middle C) say, Lok igjen! (Shut the door!) I actually believe that this very familiar expression dates back to that table catastrophe of Fido.

We shall now have to leave Fido for a while and turn back to the first great event that I am able to remember which took place in our family. It was while Nehemias, the traveler, was making his advent among us. Lewis and I were supposed to be sleeping in our trundle bed, but the racket and excitement caused by this fellow woke us up. I can remember asking Lewis, "What is the matter?"

And he answered me promptly: "Aa stora fastero a her aa helle paa aa stikke mamo i fotno me knappa naaler" (Father's big sister is here and is sticking Mother in the feet with pins).

Right then and there I got a grudge against *stora fastero* which it took many years to live down. The next morning we were surprised beyond description when we beheld our little brother. This took place on the 28th day of March 1868. We were led to believe that he was rescued from some marsh somewhere and brought to us by *stora fastero* for safekeeping. We made a vow that we would fight to the last ditch if anyone should come and try to claim him.

After Nehemias got to be about three years old his roam-ing nature already commenced to assert itself. His first trip out on his own hook came very nearly costing him his life. It came about in this manner: Father, like the rest of the early settlers, hastened to plant willows around his farm. Their idea was to get a high hedge that would answer for windbreak and fence, as well, and who knows, they might even someday come in handy as firewood. Well, a local prairie fire was approaching some of Father's fresh shoots, and he started out posthaste, his manly vigor fairly brimming over, to put in his best licks in defense of his property, not knowing that this little urchin of a traveler sneaked away from Mother, bent upon nothing else than following Father to the scene of action.

It was so ordained that this fire was not very far away from our schoolhouse where Lewis and I attended school. We were supposed to be busy with our lessons, but we were not so much taken up with our studies that we could not look through the windows once in a while, although it was prohibited. While performing one of these unlawful acts we noticed Father fighting the fire, took in the whole situation at a glance, and by a common impulse jumped out of our seats and made for the door without as much as asking permission. Lewis, being much fleeter of foot than I, soon left me behind. I plodded along the best I could and got there just in time to see Nehemias walking along unconcerned through the tall prairie grass right in front of the fire, which was traveling along at a rapid rate. I started to yell and bawl at the same time, thinking that I might be able to attract Father's attention, but he could hear nothing through that raging fire. I knew what I had to do and that I had to do it quick. I had to run around the east wing of that fire.

It was easy to run where the grass was burned away, but when I came to run in front of that fire through the tall grass it was entirely a different proposition. I was noted for being very clumsy, and the slightest obstruction in my path would, as a rule, be enough to cause me to meet the earth, not halfways, but fair and square and at full length. But this time, for a wonder, I did not fall more than about a half a dozen times before I got within reach of Nehemias. I grabbed him and started to run. The first thing he did was to fall down. I did not have time to raise him up, but I had to drag him. Now we both cried so that tears blinded me, and it was just as well, because the fire was gaining on us fast. The tongues of fire made some desperate lurches as if to grab his gingham dress, but just then without knowing anything about it, I backed right into a pond and we were safe. After the fire had swept everything clean around us, Father noticed us in the pond. The willow shoots were very abruptly left to the tender mercy of the flames, and his whole attention was given to his own tender shoots, which looked to him as though they had grown right out of the pond. His first care was to get us home as soon as possible, so as to not give Mother time to worry. The willow, of course, was burned to the ground, but the next spring brought forth new sprouts from the roots, and after a few years they were restored back to their normal condition.

I might add that this willow hedge is yet standing on the Follinglo Farm. This adventure brought back sad recollections to Father's mind. He brought forth a letter written to him while he was yet in the Fox River settlement by his highly esteemed brother, Store Per, who had moved out to Iowa and settled out on the prairie about five years before Father's coming, which stated that his daughter, about twelve years old, had been overtaken by a prairie fire and burned to death, not over eighty rods away. I can remember that the reading of this letter made us all feel very sad.

Right here I think it would not be out of place to chronicle a few of the feats performed by this remarkably powerful man, Store Per, a man who was loved by all the pioneers, a man whom the few remaining old settlers and pioneer boys never grew tired of talking about and the younger generation never grows tired of hearing about. Per was a very large, well-built, muscular man, very easy going but brim full of humor. It has been said about this man that no one ever saw him angry or even out of humor. He was a God-fearing Christian gentleman that never showed his strength unless it was highly necessary, but then he would show it in a manner that would generally leave an impression. He was also very musical and would on suitable occasions delight his friends by performing on the violin. At one time his violin had to be resorted to in the wild woods of Wisconsin to help him and others out of a scrape with the Indians, who were then on the warpath.

In the early days a man was measured very much by the bodily strength he possessed. There were about half a dozen

Fido

Hoosiers, typical rail-splitters, and a few Irishmen living along the Skunk, stout, wiry fellows who considered it a part of their religion to measure their strength with each other and everybody else who seemed to be blessed with a robust physique. Among these men was a big stout man by the name of Walter. He was recognized beyond any question of doubt to be the champion, so that when Per arrived among them this Walter eyed him with very much interest and thought to himself that he must feel of him someday and find out what kind of stuff this well-built Norseman was made of. All kinds of plans laid by this wily Yankee to engage Per in a tussle with him failed. Per tried to make him understand that there were other ways of measuring a man's ability and usefulness than by mere brute strength. Whatever surplus strength he might be in possession of at the present time might be put to better use. But he desired to have him distinctly understand that, if anybody jumped onto him unawares, he considered it his duty to defend himself. Then Walter told himself that if that is the only way I can get a chance to test him, then that must be the course to pursue. The opportunity offered itself in the following manner.

It was at a log cabin bee where all the settlers lent a helping hand piling up a log house for an Irishman by the name of Riggen Walter, and Per, of course, was there. Now or never thought Walter to himself. Today it must be decided which one of us two is the champion of this neck of the woods. They were called to dinner and started to walk, when all of a sudden Walter sprang up from the rear, jumped up behind Per, set his knee right in the small of his back, reached his hands around Per's throat and locked them, but to no avail. Per not only stood his ground and kept himself from falling, but he coolly and deliberately reached his hand behind him, grabbed hold of the seat of Walter's pants, turned the other hand so that he got a hold of his neck, and then by main strength tore him loose and flung him just like a limp rag at least one rod ahead of him, where he landed smack on his face and stomach on the grass. Walter got up very much subdued, made a beeline for home, and left his portion of the excellent dinner for somebody else. Per walked right along, never as much as alluding to the short but very decisive scrap.

Another incident which goes to show the humorous side of this noble character happened once when he, together with a number of settlers, clubbed together and took some loads of wheat over to the Boone River mills to get it ground into flour, a distance of about twenty-five miles. They reached their destination towards evening. This mill was supposed to run night and day. Imagine their disappointment, for no sooner had our settlers brought their sacks of wheat into the mill and put their horses and oxen away for the night before the machinery stopped and the miller shut down for the night.

This was quite a serious matter for our friends, who were not prepared for so long a stay. Their provisions were not figured out to last for more than one day and night, and the feed for the horses and cattle was limited for the same length of time. And not only that, some of the housewives at home did not have enough flour from which to make a single cake or biscuit. They talked, begged, and implored the miller to start that mill and run their wheat through, but he turned a deaf ear to all their entreaty. All this time Per had been quiet, but he looked as though he was revolving some plan in his mind. All of a sudden he walked over to his sacks, satisfying himself first that the miller took note of his actions, stooped down and took one sack between his teeth and one sack in each hand and walked coolly over to the hopper and set them down with a heavy thud, causing a slight quaver in the whole structure. He then started to untie the strings preparatory to pouring the contents into the hopper, when he was hailed by the miller who asked in no gentle manner what he was up to. Per answered him in his usual quiet manner, but he laid heavy stress on every syllable, "I am going to grind." And that mill was started without any further delay on the part of the miller.

The following is a story told by old Linsey Sowers, who was one of the actors in the story. It was while hauling logs to a sawmill down in the woods. This mill was located about due east from where Story City is now located. Mr. Sowers and three other Hoosiers came in, each of them with a load of logs. Per had come in ahead of them and stood waiting for someone that was ahead of him to get unloaded. Of course he was next according to all rules, but the Hoosiers thought they would play him a trick and get into a fair and square fight

Fido

with him. They reasoned like this: four strapping Hoosiers ought to be able to handle one Norwegian. They drove horses and had rather light loads on, while Per had his oxen. They drove up and slipped past him before Per's oxen had even much as pulled the slack out of the chain attached to the ponderous load behind them. They expected an immediate onslaught, but Per, instead of demanding his right as they had been looking for, let the Hoosiers have their own way and ordered his oxen to come to a halt. He stood there patiently waiting until they were through. Then he drove up to the place and commenced in the coolest kind of a manner to unload his terribly heavy logs. "But instead of putting them where we expected," says Mr. Sowers, "he rolled them right over our logs to where they really belonged. That took the fight out of us, because I doubt very much if all of us could have rolled one of those logs over those piles. Right then and there we made up our minds that a man who could control his temper like that and at the same time show us in the handling of those logs what he could have done to us, if he had been so inclined, was a man whose friendship it would be to our advantage to cultivate."

Another time when his great strength and cool mind came in good stead was at a barn raising at Lars Ostebo's place. All heavy dimension lumber in those days was hewn out of logs found in the timber. This was cut and mortised together where a barn was to be built, the framework was made ready into sections, and then a dozen or sixteen men were invited to the barn raising, and each section was raised and securely fastened. In this case, however, one of the sections was not secured sufficiently before the men let go of it. The natural result was that it started to come down. The people got panic stricken and started to scurry away from the terribly heavy section that it had taken sixteen men to raise; Per, however, had full control of his senses and the rest of his body as well, and knowing that if that thing was allowed to come down, someone would certainly get killed. He braced himself to meet it and held it all alone, and in his easygoing, well-calculated way of speaking said: "Don't get scared fellows, I've got it."

I might go on relating about this favorite uncle of mine,

telling of his exploits on water as well as on land because he was also an expert swimmer, but I shall wind up my anecdotes about him by telling how he rescued one of his neighbor's cows, which was mired in a soft spot on the prairie. The owner of the cow and some other men with him had worked and hoped against hope to get her out, but they had to give it up and were just planning on putting her out of misery when they espied Store Per coming along. He was not rigged out to meet the demands of the occasion because his footgear was a pair of wooden shoes of his own make, and they were not quite the thing for a quagmire. When he came up to them, they told him the hopelessness of the case and of how they had worked, but it was their opinion that the cow was doomed and that there was no use in wasting any more time and energy out there in that mud. But Per answered them that he did not know if he could do anything, but he had a good notion to try, and after having uttered this remark he took himself, wooden shoes and all, over to the poor helpless brute, figured out where he thought he could get the best footing, bent down, got a good hold of that poor cow, and lifted her clear out of the mire. But the same power that brought that cow up forced him down, and we need not guess how the wooden shoes fared. He did not even try to recover them. He said he could make a new pair easier than dig those out.

Meanwhile what has become of our Fido? That was just exactly the question we put to each other many years ago. One evening late in the fall Mother prepared Fido's supper and carried it out and gave the usual signal that Fido understood so well, but he did not answer to the summons. We all went out and called till we were hoarse, but still there was no Fido to be seen. Lewis and I cried because we had a foreboding that something must have happened to him and that we would never see our faithful Fido again. Mother tried to console us and told us we had better go to bed and by tomorrow he would probably be back and, if he did not come, Father would go and look for him. We went to bed with heavy hearts, and it was a long time before we finally went to sleep. When we woke up the next morning the first thing we did was to inquire about Fido, but we soon found out that his supper had been left untouched. Father, true to Mother's promise, started out to search for him, but search as he might he could find no trace of him. This was truly a hard blow to us boys and to Father and Mother as well.

This mystery was finally cleared up in the following manner: out on the prairie about two miles northeast from our place a Yankee by the name of Daly had squatted down just shortly before this tragedy. This man was nursing an antagonistic feeling against the Norwegians. He was always trying to pick a row with them, and it was always his desire to settle any grievances with his fists. His boys, yes even his girls, would instinctively double up their fists whenever anything went slightly against them on the playgrounds while attending school. This antagonism went so far that the dogs had to forfeit their lives to pay the ransom for some imaginary grievance. This, then, was the way our poor Fido passed away from among us.

Fido the Second

Among the first recollections from childhood, none of them can equal the pleasing and lasting effect of Father's and Mother's singing. They were both very musical. Mother had an excellent soprano voice, while Father's voice, although it might have been found lacking in volume, was amply counterbalanced by the taste he possessed. The memory of those good old songs is just as plain as if they had been rendered yesterday. I can remember just exactly how they looked seated on their chairs holding a book between them called Harpo (the harp) while we boys were squatted on the floor right in front of them eagerly drinking in and absorbing everything at those rehearsals that seemed to us entirely too rare.

After Lewis and I had grown to be big enough to be trusted alone upstairs, I can remember how, after we had quieted down and gone through our usual pillow fight and other fights, they would often sing. If at first we felt a little skeptical in ascending the dark stairway where our imagination pictured to us whole legions of wolves, skunks, and hobgoblins of all descriptions that were lying in wait for us, Father's and Mother's singing would make us feel secure. We thought that everything belonging to the animal and hobgoblin kingdom would have to take to their heels immediately upon hearing the beautiful strains that were being wafted to us. The effect that naturally followed was that we were soon landed safely in dreamland. I always used to pity children who were so unfortunate as to have parents who could not sing.

I can just barely remember one evening when we were expecting Father back from Nevada (that being our nearest marketplace, a distance of about twenty miles) we went outside every once in a while to listen if there might not be some sign of his coming. In those days out in the still prairies, the rumbling of a lumber wagon would be heard at a great distance. Our ears finally caught the welcome sound. Of course we were in doubt for a while, because there was a possibility that the wagon we had heard might belong to somebody else.

Now the reason why we were so uncommonly anxious this time to see Father coming home was because we had heard it rumored that he was going to bring home a clock. So far, the sun had been the only timepiece at our home, and in cloudy weather everything pertaining to the passing of time would have to be guessed at. True enough the wagon turned in at our place, and we were not slow in running outside. We surrounded the wagon firing questions, entirely too numerous to stand even a ghost of a show of being answered, studiously avoiding any questions relative to the clock, for fear of being disappointed. The fact of the matter was that we had never seen a clock. Little wonder then that we were excited. Lewis told me, however, in an undertone that he thought he could see a box in the wagon. With this slight encouragement we walked into the house and waited until Father had unhitched, unharnessed, rolled, brushed, watered, and fed his horses and had made a round or two to ascertain if everything was all right in the hog sty and cattle yard. Then and not until then did he come up to the house where Mother had a good warm supper for him.

He was usually in a hurry in whatever he undertook to do, but now he seemed to take his time telling Mother the news of the day, for bear in mind, in those days there was no daily paper. The only news from the outside world was such as could be picked up when at Nevada or Iowa Falls. It was not unusual after having returned after such a trip to sit up a goodly portion of the night telling the anxious neighbors what was going on in the world. A person would frequently be halted on the road by someone who would holler at him, "What's the news?" But be that as it may, Father got through with his supper, and the box was taken into the house. The clock was carefully lifted out and set on an improvised shelf, given a gentle push, and started on down the stream of time, where it has faithfully been ticking its way ever since, yes, even up to this time.

But was that the whole content of that remarkable box? No. Father had prepared a surprise for us, and out of that very same box came an accordion, one with two rows of ivory keys, a grand instrument of its kind. I doubt very much if I could be more happily surprised now if Thomas's orchestra or Sousa's band could have been fished out of a box and immediately set to render some of their best selections. Father was quite an expert on this instrument, and that very evening he was compelled to go through his whole repertoire. This was the first musical instrument, excepting Per's violin, in this section, but it was not the last.

But we must get back to the dogs. It was late in the fall, drawing towards Christmas, and there was enough snow on the ground for sleighing and coasting. We had received an invitation from Uncle Nils, something that was always looked upon as a great event by us boys and well might it be, for such dinners and such hearty welcome! 'Tis true they lived in a log cabin and a small one at that, and their chairs were made out of hollow logs split length-wise, under which was set four legs and behind which was a very perpendicular lazy-back. They were not very comfortable chairs, but when you got inside that log cabin and sat down in one of those chairs (*krakkar*) you felt at home, and you did not feel as though you were sitting on mortgaged property either. Uncle Nils could say like Terje Viken, "It is simple but it is mine." Well, the morning for our proposed visit dawned. When Lewis and I got out of bed, Father had just come in after having fed the horses and cattle. He shook his head and said he did not like the looks of the weather a little bit; he was afraid we would have a snowstorm, followed by a blizzard. This boded ill for our plans.

Among other things, the main attraction this trip was to try some new sleds that Father had made for us on those hills at Uncle Nils's, the most ideal place for coasting. We had also heard that our cousin Lewis had a pup. Now after our Fido was gone we had a yearning in our hearts just to see this pup, even though we did not have the slightest reason to believe that we would get him. But now we were suddenly confronted with the grave question: Will the weather hinder us from going?

Mother, who was a genuine diplomat, came to the rescue with the following argument: "I think we had better get ready, and if we see that it won't be safe to start out there will be nothing lost by it." We got ready. So far so good.

Fido the Second

Meanwhile, Father had hitched the team up to the sled and had brought it right in front of the house saying: "Let's get in and start out, but take lots of wraps along, for I am of the opinion that we are in for a blizzard." Our little sleds, of course, were taken into the wagon box. Father chirruped to the horses, who immediately responded, gradually gaining speed until they struck their even brisk trot, which had the tendency of bringing us to our destination long before we realized that we could have covered that distance.

We were welcomed by the whole family. Uncle Nils said, "Eg kjende de paa meg atte de kom" (I was sure you would come).

Cousin Lewis said, "Utor me sleadne, bakjen e just saa haale saa glas" (Out with the sleds, the hill is as smooth as glass). This meant immediate action. He ran for his sled, and we were off for the hill at once. After Father had given the finishing touches to our sleds, it was impossible for us to find anything in the shape of a rope or strings by which to draw them. We hunted high and low but could raise nothing. We came into the house very much disgusted and a little bit cross. Mother noticed our dilemma and told us in her own peculiar, pleasant way, "Aa de laga seg nok" (Oh there will be a way). This only riled us up so much more that we even told her that there was no one, herself included, that was endowed with the power of creating things. When I think about this I feel ashamed to this day that we should talk to her like this, but she got the best of us then as on all similar occasions. She stooped down, untied her long *saaka band* (garter), and handed it to us saying: "Run away like good boys and play with your sleds." This taught us a lesson, never to say die before we had to. These were the strings we had upon arriving at Uncle Nils's that day.

Well, we were headed for the hills. The first slide we made down that memorable hill I can never forget. Just below the hill was a fringe of snow, we could almost call it a snowdrift. Into this drift we plunged headfirst, almost disappearing in the snow. And what helped to make things still more comical was the fact that cousin Lewis, who was by nature a clown, insisted on taking on board his sled a black cat that was purring and rubbing himself around his legs just before embarking. He went down just like a rocket, boy, cat, sled, and all, dived right into the snowdrift, and was literally enveloped in snow. First Lewis got out and shook himself, because he was on top, then came a black cat, which was now white, but by severe shaking and scratching gradually melted back into his original color. Cousin Lewis picked him up and helped him out at arms length, saying: "velsigne deg stakkars elendige kryp" (Bless you, you poor miserable creep).

Thus we kept on till *litla fastero* (father's little sister) called us for dinner. I know that we had worked up an appetite. And I furthermore know and declare that we did full justice to the excellent dinner. By the way, just to have the privilege of seeing Father and Uncle Nils eat *torsk* (cod) was a treat in itself and to hear Uncle Nils say, after he got through, "Den tosjen va saa salte atte eg trur eg kjeme to drikka meg spent i hel" (That cod was so salty I think I will drink myself to death).

We boys had to stand up during the dinner exercises, because Uncle Nils had as yet not made *krakkar* enough to go around. The best part of it all was that after we had eaten so much of the excellent viands we were actually in misery. Uncle Nils declared up and down, "Dei gutadne har vist ikje smagt mat" (Those boys must not have tasted food). After this grand feast, we were off for the dog kennel to view the pup. Cousin Lewis could undoubtedly see the coveting looks in our eyes. Immediately elaborating upon our great loss we wondered where we could secure another dog that might fill the place that Fido had left vacant. We made thundering speeches on the degeneracy of mankind. Who could stoop so low as to deprive people of their dogs? These oratorical efforts were not without effect in our generous cousin. He turned to us a very sober face, in which we could plainly read that he was determined on making a great sacrifice. His lips commenced to twitch and his chin puckered slightly, but he managed to say: "Seeing that you are dogless (*hondalause*) and since that our old dog is of the kind that may bring me another dog, I am going to give you this pup, aa tvi vere den vippe veren saa jere han naake ske" (and woe to the whipper-snapper who would do him any harm).

We thought this was too much of a sacrifice on his part. We looked at the pup and then at him and asked him at least half a dozen times if he really meant it, to which he answered promptly and emphatically, "Yes sir." Now all that remained to be done was to run into the house and tell Father and Mother and Nehemias what had taken place. Then it was some more coasting. Talk about fun! I almost believe I could take keen delight in this kind of sport yet.

Well, we kept it up until we were invited in to lunch. After this second repast, Father took a turn outside to see what had become of the snowstorm that he promised us in the morning. Shortly afterwards he came pell mell into the house and ordered us to get ready in the quickest manner possible because the storm was coming. And come it did, a genuine old blizzard. There was hustling and bustling to get us all, the dog included, into the sled. After we were all tucked in, Uncle Nils gave a finishing touch by putting over us an *aakle* (blanket). It was under this blanket, while on our way home through that blinding snowstorm, that we came to the unanimous decision that Fido should be the name of our new dog. To us who were under the blanket it was all great sport, but it lacked very much being sport for Father, who had to brave the storm without any protection whatever and on whom the responsibility rested of piloting us through that wild swirl of icy particles. Anybody who has been out on the prairie during a blizzard can imagine his position, but nobody else. I remember that, when he ordered a halt in front of our house, we all felt happy.

After Mother got a good fire going in the stove and Father had looked after the comfort of all the animals on the place, the hardship of the drive home was soon forgotten, and we boys, considering the great acquisition which we had made, had, as we thought, good reason to believe that it had been a great day indeed. Considering the great sacrifice on the part of our cousin Lewis and the great delight we took in bringing home and installing our new Fido, I am exceedingly sorry to have to chronicle that the reign of Fido the Second was destined to be of very short duration. As I remember him, he was about the size of an ordinary Scotch collie, black, with the exception of a white three-cornered spot on his breast, disposition gentle, very much on the playful order. What breed he was a representative of, I don't know. If I should venture to guess that he was a mongrel, I believe I would strike it very close.

Well, poor Fido the Second took sick, and we noted to our great sorrow that his strength was slowly but surely ebbing away. We tried all kinds of home remedies, among other things a remedy prescribed by Mrs. Frank Wier, Sr., which consisted of one slice of bread covered generously with butter and copperas (vitriol), this to be given once a day until cured or killed. But try as we might, poor Fido was slowly and surely on the decline. Father and Mother held a consultation, of which the outcome was that Mother was appointed to perform the painful duty to apprise us in a gentle manner or, in other words, gradually make us familiar with the idea that a merciful blow would have to be dealt unto poor Fido in order to relieve him of all his misery. With this end in view Henry Henderson was consulted. He was the owner of an army musket, and he was also the secretary of the school board at that time.

In those days when the board of directors had their yearly meetings, they always met at the home of one of the members of that body, and well they might, for at the time of Fido the Second there were as yet only three schoolhouses in Scott Township. The Sheldall schoolhouse, the Pierson, and the Phillops. Since Father was a member of the board, it chanced that the meeting that year should be at our home. At 10 o'clock A.M. the first Monday in March, according to previous notice, the directors arrived, and so did the secretary, Henry Henderson, but in addition to a package which contained his books, he carried a musket. We eyed this with a little suspicion, but we soon forgot all about it because Henry was such a pleasant body and had a way of drawing our attention in other directions. After the men had gotten fairly settled, and after exchanging views on several subjects such as the weather, prairie fires, and other matters, Henry seemed suddenly and mysteriously to disappear from the crowd, very likely for the purpose of putting his horse into the stable. The fact of the matter was we did not get time to figure out anything before we heard the report from his musket, and that was the end of poor Fido the Second.

Tige

Very nearly three-quarters of a mile south and west from our home on a picturesque spot, situated close to a graceful bend on the Skunk River and very nearly screened from view by a beautiful grove of oak trees, stood a log cabin in which lived our old and tried pioneer friend Syvert Meltvedt (the Yankees called him Sam Knutson) and his family. This man will always be remembered by the growing generation of that time for the simple reason that he loved to play and associate with the little folks of the community. Wherever there happened to be a cross baby or child that was sorely trying the patience and taxing the mother to the limit, if Syvert happened along it was always considered a godsend. His presence worked like magic on the little one. I don't believe there ever was a baby that would hesitate in the least to go to him when he reached out his strong toil-worn hands and arms to receive him. But those brawny hands had just as delicate and tender a touch as the heart that gave them their impetus and feeling. Our youngest brother Nehemias was one of those unfortunates to whose lot it fell to do a lot of crying. He was rather puny and never felt just right. This gradually paved the way for a nervous disposition, and this in turn, probably urged on by a gentle hint in the form of teasing from his older brothers, caused an abnormal amount of crying.

After having lived nearly half a century I can still close my eyes and see how Mother used to lug this poor child around while performing her household duties, but the worst part of the daily program was when the water pail needed replenishing. She could not leave him in the house with us but had to wrap him up and carry him on one arm while she carried the pail with the other, and after getting to the well (which was just a hole in the ground, with a substantial cover on top) she had to lay him down on the ground while she hoisted up the water with a crude implement termed a well hook. During this performance Nehemias was not idle. He was furnishing music on the rhapsody order, while his hands and feet were diligently going through the movements of the modern kettle-drum. Even this little fellow in his grouchiest moods could not withstand the pleasant countenance and winning ways of Syvert. The crying would gradually subside, and after some facial contortions twixt tears and smiles, leaving you in doubt for a while as to what power would gain ascendency over the other, out would crop his real nature, which was by no means bad. Syvert had gained his point, and there was happiness and pleasure all around.

I can remember one day after Nehemias had reached the age where he was able to understand talk, Syvert was here helping Father with his wheat stacking. It was, by the way, a memorable stack, a monster, which it took four days to erect and no time at all to fall down again, and then another four days to build four reasonable-sized stacks out of the ruin. It was after this catastrophe, upon coming up to the house, that Syvert found Nehemias in no gentle mood. He had one of his protracted spells of crying. Syvert got his attention, puckered up his face, and acted as though he was in the greatest misery. He told him that he was suffering from a terrible earache and that this crying made it ever so much worse. The crying and earache were cured at once, for come what might he was not going to hurt Syvert.

Invariably when this man came to give us a call he would squat right down on the floor and lean his back up against the wall. On a breezy evening in the summertime his favorite place would be on the doorstep. He was a tall, well-built man of the real pioneer type. He never wore suspenders, and in the summertime his shirt sleeves would always be rolled up to his elbows. His headgear would never vary from a wide-brimmed felt hat. But you would never find him anything else but neat. His movement was graceful, easy, and well measured. One of his stunts would be to take any little baby, even if they were so small that they could not sit erect on the floor, place them on the palm of his hand, hold them out at arms' length, and then sing and dance to the tune. And what was more, children would have confidence enough in him to stand on his hand while going through a similar performance.

Another thing that helped make this man famous among

the pioneer boys and girls was his orchard. He was a pioneer among the pioneers when it came to planting apple trees. It actually seemed to us that his love would coax the delicious fruit from somewhere and place it on an especially allotted branch only to be kept there in reserve for the children of the community.

Who can forget Syvert, his orchard, and his apples? Little wonder then that when this man said that he had a pup that we might have for the asking, provided we would call and bring him home with us, that we fairly jumped and accepted the challenge at once. The next morning bright and early found us at Syvert's cabin surveying our new dog. He had the markings of a Bengal tiger, hence our friend suggested to us that Tige would be a very suitable name for this particular dog. Of course this was considered by us to be a splendid name, and after we got home all were given a voice in the naming of the dog and Tige stood the test. We shall now leave Tige in his puppyhood and give him time to develop into a dog.

Meanwhile we shall turn our attention to other things that took place at that time. The 23rd day of May 1871 was a perfect day in every respect. It was during the afternoon of that day that something mysterious seemed to take possession of the place. Father and Mother talked in subdued voices, and all of a sudden the door was darkened and filled to overflowing by our massive aunt, *stora fastero*. Shortly after, Lewis, Nehemias, and I were asked to go down to the haystacks to play hide and seek and to stay there until we were called. Father had just hauled home some lumber which he intended for a cattle shed (previous to this time), and he had laid it out in the old three-cornered style for the purpose of getting it thoroughly seasoned before using it in the walls of the intended shed.

We left good enough alone for a while and played inside of the three-cornered enclosures, but soon this became stale and Lewis conceived the splendid idea of stringing out the boards in such a manner that we had sidewalks strung out all over and beyond the backyard. Of course if we had had any forethought at all, we ought to have known that we were running great chances in tampering with those lumber piles and that drastic measures would likely be resorted to in getting those boards back to their respective positions in the three-cornered piles. The crisis might have been put off for a while if it had not been for Nehemias, who all of a sudden got tired and made for the house, disregarding entirely the instructions we had to stay outside until we were called.

Of course we were not surprised to see him promptly come back, but we were surprised when we heard what he had to tell us. It was namely this; that in the house was a little baby, and they told him that he was our brother and that we were not at liberty to come in and see him. He had seen him and he was just all right, he said. Well, we forgot all about the lumber for the time being and scooted for the house, but I can very distinctly remember that we were reminded of it later. I believe though that I can truthfully say that if it had not been for this little brother that the reminder would have been of such a nature that we would have had a still more vivid recollection of same.

There must have been something soothing in connection with this little fellow, in fact I believe I am not saying too much when I say that ever afterwards just to be near him always did give a soothing impression. Well now, there were four boys in the family. When Nehemias brought us the news we thought that if he could have said sister instead of brother it would have sounded a good deal better to us, but after we had seen him and after we had accepted him as one of us and he had been initiated, as it were, we would not have traded him off for all the girls in Christendom. The news reached all our neighbors in an incredibly short time. The result was that the good neighbor women took a day off just to see the new baby and incidentally took something good along as an offering to the little one and the mother. As a rule they got very little out of it though, as it generally fell to the bigger ones. Every morning we would smack our lips and wonder who and what would come next. This, remember, in the good old honest pioneer days lasted at least for a fortnight.

One Sunday after Mother and the baby were considered strong enough to be out, we all piled into the lumber wagon and went to the old country church where our little brother was baptized and given the name Helge Mathias. We always called him Henry. In the good old days, the people had more time to spend among each other, and whenever a slight occasion suggested itself there would always be some doings. So it came to pass that this occasion was duly celebrated. The sponsors together with the nearest neighbors were invited home from the church, and we indulged in what we thought was a great dinner. It was not served in courses like it is now, but it coursed merrily down our throats and answered very much the same purpose as do modern dinners.

After the usual *tak for maden* (thanks for the food) and the wish that the Lord would bless the little one, the men would seek out some comfortable place on which to recline, and the conversation would invariably drift onto the burning question of that time, the rupture that was going on in our church, how to check it, and how to manage to get some effective stumbling blocks or pitfalls in the way of Elling Eielson, the walking apostle, who seemed to have such a hypnotic power over some people that he could make them believe that schools and institutions of learning, as far as the training and education of ministers of the gospel were concerned, were nothing but broad highways and wide portals leading to hell. Furthermore he sought to instill into their minds and (I am sorry to say that he partially succeeded in making some of them believe) that it would go easier with Sodom or Gomorrah than it would with our learned ministers. After having exhausted this subject pretty thoroughly, there were more refreshments, and the company dispersed.

It was a similar gathering, although some years later, after having listened to a lengthy speech given by Rev. Estenson, the dissenting party's minister, where he was supposed to give a clear explanation on the difference between the two factions and the reason why they had found it prudent to leave us and organize a church of their own, that Uncle Nils gave birth to an expression which toes the mark to perfection and is well worthy of being remembered. It came about something like this: Estenson got up, placed an enormously big Bible on the palm of his right hand, and at once commenced to swing it around in half circles, holding it out at arm's length and once in a while giving it a slap with his left hand whenever he thought he had an argument that he wanted to drive home.

He started out in this manner (let us not forget the rhythmic swing of the Bible): "Vi Hauge Synode trot og bekjender" (We Hauge Synod people believe and confess) — but the trouble was, he studiously went on without mentioning questions which had caused the mischief but went on elaborating on truisms which no one would or could gainsay. In fact, he said nothing on the subject that he was supposed to talk on. Uncle Nils took exception to this kind of oratorical effort and at once set about ridiculing it, putting on a voice which sounded as though it might have issued from the bass section of a calliope and said, "Vi Hauge Synode trot og bekjender atte revo e bak!" (We Hauge Synod people believe and confess that a man's backsides are behind him!) This is equally a truism; nobody can deny it, my statement is correct, and so was his, but neither of them had any bearing on the subject. The bitter feeling which this division naturally caused was very sad indeed and was detrimental in ways more than one.

But I must leave this heavy subject and go back to where I started to say that the people in those days had more time to spend in mutually wholesome enjoyment then the present generation seems to be able to spare. It was nothing unusual in those days for the people to take a day off and gather down in the woods to view the trees and for us boys to outline all the fun there was in store for us when the next nutting season would appear. We would calculate the possible yield of the different tufts of hazel brush, viewing with great wonder and respect those magnificent black walnut trees, picturing in our minds the sport that would be ours in gathering walnuts from under them in the fall. Yes, and those grand hickory trees just as straight as an arrow, towering above everything else! What were they not capable of doing?

The old settlers loved the trees. Little did they dream that the greed for money should so far take possession of their successors that what they would have considered little short of murder would have taken place. When I recall how the grand Skunk River timber looked then and look at the half-rotten stumps of today it calls forth a sad feeling. After a downpour of rain, the people, both young and old, would take another day off for the purpose of watching the rolling and tumbling of the waters of the Skunk River on its mad race towards the Father of Waters. Then some of the old tars would tell stories from their life on the ocean. Others would tell stories of narrow escapes in crossing streams and rivers.

I can remember two such stories, and the reason why I can remember them I suppose is because my favorite uncle, Store Per, figured as the hero in both of them. The first one was told by Stone Charlson. He said it happened while moving from Illinois to Iowa. "There must have been at least twelve prairie schooners in the caravan, and we had a drove of cattle of which I was one of the drivers. When we got to the Mississippi River at Davenport, which was at that time a small place, we had to get all our effects onto a ferryboat in order to get to the Iowa side. Everything went well until we got nearly up to the wharf, when all of a sudden one of our cows plunged overboard and into the water. We immediately commenced to lay plans for rescuing her in the shape of ropes, tackle, boats, and cant hooks, but Store Per was there just at the right time and in his own peculiar cool manner simply reached out his hand and grabbed the poor cow by the horn. He then got down on his knees and by sheer bodily strength lifted her right out of the water and planted her right back on the ferry without saying a word.

The second story was as follows: Right close to where the Grindheim bridge is at the present time, about eight rods farther north, was the ford where the early settlers used to cross the river. One morning Store Per drove his oxen hitched to a wagon across the river at this place. He noticed that the water was slightly above the normal watermark and indications were that the river was rising, but he thought by shoving his oxen along a little faster than usual he could make his trip and return before there should be any danger in recrossing the river. But when he came back he found to his great surprise that he had misfigured. The water had risen to such a height that the only way to get across would be to swim his oxen, and cross he must. Before plunging in, he lashed his wagon box securely to the truck, then got into the wagon and gee-hawed them right into the current. Everything got afloat, Per was balancing himself in his awkward craft, the oxen were worming themselves along at a seemingly satisfactory rate of speed, when all of a sudden the ox on the near side got tangled up in something and immediately keeled over and in so doing got

Tige 37

under the wagon tongue, the off-side oxen thus threatening to make a complete wreck out of the whole rigging.

Per had the reputation of being the owner of the finest yoke of oxen that hit the trail for Iowa out of the Fox River settlement. Was this to be the final windup of Buck and Pride? No! Not as long as he could help it. With this thought uppermost in his mind, he made a dive right under the tangled mass where the oxen were churning the water most frantically. Right here again, his Herculean strength was given the most severe test. It was not a matter of minutes, not even seconds, that would have to decide the fate of that poor ox under. He grabbed one of its horns and applied his strength towards getting him released from the yoke. This, of course, was accomplished quicker than can be told. After Pride was released from his moorings, he immediately came to the surface, and the current started him puffing, snorting, and coughing downstream. This left Buck and Per in charge of the wreck, which was also gradually drifting away from the landing place. Right here, Per did one of his famous stunts. He took Pride's place in the yoke and, with the united efforts of both himself and Buck, swam ashore with the wagon. He did not consider it worthwhile to put Pride back into the yoke; he, by this time, had scrambled up the bank. Per continued on home, a distance of about two miles and a half, drawing the wagon and some other effects, while Pride came trudging along on behind.

There were many stories and experiences told at those impromptu gatherings which would have been of interest if we only could have had them stored away, but this was before the time of capturing and storing away vibrations in the form of phonograph records. Suffice to say, they had wholesome fun and amusement in abundance and well they might, because they had such characters as Lars Boe (Bo) and Owen Soken right with them.

Lars Boe was one of those phenomenal designs in general makeup which would bring an involuntary twitter in the region of the seat of mirth just by looking at him, let alone when he opened his head to give utterance to words. It would generally act like spontaneous combustion. As I remember him, but I will not vouch for its correctness as it is only a vague recollection, he was a tall, slim man. He had a beard like a billy goat, had a kind of sepulchral voice, and moved and acted more like a minister of the gospel than anything else, and his face was just as immovable and unchangeable as that of the Sphinx. His connection with the ministry, however, would immediately be banished from your mind upon hearing him talk. Owen Soken was his nearest neighbor. This man was noted for his good, hearty laugh. These two men spent a good deal of their time together, and a splendid combination it was. One was the source of all kinds of mirth, and the other was always in readiness with his good, hearty laugh. The old vulgar expression, "I thought I should have died laughing," came very close to the point of being acted out to perfection in this man's case.

It came about in this manner: Mr. Boe and Mr. Soken were hauling hay one day. Soken did the pitching, and Boe built the load. After the load was finished, Soken made the remark that the load was heavier on one side than on the other and that he was very much afraid that the load would tip over. To this Boe answered positively that he just couldn't build a load that would tip over and that he should come up and they would drive home. He furthermore added that even if his loads did look lopsided they were made to stick. But Soken said he did not propose to risk his neck on top of that load but would walk behind. To this Boe promptly answered: "All right you walk and watch me. I'll demonstrate to you that I am an expert at this business."

After having uttered these words, he clucked to his horses and started off, all the time vociferating on his skill and infallibility in shaping loads of hay so that they would stick. This kept Soken continually in a laughing mood, so that the slightest change now to the worse would be sufficient to start him roaring. He did not have to wait long either because all of a sudden the front wheel struck a little rut and down came hay, Boe, and all. The lecture on top of the load ceased. Soken fell to the ground in a heap laughing so that Boe actually gave him up as dead. If it had not been for Mrs. Soken, who happened along with two pails of water which she promptly poured over him, he would not have survived. It was fortunate for him that this happened right between the spring and his cabin and that his wife just at that time thought it necessary to fetch home some water.

I presume by this time that Tige has a right to demand our attention. He is now in position to grapple with any and all problems that might beset him or any of the rest of us. The first trophy gained by him was the complete subduing of Anders Kallavaag. This man lived about three-quarters of a mile across lots from our home. He was a rather eccentric character but honest as the earth! He had an ingrown antipathy against dogs and, in fact, he was afraid of everything, even his own shadow. He measured time in the afternoon by his own shadow, and it was never allowed to become very long before he made for the house, locked the door, and went to bed.

This man had been a fearless sailor for many years. He had rounded Cape Horn and the Cape of Good Hope many times. He was familiar with Chinese ports, Japanese and Hindu as well; he had touched on Australian shores many a time, sailed through the Suez Canal, passed through the Strait of Gibraltar, the Mediterranean and Adriatic seas, been to the Arctic and Antarctic regions, had hairbreadth escapes from icebergs and floes, lived through the gold fever excitement in California, and acted as a bartender in the awfullest places, namely the saloons of the gold-digging regions. He had been chased by grizzly bears in the deep forests and wilds of Oregon and lived through it all fearing nothing, but here he comes, settles down on a peaceable forty-acre tract on the Iowa prairies, and is, above all things, afraid of our pup.

This is a rule that seems to apply to all old retired sailors and has always been a conundrum to me. Our friend Anfin Anfinson and I, with our own peculiar way of reasoning, have, among many other ways, sought to solve the problem in this manner: The tissues forming that part of their anatomy called fearlessness have constantly been drawn upon to such an extent that there is little or nothing left, while that part of their organism called fear is yet like the virgin soil of an Iowa prairie, untouched, and when this dormant mass of tissue is given the slightest chance of developing, the whole anatomy gets unbalanced and everything turns into fear.

I can remember one morning, one of the first days of May,

when we heard someone calling and the dog barking. In looking out through the window, we saw Anders Kallavaag on the east of a little pond and Tige on the west side addressing each other in a way that was not suggestive of the very best of brotherly feeling. They were both talking at once, ignoring entirely any and all rules of etiquette, and once in a while Anders would let loose a shout that would echo and re-echo back from the Skunk River woods. Father, of course, at once betook himself to the scene of action. He considered it his duty to get the pup silenced and sent up to the house. Then he turned his attention to Kallavaag and invited him up to the house.

The only answer he received to this was: "Ka i vero vil de me den raatne hoen?" (What in the world do you want with that rotten dog?), after which he added: "This is as close to that brute as I want to come this morning, and I shall state my errand very briefly. I want one of your boys to come and help me plant corn this afternoon and tomorrow. I shall pay ten cents per day."

To this Father answered that he would do the best he could to help him out, but the boys would have to be consulted before giving a definite reply. Father feared that we would be a little bit skeptical in considering the proposition, as he had been resorted to as a sort of bogeyman to scare us children with, saying for instance: "If you do so and so we will give you to Kallavaag." But money always has had a great power over the human race, and there was no exception in this case.

Ten cents a day looked big to us. Why, ten cents would buy all we would need to celebrate the Fourth of July in due style, an event which we looked to with great anticipation. This decided us. After a lengthy colloquy I was the one decided upon to cast my fortune with Anders Kallavaag. I must confess that I started out with a heavy heart, but my fears were all thrown to the four winds as soon as the bighearted and kind old Mrs. Kallavaag admitted me into the house and offered me a cookie.

Shortly afterwards Kallavaag, armed with a hoe on his shoulder, and I, with a little tin pail filled with king corn in my hand, started out towards the scene of action. The field had previously been thoroughly prepared and marked off into squares of about three feet, eight inches. I was supposed to drop just exactly three kernels of corn, precisely in the cross made by the marker. If this was not done just so, I would immediately hear from the man behind me, who was vigorously manipulating the hoe, in dangerous proximity to my bare heels.

Thus we would go back and forth over the field until Mrs. Kallavaag would bring us a splendid lunch. Then we would sit down and rest, talk, and eat. It was during these moments that I got acquainted with this queer man, who, I found to my great surprise, had a heart that was just as true and noble as anybody's. From that time on we were fast friends and differed only on the dog question. He wanted me to distinctly understand that he positively had no use for dogs.

Another experience that I can remember in connection with Tige, and I cannot think about it without shuddering, happened one day just after a heavy rain. Lewis and I asked Father and Mother for permission to go and see the river. After some consideration they rather reluctantly gave their consent but cautioned us (and of course we promised faithfully) to keep at a safe distance from the bank. After getting there we found the water a good deal higher than we expected. The whole bottom was in a mad swirl. We sat down on a log and admired the wonderful works of nature for a while, but this soon became tedious, and we had a longing for something more exciting. We accordingly sidled down to the bank, although we felt something tugging away at our conscience. But we would be careful and would at least live up to that part of our promise.

In spite of this, we found ourselves on the very edge of the bank looking straight down into the mad current, which was only about two feet below us. Suddenly a bright idea struck us. Tige ought to be given a few lessons in swimming. We accordingly set about laying plans how we could induce him to jump into the river. But the throwing of sticks and every conceivable plan of inducement would not fetch him. He very evidently had a whole lot more common sense than we. Now since he seemed so stubbornly to thwart our well-meaning plans, we fell to reasoning like this: It won't be well for his future career as a faithful dog to let him off as easy as this. We must take him by main force and throw him in. He will enjoy it after he once gets started. We therefore grabbed poor Tige and after a fierce struggle finally succeeded in dumping him in. But no sooner had we gained our point before we commenced to feel bad. He made a dive, and when he did come up to the surface he sniffed and whined most pitifully, struggling against the stream because he wanted to get out just precisely at the same place where he went in, and he very naturally looked to us to be just as zealous in getting him out as we were in getting him in.

The bank was perpendicular for quite a ways down, and if we had had sense enough to have walked downstream until we could have found a decent landing place, it would have saved us whole lot of worry. But there we stood glaring and far from admiring our own handiwork. Something would have to be done and without much delay because he was already showing signs of fatigue. Lewis said: "I am going to try if I can't grab him." And suiting the action to the word he dropped down on his knees on the edge of that rotten crumbling riverbank, stooped over, and grabbed him by the neck. Now came the tug of war, and we began to realize that we were in danger. Lewis yelled to me, "Grab a hold of my coattail quick." I obeyed and instinctively got one hand locked firmly over a sapling just within my reach. The dog was heavy, but Lewis had a good grip and the coattail was homemade, manufactured out of cotton jean, and stood the test, and the outcome was that the dog came out. But if there ever were two boys who felt that a just punishment had been meeted out to them we did. We even cheerfully took the thorough drenching that Tige gave us in shaking himself right under our nose.

This was about the middle of June. Father was plowing corn with Charley and a single shovel plow, an implement that had never been known to scour. Lewis, Nehemias, and I were attending school. Before and after school hours Lewis and I were supposed to pull weeds from among the corn hills. It was while thus engaged that we already began counting sleeps between the above-designated time and the Fourth of

July. Looking at it from an economic point of view, we were well fixed for the occasion. We had all that Kallavaag money, which amounted to five cents apiece.

We had already gained permission from Father and Mother to attend the celebration, but this included the provision that we must be back in time to fetch the cows home from the prairie. This cow-fetching business was always looked upon as more or less of a gambling proposition because sometimes we would find them and sometimes not. We may touch upon this later, but be that as it may, the Fourth of July dawned, and we were up bright and early making our toilet, which was not very elaborate. We did not even bother with shoes and stockings in those days, just a pair of pants and a shirt and a hat just clapped over our noodles, and we started out in full array. The only thing that bothered me and made my heart feel sore was the way Nehemias pleaded, but in vain, to go along with us. But sentiment was dispelled and thrown to all winds as quick as I began to nose the firecracker fumes and heard the din of battle occasioned by the firing of an old cannon, alternating with the tiny spitting of firecrackers and, at reasonable intervals, an explosion from a pair of anvils.

On an elevated platform stood Dr. B. F. Allen laboring away at the Declaration of Independence, and seated right close to him was the speaker of the day, brimming over with enthusiasm, while on the other side sat the singers, who were just then clearing their throats preparatory to giving us "Columbia the Gem of the Ocean." We swerved neither to the right nor to the left but made a beeline in the general direction from whence a hoarse voice wheezed out the following: "Here's where you get your money back — ! Firecrackers five cents a pack. People! Help — help — yourself!" We had heard enough. Firecrackers were all we wanted, and there was no slacking of speed on our part before we had reached the stand and pulled out our Kallavaag money, which consisted of a crisp ten-cent greenback, and ordered, in a businesslike manner, two packages of firecrackers.

We immediately set to work to add our mite to the already overdone racket. It was a wonder how fast our long-coveted firecrackers disappeared, and it was with heavy hearts that we fired the last one. Now what would we do in the way of amusement? Lewis, who had an eye on business, soon solved the problem in the following manner. The man who was serving lemonade at five cents a glass announced that his water supply was running out and called for volunteers to carry water to his stand and that the compensation would be five cents a pail. Lewis jumped at the liberal offer at once and, after seeing me stationed safely, leaning up against a tree, and after cautioning me not to stir an inch for fear of getting lost, he took the big wooden pail handed him and struck out for the nearest well, a distance of about half a mile at Nils Uttaaker's place.

As I stood there leaning up against my tree, thoughts like these came coursing through my mind. "I wish I had something to eat — I wonder when Lewis will be back — That pail of water will be too heavy for him to carry alone — Why didn't I go along? I might have helped some." Then my imagination fell to drawing pictures of the darkest hue. "Supposing he should get lost; perhaps he is at this very moment walking in the wrong direction — or suppose he should fall into Nils Uttaaker's well!" Things from the dark side were crowding fast in upon me. I tried to recite poetry, but the only thing I could think of was Casabianca, "The boy stood on the burning deck." The upshot of the whole thing was that I soon found myself crying lustily. But when things came to that stage where I thought something should be done, all worry and forebodings were suddenly swept away for there right in front of the stand stood Lewis with his pail of water demanding his five cents or rather its equivalent, a bunch of firecrackers.

When I came to him in my bedraggled condition, he was just negotiating with the lemonade man about making another trip, which also should be paid in like manner, a bunch of firecrackers. This time I made known my desire of accompanying him, to which he answered, "What's the use? You would only fall down and spill the water, and then what would we have for our trouble?" I thought this falling down business was by this time getting to be an old chestnut, but, nevertheless, upon second thought I could see that his argument was not unfounded, because that which had happened so many times before might, through some unlooked for accident, happen again. I then most graciously acquiesced, upon which he handed me the bunch of firecrackers for safekeeping and ordered me back to my tree. Now while standing there during my second installment, my attention was called to the fact that the people were streaming by in a general northwesterly direction, and my ears caught a sound which resembled very much the wailing of a cat in great misery.

This, thought I, is something that will have to be investigated as soon as Lewis comes back; therefore, promptly upon his return, after having delivered his cargo and received his pay, we found ourselves in hot pursuit of the crowd that surged past my tree. After coming up with them, we found them massed around a floor made out of rough planks. On a raised platform about five feet high, built right close to this floor, sat old man Doolittle on a chair holding in his hands something which we afterwards learned to call a fiddle, and bolt upright, just as sober as an owl, six feet three inches tall, close to Mr. Doolittle, stood our friend Mr. Nash from Starvation Hollow. On the floor, arranged in splendid order, forming a circle, were about one dozen typical Hoosiers, men and women from the same hollow, just waiting for the word, "Hop to it," from Mr. Nash, who was to do the calling off, and they plunged wildly into what was called a square dance.

Mr. Doolittle started out playing his only tune, "The Road to California." (We have ever afterwards called it the Doolittle tune.) Mr. Nash cleared his throat and yelled out, "Bow — to — your — partner!" After this order had been duly complied with and performed, the following order was issued, "Balance — all — 1 — 1 — !" Upon hearing this, a new life seemed suddenly to take possession of the Hoosiers. They commenced to trip around in front of their partners, bowing nearly down to the floor, but meanwhile beating a more than lively tattoo with their boots, sometimes backing and then again coming forward but all the time aiming to keep time to "The Road to California." To me it looked as though they were all the time stepping on red hot coals. This performance was kept up until the call, "Swing — your — honey — " rent the air. Then you ought to have seen them. "The Road to California" increased in tempo, the long-legged Hoosiers started to swing, the speed all the time increasing until the velocity, it seemed to me, had the same effect on those boots as speed has on the governor of a steam engine.

Well, we listened to "The Road to California" until we could stand it no longer, being afraid it would drive us crazy. We then turned our attention to our firecrackers and had made quite an inroad into our second supply when all of a sudden an idea struck Lewis, who was by nature very generous, that we must save some of them for Nehemias and Henry. This at the same time reminded us of home and that we were terribly hungry and the prosaic duty which awaited us at home, namely the fetching home of the cows. We now took a formal leave of the place where we had celebrated the glorious Fourth for the first time in our lives on our own hook, and on our own resources, and started for home.

In going home we took another route from the one coming down. This route took us right by old man Baar Beroen's place. While nearing the place I noticed his pump, and, since I had not tasted water nor anything else since leaving home early in the morning, I was actually suffering from thirst. Lewis, of course, had had all the water he wanted at Uttaakers. We walked right up to the pump and helped ourselves. We had no scruples in so doing, for water was, as a rule, considered common property.

While we were thus engaged, all of a sudden the old man stood right before us. This man resembled very much the picture we had seen in the old family Bible of Moses or Aaron; his beard reached nearly down to his waist and was white as snow. He had the reputation of being rather penurious, and the feeling of fright took possession of me at once. Perhaps he might think that we were being a trifle too familiar in taking the liberty of helping ourselves the way we did. But not so. He greeted us and talked to us kindly. After he learned whose boys we were, he said that our grandfather Nils Murar and he had been great chums in the Old Country, and he tried to gather as much information about him as possible.

After this topic was exhausted, he asked us where we had come from, and we said without reserve that we had been celebrating the Fourth and had had a splendid time. But then is when we caught it. He was a true disciple and follower of the before-mentioned Elling Eielson and had some queer ideas. He told us that this celebrating of the Fourth was nothing short of the Devil's work and we must never do it again. He said that powder was invented by the Devil himself for no other purpose in view than to kill people and then drag them into his storehouse. Then he told us about his son Henry who enlisted and went to the war and was killed on the battlefield. The poor old man was moved to tears while relating this sad story yet so fresh in his memory. When he was through, we bid him good-bye and started for home, feeling not quite as lighthearted as we did when we left the celebration grounds. We arrived home according to agreement, and Mother had a splendid spread awaiting us. After having appeased our hunger, we showed our skill in handling firecrackers to the great delight of Nehemias and Henry.

The country around here in those days was known as the east prairie and the west prairie, the Skunk River being the dividing line. The west prairie extended without a break clear out to the Des Moines River. The intervening space had such lakes as Clear Lake, Wall Lake, Mud Lake, and Goose Lake. Farther south were the everglades of Story County, a most ideal place to get stuck. For fear of being able to reach far enough with this narrative of mine to cover some of our experiences as they come in their natural course of time, I want to say that on our way home from the Squaw Creek coal mine with two loads of coal, Father and I got stuck fast in the mud seven times during one afternoon. We saw no less than seventeen wagons loaded with coal anchored in those swamps. I do not care to dwell on this subject as it gives me a nightmare simply to think about it. The east prairie on our side reached from the Skunk River woods and on east, I do not know how far, broken only by creeks such as Long Dick and Bear Creek but, thanks to Providence, minus the swamps.

This, then, was the arena upon which we were to do some of our acting, and mighty glad am I that I have had the great privilege of living through that era that has wrought such great changes in central Iowa from the winding cattle paths to the modern highways on every section line, from the scrub cow that could travel twenty miles a day in quest of choice tufts of grass (and in the evening not feel any the worse for it) to the grand shorthorn cow of today. We will now go back

Tige

The earliest known likeness of Ole Andreas. From a tintype.

Ole Andreas and Martha Karina. From a tintype dated 1875.

Lewis (ten), Nehemias (four), and Peder Gustav (seven). Martha Karina made these suits for her three oldest sons in 1872. The family then went to Ames where the boys sat for this tintype. Thereafter Ole Andreas paid 10 cents to treat his family to ice cream. This outing formed one of Lewis's favorite childhood memories.

Lewis and Peder Gustav, ca. late 1870s.

Martin and Henry, early 1880s.

One of several instrumental groups composed of Tjernagel brothers and other young males of the neighborhood. Peder Gustav is second from the left.

Martha Karina and Ole Andreas flanking their adult children. On ground, Bertha and Martin. On bench, Henry and Lewis. Standing, Nehemias, Peder Gustav, and Gustav Adolph.

Peder Gustav (left) and Martin laying drainage tiles, ca. 1890s.

Lewis, 1911.

Martin in his band uniform in the Flanders, 1912.
Hayrack and barn in background.

The wedding photo of Peder Gustav and Jennie, 1895.

The children of Peder Gustav and Jennie, 1905. First row, left to right, Herman, Martha, Elizabeth, and Erling. Second row, Alfred and Otto.

Left to right: Otto, Herman, Erling, and Alfred, ca. 1908, with the same children in reverse order and their cat on the right half of the photo.
A blending of two exposures by Clarence Tjernagel.

Peder Gustav standing on one of the concrete corner fence posts he designed and made. He likely assumed this out-of-character, soldierly pose at the request of his nephew Clarence Tjernagel, who experimented with photography during visits to Follinglo Farm.

Jennie and Peder Gustav, ca. 1915, with their then surviving children, from youngest to oldest: Peder Julius, Olaf, Martha Karina, Alfred, Erling, Elizabeth, Herman, and Otto.

The youngest and the oldest residents of Follinglo Farm in 1917. Sigurd, youngest child of Peder Gustav and Jennie, and Ole Andreas.

In old age Ole Andreas kept busy north of the farmhouse cutting and chopping firewood. On Mondays he fueled the kitchen range to ensure an adequate supply of hot water for washing clothes.

The sons of Peder Gustav and Jennie with their cousins, dogs, and watermelons by the concrete corncrib, World War I era. Photo by Clarence Tjernagel.

In 1923 a contingent of Tjernagels traveled by truck from Follinglo Farm to Saude, Iowa, to visit relatives and possibly for an engagement of the Follinglo Orchestra. They are on the grounds of the Lutheran church and parsonage where H. M. Tjernagel was pastor. He is near the center of the picture holding a child. Peder Gustav, wearing a black hat, is near the rear of the truck, below the boy on the ladder. Jennie is at the left in the front row holding her coat. The truck owner stands, hands on hips, on the far right.

The farmhouse at Follinglo during the reign of Noble, who is in the foreground.
When horses working in the fields heard the bell on
the far right, they knew it was time to head for the barn.

The cattle barn. Peder Gustav's woodworking shop was on the second floor of the
south end of the structure. Photo by Clarence Tjernagel.

(Opposite) *The music room at Follinglo Farm in 1925. At the far left is Peder Gustav. Electricity has recently arrived at the farm. A light fixture patterned after a Norwegian* stabbur *hangs from the ceiling, with light bulbs wired to its gargoyles. An illuminated cabin is on the wall. Olaf M. Norlie used this photo in his* History of the Norwegian People in America. *"This is the 'Follinglo Orchestra,'" he explained. "Its members all belong to the Tjernagel family living on farms east of Story City, Iowa, brothers and their children. The musicians meet in the music room on the Peder Tjernagel farm. All pieces of furniture in this room except the piano and the organ were made by Mr. Peder Tjernagel (the cellist) from black walnut grown on the farm. The seats of the chairs have the shape of violin-bodies, the backs that of the antique lyre. The music desks are carved in Old Norse design. The large music cabinet [behind Peder] contains drawers for music by Bach, Beethoven, Mozart, Mendelssohn, Grieg, Tschaikowsky and others, besides a special drawer for operas. The Tjernagel brothers have named the orchestra after their mother who came from Follinglo, Valders, Norway. Their father came from a farm north of Haugesund, Norway. This family has meant much to the musical life of Story City and vicinity."*

The seed house, or stabbur, *upon completion in 1916, with gargoyles at the eves and the* gabelspir *at the peak. Compare with the music-room light fixture.*

The Universal Portland Cement Company distributed this photo in flyers and ads with this text: "One of the most unique corn cribs ever built stands on the farm of Tjernagel Brothers of Story City, Iowa. The building is quite imposing, 48 feet long by 31 feet wide, has two cribs 8 feet wide, the full length of the building, and is 22 feet high up to the purlins of the roof. . . . Bins above hold about 4000 bushels of oats. The walls are of concrete, consisting of solid 16-inch columns . . . The owners planned the building and put it up with their own labor, paying only $550 for lumber and cement and $35 for reinforcing material."

A steel-reinforced, concrete fence post designed, manufactured, and installed by the Tjernagel brothers. Some of the massive corner posts survive at Follinglo Farm.

The Tjernagels owned the first American Manure Spreader in the neighborhood. Penciled on the photo: "in use Sept. 1917 Hermans up." When it was his turn to spread manure, Herman took measures to protect the horses from flies.

"Follinglo. Stacks on North East field 30 acres," reads the back of this photo, ca. 1917. Peder Gustav stacked grain bundles to shed water until threshing time.

Until the arrival of the mechanical corn picker, corn picking changed little at Follinglo Farm. This photo is from the mid 1930s. Note the bang boards on the wagons.

The residents of Follinglo Farm and visitors during World War II. At the point of the V (for victory) is Amanda Tjernagel, the youngest of Jennie's grandchildren present. Unko, senior member of the group, is on the far right.

*Adolph M. and Martha Karina (Tjernagel) Harstad with children
Mary, Margaret, and Peter.*

Nehemias in the mid 1950s sitting on a kubbestol *at a table made by Peder Gustav
for items Nehemias collected in the Holy Land.
Below are North American antlers, tusks, and fossils.*

An aerial view of Follinglo Farm, 16 September 1968. The horse barn is out of view to the east (right).

and follow up that great traveler, that wonderful sprinter, the scrub cow of about forty years ago, and we will have to depend on the barefoot boys and girls of that time to do it.

Among our cattle there was a black cow with a white band encircling her middle which had, somewhat, the shape of a saddle. On account of this mark, Mother gave her the name Salrei. This cow was a leader among leaders, and nothing would satisfy her but to get as far away from home as possible. She would always take the lead, and the rest of the cattle from our locality would, as a rule, follow in her wake. It occasionally happened that she broke away from the rest of the herd, after having first interested some of her most intimate friends among our cows to take part in some lengthy tour of inspection because it seemed to devolve on her to seek out the places where the herd should graze the next day. It was when such expeditions were on that Lewis and I were in for it. It was hard to have to part company with the other boys and girls to go in quest of the stragglers, especially if the sun was just setting behind a bank of clouds, the usual sign of a coming storm.

We would usually assemble right after school. There was Syvert's Andrew, Christian Aabe, Jabob's Anna or Jakob's Kittle, Baara Gurrina or Lena, Kittel's Bella or Kittel's Ola, and Lewis or I or sometimes both of us. The first thing was to go a little better than one mile east of our place where we would ascend a big hill called Springa Hauen, which derived its name from the many natural springs in its close vicinity. There we would scan the horizon in quest of some sign pertaining to the whereabouts of our cattle. In most cases we would be able to locate them from this hill, but if they were too far to the northeast they would be hidden from view by Taalige (quiet) Lars Hauen, a hill or rather a ridge that was higher than the hill on which we were standing. If they were to the southeast they would be swallowed up by the colony of hills which is known now as the Phillops south quarter.

In such cases, where there was nothing in sight to give us a clue, a council was held, and the drawing of lots was even resorted to. The method adopted by us was the wet or dry method. We would find a flat stone, spit on one side of same, fling it up into the air, and holler out wet or dry, and, if it

Tige

struck the ground with the wet side up, we would holler out, "The wets have got it." Then it would be to start out in due order, single file, following as much as possible some cattle path and avoiding stepping outside, because the stubble after the last fire was sharp. So we searched for the cows that would give us the milk out of which we would churn the butter that would, if we succeeded in wallowing through Jermund's Lane and Utlø Lane and then through the everglades, down the dangerous Amesa Bakjen, and over swollen streams into Ames, bring us five cents a pound, providing quality was good.

If we were fortunate enough to find all our cattle at or near the same place so that we could all go home together, we rather enjoyed it. But it was far from fun when we became separated and had to shift each one for himself out on the endless prairie. I can remember one evening that Lewis and I had to see our companions start out for home with their cattle, and we in turn had to strike out in just the opposite direction which was bringing us farther and farther away from home. It was, of course, Salrei and some of her chums that were missing. We walked and we ran, circled to the right and to the left, but found nothing. We then made direct for the Lone Tree, a magnificent elm tree standing alone out on the prairie, a wonderful landmark, indeed, but we reaped no reward even there.

The sun had now sunk below the horizon, and daylight was changing into twilight, and fog was forming along the creek bottom. The evening bugs had started up their doleful chorus; fantastic figures were beginning to take form, and, if we had dared own up to each other, the truth would have been that we were scared nearly out of our wits. The conversation was now carried on not above a whisper. We were now fast becoming enveloped by the much dreaded darkness. And there we were, at least five miles away from home and still no sign of the cows. Who would blame us for feeling discouraged? But we trudged on with no particular end in view as to where we were going, but we thought that we might accidentally stumble upon them; and for a wonder that is just exactly what happened.

There was Salrei herself with head erect and just as proud as a peacock, in full tilt headed for home. We were only too

Tige

glad to fall right in with the procession. By this time it was pitch dark, but we could hear the rattle of their hoofs as they pitched along ahead of us following in single file the winding cattle trail. These trails were laid out carefully along the ridges, avoiding as much as possible the low places. Thus it became necessary to make long, circular detours. This constant shifting from one direction to another soon had its effect upon us. Since we were walking along in total darkness it was not to be wondered at that we got thoroughly muddled on directions. The painful idea was soon fixed in our minds that we were drifting in the opposite direction from the one we fancied should lead us home. Now the second spell of gloominess was on, and we admitted freely to each other that we were lost. Meanwhile Salrei rattled on with seemingly no intention of changing her course, and we could do nothing but follow.

While in this gloomy condition a bright idea struck Lewis, namely that we should sing. It was more than likely that Father was out on the prairie searching for us, and in this way we would apprise him of our whereabouts. Our first attempt in trying to raise our voices was a complete failure. In our frightened condition nothing but a gust of wind passed through our throats. There was not force enough behind it to cause any vibration whatever. But our second attempt was better. As soon as we heard our own voices, we found ourselves singing, "Come ye sinners poor and needy." We were all the time increasing in volume, but not until we struck a high, high pitch and sang, "There is a happy land far, far away," were our efforts rewarded. Then we heard a shout cutting through the darkness, which was soon followed up by the stalwart figure of Father himself. Talk about a happy reunion; this was one of them. We soon found that Salrei was right on directions and that we were sadly in the wrong. I believe I can to this day point out the very spot where Father found us that evening. After getting home, we found that we were just terribly hungry, but Mother had a remedy for such things. We were tired, too. That was also remedied, for Mother tucked us snugly into our trundle bed, where we soon disremembered everything in connection with our recent adventure.

Another incident from the time of the prairie which took

deep root and still clings to my memory is the following. One day Father had to make a trip to Nevada, and we were supposed to help Mother look after things at home and in the evening, as usual, fetch the cows home. It was decided this time that Lewis should go alone and that I should stay at home with Mother. He started out with the before-mentioned company, but this time it was Kjittel Grove instead of his sister Anna that represented the Groves. After they had been gone a reasonable length of time, Mother began to cast uneasy glances through the east window in the direction of the expected cows because there was a storm brewing. We heard the dull rumbling of distant thunder for quite a while, and now all of a sudden the sun was overshadowed. She also hoped that Father would be back soon, since he had made an early start. As a rule his weather eye was always cocked, and she knew that the fast-approaching cloud bank in the west was being duly noticed by him and that he would urge his horses on to full capacity.

Upon looking through the window again she noticed the first cow coming over the hill, Store Hauen, but it was not Salrei, and she knew what that meant; if she was not in the lead, she was not there at all. After the cattle came up with us, we noticed that Kjittel was not there and that the Grove cows, at least Guld Dokka, were missing. We consoled ourselves by saying that Lewis was not alone out on the prairie. The onslaught of the storm was quick and furious, and the downpour of rain was simply tremendous. The first gust of wind broke one of the windows and flung it clear across the room. The crashing of the thunder was terrific, and through it all we knew that Lewis and Jakob's Kjittel were out on the prairie right in the path of the storm and Father on the road somewhere between us and Nevada.

The storm soon passed over and the sun came out just before setting, and everything looked just as natural as ever with this exception that water seemed to have taken the place of land everywhere. To say that we were scared is putting it very mildly. I cannot now recollect how long we were kept in suspense regarding how Lewis and Kjittel had fared out on the prairie, but I can remember that it was yet daylight when we heard Salrei give the signal that the stragglers were approaching and that immediately after the last cow came over the hill two very wet boys came into sight.

I believe I shall let Kjittel describe this adventure out on the prairie, but first I want to describe him. He was a lad that was brimming over with humor, and I believe with the proper training he would have stood up with Mark Twain, Bob Burdette, or Eli Perkins any time. In quick wittedness he was second to none, even from the Green Isles. He was perhaps given a trifle to exaggeration, but take it all-in-all he was a loyal friend and a splendid fellow. His hair was red, and this caused him a whole lot of worry because some unscrupulous fellow had told him and caused him to believe that red hair had quite an attraction for lightning, and he thought that the lightning would get him someday.

On this particular day he thought his time had come. He described it like this: "Naa stormen kom saa blei me klapsa ner i markjo saa naage panne kager aa saa greib me henno fudle me gras aa laag aa pin hilt os aa me torte inkje sjaa op for de ringde saa gormalige atte me vilde draunda i logtro aa lynil hilt paa aa spratla aa gneista i disse stakkara haar stobadne mine saa skrekelige atte eg trude eg hadde laada je an" (When the storm came we were clapped down on the ground like pancakes, and we grabbed our hands full of grass and hadn't dared to look up before it rained so prodigiously that we could have drowned, all the while the lightning kept on crackling and sparkling in these miserable stubs of hair of mine so forcefully that I thought I would have to give up). Well, all's well that ends well. The boys none the worse for a scare and thorough wetting were all right, and Father came home shortly afterwards. He had stopped at Marselius Olsen's place, not very far from where Roland now is located, while the storm was raging.

The following adventure in which Lewis was the sole actor is entirely of a different nature, inasmuch as he was forced into it. But there were others that were very much forced into it before he got through. It came about in this way. Salrei had been on one of her extensive exploring expeditions, hence it became necessary for Lewis to separate from the rest of the cowboys. He struck out and was fortunate enough to come up with the missing one sooner than he expected but not soon enough to be able to catch up with the rest of the herd. In going home he crossed over a vast stretch of prairie which had escaped the last prairie fire. The thought struck him at once that, if this old grass was burned away, the new grass would tempt the cattle to stop and feed right there instead of straying so far away. Now he thought if I only had a match I'd change the face of the prairie in a jiffy. But he had no match, hence it was out of the question, but what happened? As he walked along he came to a place where a fire must have been started recently but squelched by someone. Right in the center of the burnt space was an old dry cow chip which was still smoldering and smoking. This gave him another bright idea. He picked it up, carried it over to a large tuft of grass, got down on his stomach, and coaxed it into a flame. The result was that he soon had a raging old-fashioned prairie fire going at full tilt headed directly for Indre Tjernagel's place. Now he began to see his mistake and wished he hadn't done it.

I can remember seeing this fire flare up all of a sudden, and it looked to us that it might be right east of Store Hauen. Father felt a little bit uneasy and started out to make investigations. There is nothing so deceiving to the eye as a prairie fire. After getting on top of the hill, he noticed that the fire was a good deal farther east, but he kept on in the direction of the fire and who should he meet but Lewis, who was in position not only to say where the fire was but how it came to be there. This only made Father feel so much more anxious to come up with it and help fight it, while Lewis walked on home, looking more like a whipped cur than anything else. They had quite a time before they got the fire under control, but fortunately there are no casualties to report unless it might be a few of Indre's fence posts that got singed.

Another incident of very much the same nature happened one Sunday after Lewis and I had become big enough to be trusted to look after the place, while the rest of the family, together with Signe and her family, who lived right across the road from us, went to church, leaving Kjittel to stay with us. The first thing we did was to go on top of Store Hauen to play monka, a game very much in vogue in those days. After having played a few games, we got started to talk about practical things and that we ought to do something worthwhile.

We thought that this grass around here ought to be burnt away because we had heard Father say that he intended to break some of this prairie as soon as the breaking season opened up, and we were sure it would be highly appreciated by him. Thus we talked and made believe that our services in this particular burning could not be dispensed with without incurring great loss to the general welfare of those whom it might concern. One forcible argument followed the other until we considered it our bounden duty to set fire to this prairie. We had promised Father and Mother never to touch matches, so in order to overcome this obstacle Kjittel offered his services, he not being bound by any such promise. He accordingly set out for the matches, but since his mother had locked the door he had to open a window and slip in, and in this manner this slight obstacle was overcome.

I can remember so distinctly just how that fire started, after having scratched the first match on a little rock, and how quickly it spread. The old saying, "It spread like wildfire," we had personified right there, and I can also distinctly remember that the grand surprise did not strike Father the way we had intended at all. There was a thing, however, that struck us that was not in the bargain when we laid the splendid plan. I am glad to report that there was no damage done this time either, thanks to the prompt action of Father and others, and I can also report that this was our last attempt at starting prairie fires.

The thing that stands forth as the most gruesome and the awfullest among my memories of the prairie were the bulls, just as spry as kittens, and on the least provocation always ready for a blood-curdling fight to the finish. Where they all came from and who owned them always remained a mystery. We could hear them blow their trumpets, which on a still evening would echo among the hills. This in turn was answered by another one and still another one, and so on until pandemonium was actually let loose. Those calls, which were nothing short of a challenge, always sent a thrill through my body. I always imagined myself as the center of attraction and then being by nature equipped with a mortal dread for bulls, I was always kept in constant misery if I chanced to be alone out on the prairie.

Another thing which I dreaded was the horses. The settlers were in the habit of turning their young horses loose in the spring and trusting to chance to find them again in the fall. The horses were unlike the cattle in this that they would seek each other's company and stay together in one herd during the grazing season. Where they all came from was always a mystery to us. They were not wild horses, but they acted very much like them because upon the least provocation they would start to run. During still evenings we could hear the thunder of those herds of horses when they were on a stampede. Their maneuvering and racing from one knoll to another was picturesque enough, but my hair always stood on end when I heard them because I had the mortal dread of being run over by them.

I do not know which I dreaded most, the horses or the bulls, but all this fear and dread were eliminated when I got so far along that Father and Mother would trust me to ride the tried and trusted old mare, Florie. Young folks in those days, both boys and girls, were expert riders. There was one summer that I rode Florie so incessantly that her back got sore. This would not have been so much to wonder at if I had used a saddle, but I had no such thing. All my riding was done bareback.

I remember one evening that I asked Father if I could ride Fly instead of Florie. Fly was a spry mare that could outrun most of the horses in this settlement. When I rode Florie, the rest of the equestrians would, as a rule, outdistance me. It even happened that we would indulge in horse racing out on the prairie. I hated to be left behind always, hence this appeal for a better mount. Father said, "All right. Take her, but you must be exceedingly careful not to tumble off and get hurt."

It chanced that this evening I had a later start than usual, and the rest of the cowboys and girls were already out on the prairie in hot pursuit of their cattle. When I got on top of Taalige Lars Hauen, I could see far to the east, silhouetted against the sky, a girl riding like the wind. I turned Fly's head in her direction and let her fly. When I came closer, I saw that it was Anna Grov, now Mrs. Vangness, riding the champion racer of the prairie, a mare belonging to our fearless rider, Anfin Anfinson. When I came close enough, I asked her if we should have a race, and to this she promptly answered, "Catch me if you can." I urged Fly on to the utmost, but that was all the good it did me. Anna left me sadly behind, and I soon gave up as badly beat. I wish the girls nowadays could ride like our pioneer girls did. I, of course, felt a little chagrined at thus being beaten by a girl, but I consoled myself by saying that Fly was not the only one that had been outdistanced by this marvelous runner.

The question might arise, "Why did not Tige take part in these cattle escapades?" That question is very easily answered. He was absolutely no good. All he was good for, and that position he filled to perfection, was to romp and play with us children. He, like so many other dogs, got into the chronic habit of following the team. Whenever Father drove out any place, Tige was sure to follow, but on one trip he had quite an adventure. Father was obliged to make a trip to Nevada and, of course, Tige had to follow. When Father had finished his business, the thought that was uppermost in his mind was to get started for home as soon as possible. It was not a part of his nature to loiter in town after his business was finished.

Somehow Tige was left behind. When Father came home and told us that the last he had seen of him was in Nevada, we mourned him as irretrievably lost. Mother tried to console us by saying that it was very probable that he would find his way home, but we waited in vain for three long days and still there was no sign of the missing one. On the fourth day Andrias Meltvedt announced to us that he was going to Nevada and that if our dog was inside of the corporation he would fetch him home. Remarkably enough, as soon as he had put up and fed his horses, John and Polly, and walked up as far as Ringham's store, he noticed Tige sitting on the steps in an attitude suggestive of waiting for someone to come out of the store. He had evidently seen Father go in but missed him coming out.

Andrias Meltvedt, being endowed with a nature which could captivate and retain the love of young and old and all the pets of the community, had no trouble in attracting Tige's attention, and with one single bound he made for Andrias and tried to cover him all over with caresses in a manner becoming to a happy dog. In my estimation there is no living thing that can do this as effectively as a dog. Our friend divided his lunch with Tige, and in the evening they arrived home, safe, sound, and happy. Who ever saw Andrias Meltvedt in any other but a happy mood?

The next great event was our trip to Store Besten (Grandpa Anderson), the before-mentioned Nils Murar. He had moved way out on the Des Moines River, where he had squatted on some river land. This meant a journey of about forty-five miles across a wide stretch of prairie and then through the Boone River woods, across another stretch of prairie, then it was Brushy Creek and its patch of timber, another stretch of prairie, and so on until the Des Moines River woods hove in sight. Right on the east edge of this timber, about half a mile north of the Border Plain post office, in a very small but substantial log cabin, lived Store Besten and Margreto and our uncles and aunts, Anders and Hans, Martha and Gurrina.

Who of us can ever forget that splendid morning when Mother called us and told us that we must get ready for an early start, Father being outside getting horses and wagon in readiness. For this occasion Father had secured a light wagon belonging to Andrias Meltvedt. He filled the box up with fine fresh prairie hay; into this Lewis, Nehemias, and I were supposed to roll, sit, and if need be go to sleep while journeying over the prairie. Meanwhile, Father, Mother, and Henry were promoted to the more commodious accommodation of sitting on a board across the front end of the wagon. This was before the time of the modern spring seat, not to mention spring wagon.

I wish I could describe our feeling on that memorable morning. I can close my eyes and see how Mother bustled around finding our suits that she had made for the occasion with her own hands without the aid of a sewing machine. We thought much of those suits, double-breasted coats with pants to match. Ah! It makes my heart warm and causes a slight twitch to my lips and gives a pucker to the chin and whatnot to the eyes when I think of it all. Father made arrangements with Signe Johnson and her boys to look after the stock and Tige during our absence. What bothered Nehemias and me not a little was the idea of sleeping away from home in somebody else's bed.

What I can remember most distinctly in crossing the prairie was when we came to a trail or road that branched off in different directions, the question would then arise, which one of these roads would finally lead us to our destination? Mother would always have to decide this all important question, and she always handed in a decision which we found to be correct. This road question caused us boys an endless amount of worry, because we naturally thought that we might get lost. When we got as far as the Boone River woods, we halted and had our lunch and fed the horses. After having rested a while and after having hooked up to the wagon, Mother suggested that all except Father had better walk behind the wagon until we reached the river on account of the steep hills. I remember falling down those inclines more than I walked; and, when the river was reached, Nehemias and I thought the end had indeed come, as far as our sojourn here below was concerned, because it would have to be forded, and we had a mortal dread of the water.

The next place of interest was Homer, where there was one schoolhouse, two churches, and a small country store where the Hoosiers were wont to congregate, sit around on grocery boxes, and talk about railroads that would all without fail hit Homer. They have been sitting there ever since, nursing the same idea, discussing the same subject. So far no change has come over them unless it might be for the worse, because then they were surrounded by fine prairie grasses while now they are bounded on all sides by thrifty cocklebur and sweet clover.

After leaving Homer behind us and after having crossed Brushy Creek, we could see the outlines of the Des Moines timber. On toward evening we reached our destination, tired and very hungry, but very fortunately for us Store Besten had caught a stray sheep the day before, which was promptly changed into mutton, and while there we lived on the fat of the river land. The wild plum season was on, and we had our lion's share of them. Talk about a glorious time! I can't describe it! We just had it.

Our return trip was marred a trifle in its splendor by small rain showers. When we came home, we found Tige and Kjytten comfortably reposing on Father's first bluegrass patch.

Father took great pride in this patch of bluegrass, hence he viewed with much disfavor this man's familiarity.

Very little remains to be said of what transpired during Tige's administration. Just his sad ending. One afternoon Father sent Lewis and me to fetch the cows home from the cornstocks, and Tige went with us. When we got over to our neighbor's line fence, Tige struck out after a rabbit. In this field there chanced to be a hunter, and out of pure meanness he raised his gun and let fly a load of shot right into the hindquarters of poor Tige. It has often been said that a man that will wantonly shoot a dog for fun is a criminal at heart. This proved to be true in this case because poor George died in the penitentiary. Tige came home and Father advised putting him out of misery at once, but we could not even bear the thought of any such a thing. He was therefore allowed to linger and suffer for about two weeks when Father, in spite of our protests, put an end to the suffering of poor Tige.

Chip

We are now entering upon a new era in which changes are being wrought in ways more than one. If the walls of the old Sheldall schoolhouse could be made to reproduce all the oratorical efforts both pro and con that were hurled at them at this exciting period, it would be worthwhile to lend one's ears. One notable discussion was about a proposed railroad to be built from Ft. Des Moines and north through Ames and Story City, and no one could foretell how close it might come to our country post office, Randall, that is, if our people would vote a tax which would be considered sufficient by the promoters. It was during one of these heated discussions that Lars Ostebo (Østebø), a man who always favored progress, uttered the undying words: "Those railroad mans is some curiosities folks." And Hans Pederson, who took the opposite view of the question, most naturally said: "Dat man tell a lie." I shall not undertake to give even the gist of those honest scraps, but the final outcome of it all was that a tax of five percent was voted. The taxpayers were to receive certificates of stock in the Narrow Gauge road. This sounded big and might have become so, but our highly honored and trusted county treasurer, Geo. H. Ship, instilled into the minds of our honest citizens the idea that their certificates of stock were worthless, but in spite of all this he would still give them twenty-five cents apiece for them. In this way he got most of them. I remember father's tax amounted to $60.00.

The arrival at Story City of the first locomotive, a flat car, and caboose was celebrated as was becoming such a great event. Lewis and I were there so I know whereof I speak. Right in front of the Tungesvik store was planted a cannon which had seen service in the Civil War. Into this was stuffed powder and brown wrapping paper, and a brave veteran, with a cigar stub stuck into the split end of a flexible stick about eleven feet long, shouted: "Look out," and reached out for the cannon. The fearful explosion which followed left us in doubt which came first, the cause or effect. He turned on his heels with an air of bravado, lighted another cigar and smoked, because a short cigar will answer the purpose as well as a long one, and the harder he drew the more he was able to get out of it before he was called upon to officiate.

Amid the din of intermittent explosions from the before-mentioned cannon and shouts from some enthusiasts there were others laboring at speech-making. But Lewis and I were there for no such edifying purpose as listening to speeches. Our attention was completely given over to the cannon and locomotive, to neither one of which we dared venture too close. The cannon was religiously guarded by the inveterate cigar man with the split stick, and, if we got too close to the locomotive, it was only to be made a target of by the fireman and engineer, who seemed to take special delight in squirting hot water and steam at us. But, be that as it may, it was a great day for us. The railroad was ushered into our community.

About this time, or it might have been a few years earlier, the long-talked-of plan of building a new house bade fair to become a reality. Father and Mother had for many years been cherishing the fond idea of someday being able to build a house that would provide room and comfort for their grow-ing family. To us boys it meant a change from the trundle bed and the cold upstairs to cozy bedrooms. They were fascinat-ing moments for us when Father and Mother would sit down to plan and talk on the all-absorbing question. Arguments for and against were thoroughly considered and disposed of one by one. Of course we could see no reason for delaying mat-ters, but Father, who had to finance the deal, had to know beforehand how he would be able to meet the cash require-ments as they came along, as it was very much against his nature to take advantage of the credit system.

On the 7th day of October 1874 something happened which was enough to give zest to everything. It was namely this: we could from that time and on say that we had a sis-ter. Her advent into the world gave a new light and color to everything.

Many resolutions were made and adopted and, if any girl was promised luxury, comfort, and protection in this world, she was. Father must have been affected in the same manner because shortly after the before-mentioned date he was known to have made tracks across the prairie for the express purpose of consulting Ola Sandness, the carpenter, in regard to the new house. After one of these visits, and after going down to the hog yard, where he had a good-sized bunch of Chester White hogs, and after having examined each individual carefully, he volunteered the information that if the price reached three cents per pound, they would about pay the lumber bill. This, together with what he believed he could get for a young team, Prince and Queen, which he thought he could spare, he believed sufficient for the undertaking without being classed among the reckless ones. That affair was now settled. Ola Sandness was forthwith engaged and was to commence operations the following spring.

In order to have things on a firm and safe basis, it became necessary for Father to make a trip to Nevada to consult the lumber dealer, Wm. Lockridge, and get the exact figures on the lumber bill as specified by Ola Sandness. I remember there was some brain-racking study as to what grade of shingles to use, whether it would be *star A* or *star A star*, but it was finally settled in favor of *star A star*.

Everything was now in readiness for the hauling home of the lumber, which would have to be done during the following winter. I can clearly remember the two first loads that were brought home. Our old friend Syvert Meltvedt and his team Polly and Jim brought one of them and Father's old Charley and young Frank the other. That winter was an exceptionally severe one, but in spite of zero weather and blizzards Father kept hauling lumber from Nevada.

I remember one evening after he got home that he told us that he had come very nearly giving in while crossing a certain stretch of prairie on the way home. He was overcome by a drowsiness that came very close to upsetting his reasoning powers. All he wanted was to go to sleep. He was just on the point of halting his team for the purpose of taking a little nap, when all of a sudden the thought flitted through his mind that this is just exactly the way people feel when they are on the point of freezing to death. This stirred him up so that he put up a pretty brisk fight for his life, which ended in shakes and shivers equal only to the ague. Another time he came home with one of his cheeks frozen.

We had no thermometer, but the way he tested the temperature was in this way: he would get up very early in the morning, build a roaring fire in the stove, and if the heat from the stove was sufficient to thaw a little on the frosted east window, he would consider it safe to venture out on his trip to Nevada. His rule was always to get started from home so early that the sun would not rise before he had passed one mile beyond Paul Thompson's place, a distance of about ten miles.

During this construction period a young man by the name of Lewis Anderson was our schoolteacher. He boarded with us and even during vacation made our place a sort of a home and good reason why, because our Aunt Martha stayed with us. Later he made her his wife. Their wedding was celebrated at our home immediately after our new house was finished and furnished. He captivated us boys by telling us stories from the wilds of Dakota, where he, together with his parents, had resided prior to his coming here and from where they had been starved out by the grasshoppers and driven out by the Sioux Indians. He was an expert at archery and taught us how to make bows and arrows of the Sioux Indian pattern. During the terms that he acted as our teacher all intermissions were given over to practice with our bows and arrows, a dangerous pastime but fortunately no eyes were lost. 'Tis true I brought Jake Weltha to earth by hitting him squarely in the temple, but he got over it soon, and shooting was resumed and kept up just as briskly as ever.

One day one of Anderson's friends from the Indian country came to visit our school. That day at twelve o'clock Anderson announced to us that the afternoon would be given over exclusively to the Indian. That was a great day for us boys and the girls as well, not to mention Anderson and his friend, who seemed to enjoy the sport as much and more than any of us. I introduce Lewis Anderson at this juncture of my history because he will play a part in some of our undertakings later.

When our little sister had reached the age of about three weeks, preparations were made for her baptism. Bertha Kjerstine was to be her name, and a good fat goose was to be awarded first honor on the day of her baptism. A dinner must needs be given in her honor that would outshine any or all of her predecessors. For this there was no sign of jealousy shown. How could we begrudge our only sister, the finest girl on earth, this rare treat, especially since we're to have a lion's share in it? Our excellent neighbor Kathrine Meltvedt was to attend to the cooking of the goose, while Lewis and I were to stay at home and lend her such assistance as she might see fit to impose upon us. We were supposed to supply the house with wood, and I can remember we helped her peel and mash potatoes.

Nehemias and Henry went with Father and Mother to church. Mr. Knutson can remember to this day the questions we had up for discussion while we were preparing the dinner. They were mostly deep theological questions treating on the baptismal rites. Some time was also taken up by translating from Norwegian to English some parts of Luther's catechism. My recollection is that we thought we had to wait an unmercifully long time before the folks and guests arrived from church. 'Tis true ministers in those days made their sermons rather long; it happened quite frequently that a sermon would last for two hours. She geared her cooking for a two-hour sermon and hit it just right.

I can remember no particulars in connection with the dinner except that I felt very much insulted because there was not room for all of us at the table and I was obliged to wait. I made some remarks which were not at all in keeping with the occasion and for which I ought to have been spanked, but I was spared this humiliation. I was subdued, however, so that I felt like a two-cent piece in Andrew Carnegie's pocket by stora fastero, who just at the crucial moment laid one of her hands on my mouth and with the other hand gave one of my ears a very gentle squeeze. Her face, which she could at a moment's notice change into expressions to suit any and all occasions, at this moment assumed an expression which was a combination between a frown and a smile. Take it all in all, this dinner, as well as all old-time company dinners, was looked upon as an event, and I for one can certainly never forget this particular one.

About this time the serious question was raised among the settlers, how to manage to see the cattle through the grazing season. The prairie was rapidly being changed into farms and homes. We had to go through a straight lane two and one-half miles long before we reached the open prairie. The only fence known was the rail fence, and it would be out of the question to partition certain tracts for pastures. For the purpose of trying to solve this problem the settlers gathered at our house one evening. The result of this meeting was that after this the cattle must be watched and herded. This verdict came right home to me with a stunning force because I knew that I was the only one available at our place that could be employed for any such purpose.

The plan was as follows. There were seven cattle owners, and each one was to put in one day out of each week to look after the cattle. Now it so happened that Kallavaag and old Gjert had no children, and it devolved upon the rest to find volunteers. Jakob's Kittel was duly examined and thought to be a likely candidate, but he was dismissed from further consideration on the grounds that he was to read for the minister the following summer. Baara Erik was also mentioned, but his father could not spare naught. Lewis was also booked for preparing for confirmation, and I was the only one left to consider. They made short work of it now. I was appointed. That night I went to bed with a heavy heart and swollen eyelids. I knew too well what it meant to be out on the prairie all alone three days out of the week and in all kinds of weather. I remember how Mother tried to comfort me by telling how she had herded sheep in Norway when she was a little girl, and if it came to the worst probably Nehemias could go with me. And then a bright idea struck her, why not get a dog?

This last suggestion had an invigorating influence on me. I just thought if I had a dog that lonesome feeling which always came over me when I was out on the prairie alone would, to a great extent, be allayed. I therefore immediately set out to try to get this, my heart's desire, appeased. The vacancy made by Tige's departure must be filled and at once, because it would naturally take some time to train a dog that would be equal to the occasion the following spring.

The first one that I took into my confidence and whom I thought might be able to put me on the scent of my much coveted dog was my intimate friend and seat-mate at school, Martin Henderson. Whispering was not allowed during school hours, and the culprits who were caught at it were most rigidly prosecuted, but in spite of this I managed to tell Martin what my mind was brimming over with. But conversation was a spasmodic effort because we were ever within the radius of Anderson's eagle eye and not outside of his range of hearing. His sense of hearing was most wonderfully developed, owing, we thought, to the fact that he was from the Indian country. This is what Martin told me: Henry Henderson's Penny was then convalescing, and the cause of the whole trouble was half a dozen pups which had been thrust upon her care, and he was sure they would be good ones because their dog, Prince, the oracle of the community, was not altogether a disinterested party.

After school that day I took the liberty of going with Martin, who said he would go with me for the purpose of viewing those pups and what was more probably secure one. I knew I would stand a good show with our splendid neighbor, Henry Henderson. He was a man who had never been known to have been out of humor, and what was still more important to us boys, he always gave the impression that he could not get away from the fact that he had been a boy himself. Perhaps for this reason we so readily fell in with him, or he with us. Another thing that raised him in our estimation and made him tower above the average mortal was that he was a champion speller, and all schools within a radius of at least ten miles were forced to consider him as such.

The schools in those days were ever on the warpath wielding big words at each other. Whenever we received a challenge of this sort the invulnerable one was always consulted, and we very frequently prevailed upon him to hitch up his mules to his bobsled and take as many of the young folks as he could carry to the scene of action. He did not seem to know when he was loaded to the limit for he would invariably say: "There is always room for one more." Talk about sleigh rides! With open prairie before him, he would head the mules directly for the schoolhouse and get them into a swinging lope, which would be highly intensified on downgrades. When we reached our destination, there would be shouting: "Hurrah for the Sheldall school!" The ranks were soon formed and filled, and then the thinning-out process began. A goodly portion of us usually went down during the first preliminary volleys. I could seldom withstand the siege very long. But what did I care as long as our champion held his own! Broadside after broadside was hurled at him, until McGuffy's spelling book was exhausted. At this stage he was usually the only surviving one. This was literally a case of the survival of the fittest. The pronouncer with an air of "I'll fix you" reached out for *Webster's Unabridged Dictionary* and deluged poor Henry so unmercifully with words that he finally succumbed. Now came our time. If we couldn't spell, we could cheer, and with an extra hoop and hurrah for the Sheldall school we soon found ourselves behind the mules and rapidly disappearing out of the hubbub.

This champion speller was the owner of Penny and her pups. Upon hearing what I wanted, he hurriedly said: "Select your pup and come and get him as soon as he can safely leave his mother." He was a man of few words, but he could spell them. The honor of selecting the pup I bestowed upon my friend Martin. He naturally favored the one that had the closest resemblance to his dog, Prince, and I will say right here that I never had the occasion to rue Martin's selection. But poor Prince, little did he dream that he was the author of a being that would become a rival, that would be more than an equal to him as a scrapper and in general usefulness.

About four weeks after the selection had been made, Henry told Martin that he thought I had better come and get my pup. Martin said nothing to me about it but surprised me the following evening by bringing him over. Mother fell in love with him at once, but Father shook his head and said he had had just about enough of this dog business. But we could see beneath the surface that his real feelings belied this statement. Mother already had a name for him. We had just at this time been reading a continued story out of the *Youth's Companion* which dealt with some sort of a pet animal, what kind an animal it was I cannot remember, but at any rate it developed into the hero of the story. The name of this creature was Chip, and it was unanimously accepted.

The first evening we put him into a substantial box and placed him in Mother's old cook shanty. We put the door up as usual, but Penny, led by his pitiful howls and yelps, made it her business to come over here every evening for at least two weeks and tear down either the door or other parts of the building so that she effected an entrance and appeased the cravings of the inner dog. She also tried to carry him away but was unable to lift him out of the box. It is believed by some that if the mother dog is partial towards any one of her pups that this one will be the flower of the flock, and anyone would do well in selecting him. Judging from the way Penny demolished that poor old cook shanty we must have hit upon the right one.

Of all the buildings we ever had or are ever likely to have on the Follinglo Farm, Mother's old cook shanty will stand as number one in my estimation. Here we sat, the string of us lined up along the wall on the elm log foundation, watching Mother as her deft fingers prepared those much sought edibles, such as fried cakes, *kringla*, and other delicacies of which we have never tasted the like since. It was there while she was manipulating the rolling pin on some piecrust or lefsa that we sat vying with each other what we would do when we became a force that would make itself felt in the financial world, each one trying to outdo the rest in making rash promises as to what we would buy for Mother and our little sister. The offerings we mostly planned on laying at their feet were sweets of some kind, never anything smaller than barrelfuls, and they would run up into the hundreds and thousands. Talk about memories that are sweet, what could equal these in sweetness?

The dimension lumber in this old shanty was made out of logs from the timber. The foundation was hewn out of good-sized elm logs and rested on four cornerstones. This structure was not provided with a floor, thus a splendid rustic seat was the outcome, although it was never intended as such by the architect. Every Saturday afternoon our beaming countenances were very much in evidence, for it was then after the floor scrubbing had been attended to that Mother's pastry work would have to be done. It was in this much adored building that Chip took up his abode. I was allowed to keep him there until the warm weather set in, when it would again be claimed as a cook shanty.

Now it was up to me to care for him in such a way that he might possibly develop into a dog by the time that the prairie should be ready to receive me and my charges. That spring the windflowers came very early, those wonderful little elflike beings of the wild prairies, just about as delicate as nothing at all. This and other signs betokened an early spring. I always used to welcome this change of season, the beautiful life-giving springtime, but not so this season. It meant my exile to the prairie.

I shall never forget that first morning when I started out with the herd entrusted to my care. I had one hundred and seven in all, nearly all of which were of the leggy type, indicative of untiring traveling ability. Salrei, who was still with us, of course, took the lead, and Plomrei, a low-down dumpling-shaped cow, always lagged behind. To secure a golden mean between these two extremes always caused me an endless amount of trouble and worry. I, of course, brought up the rear, and a very cheap looking article I was indeed. With tear-stained eyes, a little haversack fastened to a strap thrown over my shoulder, into which Mother had tucked as many dainty morsels as she could lay her hands on, and my catechism. In my right hand I held a twine which was tied securely around Chip's neck. I had made up my mind fully on one thing and that was that I would never let go of the twine, come what may, before I had him safely home again.

When I reached the first crossroad, I received my last consignment. The one who brought them was no less of a personage then Kallavaag himself. The first thing he accosted me with was, "Ka i vero vil du me den hoen (What in the world do you want with that dog)? You must not allow that whelp to chase the cattle, it would be their ruin." With these words ringing in my ears, I was cut off from mankind for the first time in my life, the full length of a day.

No sooner had I reached the open prairie before the much dreaded bulls commenced to bellow defiance at each other from all directions. This opened up the sluices of my tear ducts again; and Chip, being accustomed to nothing outside of Mother's cook shanty, tried to cuddle up between my legs while I was in the act of walking. This impediment of dog and twine between my legs had the blessed tendency of distracting my attention from the bulls for the time being, but this soothing spell was not mine for keeps. The huge monsters soon hove into sight. What puzzled me not a little was how my cows could view this onslaught with so much unconcern. This gave me another soothing spell. But when they set aside all conventions and plunged right into my herd snorting, puffing, and bellowing, tearing up the ground with their hoofs and horns, and then knowing from former experience that this was only an introduction to the real drama, because the fight had yet to follow, I was on the point of breaking down completely. But I rallied again upon seeing how completely my cows ignored the whole fuss. It did not even seem to affect their appetites in the least.

Chip and I got another respite which was just long enough for us to form the following resolutions: First, we must bow to the inevitable. Second, we must grin and bear it. Third, this is the way we are supposed to be initiated. Fourth, we shall get used to it. And then the bulls clashed their weapons, and the battle raged in all its fury. It must be decided then and there which one should be the champion for the season.

I might as well add right here that I could never get used to those bullfights. But not so with Chip. He not only got used to them, but he saw to it that none of them took place in his vicinity. That first day I thought the cattle would never settle down to business. They did not seem to understand that they belonged in one bunch. Salrei was always on the lookout for new worlds to conquer, and Jone Graav's Gulddokka seemed to have the same ambition but always in a different direction. Others were similarly bent, and still others had no ambition at all but fell in with the different leaders. Others again, such as Plomrei, cared for nothing but rest. Thus I was kept on the go all day long, hampered not a little by my dog and twine, for I never dared let go of him for fear of losing him. I did not know it then, but I realized later that I was pursuing the correct method in the training of my dog.

Owing to the restlessness among the cattle, it was quite late in the day before I dared unsling my haversack and think about our dinner. I believe I could at this very day, in spite of corn- and grainfields, locate the very spot where Chip and I made our first attempt at dinner on the prairie. I can't say that I enjoyed it, because there was a lump right above the region of my stomach that had the mortifying art of communicating something to the brain which in turn would affect the gland which furnished the liquid to the tear tank. This sympathetic action of all nerve centers made it next to impossible for me to swallow anything that day. The splendid lunch that mother had taken such pains to fix up for me had to go very nearly untasted.

I thought that first day would never come to an end. I kept my eye on my shadow all the time, for I was waiting for a certain angle to determine the time of day suggested by Father for my return home. Hardly had this angle been reached when I thought I was justified in rounding up my cattle. Now I worked with a vengeance. The first move meant that I was on my way home. The provoking lump disappeared. Appetite asserted itself, haversack was ransacked, favorite melodies rent the air, even shapeless cadences were resorted to.

What mattered anything now? I was on my way home. Cows and strange bulls were all gathered into the same fold. I wished that I could have shaken off at least some of those bulls, but they all stayed with us. What would Kallavaag say if this troop of actors should decide to escort his cows home? In fact what would anybody say? If they were left outside of the cow yard, they would break in; and, if taken into the yard, a man's life would be hanging in the balance while milking the innocent cows that brought them there. And not only that, but in their deadly struggle for supremacy they would bump up against the fence and break out. And last but not least, the free reign of pandemonium would absolutely prohibit sleep as the bulls tried to escape. All this material for a free entertainment I was bringing home with me, and who would it strike?

After this nerve-racking day's work, I was so tired that I could hardly stand on end, but I was proud that I had lived through it and that all my charges were brought back safe and sound. After depositing my tired dog in his box, I managed to tell Mother that the next day Nehemias would have to go with me or I should be compelled to throw up my job. I said I could not see how I could live through another day like this one. Nehemias was consulted, and an agreement in my favor was reached. That night my sleep was disturbed by dreams in which bulls of all descriptions figured.

The next morning Chip was attached to the twine again; and, after the whole herd had congregated, we three set out to spend another day on the prairie. When we reached the crossroad, we were doomed to listen to a long lingo from Kallavaag and *gamle* (old) Gjert, who both appeared in person and entered their complaints in regard to the aggregation of bulls which must have given them not a little worry the night before. In reaching the crossroad the evening before, I was fortunate enough in shaking off most of them, among which were all the champions. This day was passed something similar to the first one, but there was less worry and misery for me because there were two of us.

Towards evening Nehemias let utterances fall to the effect that he had had just about enough of it already and that I must not be a bit surprised if he should insist on staying at home the next day. This piece of information gave me the heart-ache, but there was one consolation. If I could manage to live through the next day, there were four days ahead of me in which I would not have to be on duty. These four I would use to good advantage in watching the carpenters who were just then busily engaged in building our new house, something we had all looked forward to with the keenest interest. Not only this, but Lewis and I had extorted a promise from Father and Mother to the effect that this season we would be allowed to go fishing. These thoughts had the effect of banishing for the time being the unpleasantness connected with my work on the prairie. Another thing that helped to relieve our high-strung feelings and soothe our nerves was that the much dreaded bulls all of a sudden took to the prairie in an easterly direction in answer to a challenge hurled at them from among the hills on the east side of Long Dick. We afterwards discovered that there was a herd of about the same size as our own over there among those hills. The bulls had to our great relief other worlds to conquer. We also noticed a horseman followed up by a dog among these cattle. We reasoned that sooner or later we would brush up against this neighbor of ours and wondered what he would look like.

The next morning Chip and I had to start out alone. The lump in my throat asserted itself once more, and tears came and went at regular intervals. The internal volcano had just about spent its fury by the time I reached the first mile limit. Right here our old friend Syvert had just established himself on a new farm of one hundred and sixty acres right at the foot of Springa Hauen. His youngest daughter Julia was just my age, and on seeing me coming, she came out to the road to say good morning. Seeing my miserable face, she must have taken pity on me; and, being of a kind disposition, she volunteered the suggestion, "Why not herd the cattle on this quarter and the south quarter; they certainly ought to be able to find feed enough for one day?" These two quarters cornered up to each other and were yet in the wild prairie state. This splendid suggestion was not thrown to the four winds. It fell on good soil.

Julia saw at a glance that her plan was accepted. She ran up to the house to get her bonnet and came back and said that she would go with me if I would let her. I was only too glad to give my consent. She then called her dog, Rover, and the cattle were headed south instead of east. We ascended Springa Hauen, where we could look down upon all the surrounding country, and then selected twelve uniform pebbles and settled down to a game called monka. After getting tired of this we played mumble peg. The day that started in so dark and dreary was changed into a day of keen enjoyment, thanks to Julia.

That evening when I came home Lewis had everything in readiness for a trip to the river, his poles, hooks, lines, and a generous supply of angleworms. It was conceded in those days that the fish took more readily to bait after dark, especially if there was a huge bonfire on the riverbank. We accordingly tried to live up to all rules and regulations. It was with some misgivings that Father and Mother let us go on this our first fishing excursion, but we had to promise them faithfully not to venture too close to the bank. Father declared without reserve that he would eat raw each and every fish — scales, slime, and all — that we might catch and bring home. Accidents might happen we thought, and it should be no fault of ours if he did not have occasion to rue this rash promise. At the bottom of our hearts, though, we were very much afraid that he would be only too safe, but this, of course, remained to be seen.

We set out after supper. When we got to the edge of the timber, the stillness of the forest had the tendency of bringing forth symptoms of my prairie lump, and I clung to Lewis just like a sandbur. He was not any too brave himself and had very little nerve to spare. Just as we entered the timber we were gradually enveloped in darkness. One halting word from Lewis would have been enough to have given me the momentum for a heedless stampede. I dare say that a single hoot from an owl would have been more than enough to have given us both the impetus, but as luck would have it they kept still and kept all their strength in reserve until the time came for our exit. There was a single trail through the thick of the woods, and we imagined that this had been made by some war party of Sacs and Foxes; but, if the truth had been known, we could very safely have laid the blame to old man Grindheim's cows. To make matters worse our fish lines got tangled up every once in a while in passing through the narrow trail, which was hemmed in closely on both sides by thick underbrush. I do believe that if a whippoorwill had not come to our rescue that Father's prophecy would have been verified. But no sooner had he sounded than our courage returned.

From this moment our poor Father was destined to get his fill. After a slow struggle that lasted only a few minutes we emerged through the brush and came into a little clearing right on the bank of the river. Here we decided to throw in our hook and try our luck. But first we must gather some driftwood and get a beacon fire by which to lure the fish shoreward. We were at first a little bit skeptical as to the safety of our fingers when it came to thrusting them under the bushes of driftwood because beneath them there might be hidden some kind of venomous reptile. What we feared most at such places along the river was the black snake.

In spite of all imaginary obstacles in our way, we very soon had a roaring fire going. By the light of this fire all fear of hobgoblins vanished. We soon had our hooks in the water and were immediately rewarded by a bite. Judging from the way that the cork was maltreated and had to bob up and down in the water, there could be nothing smaller than a whale at the other end of the line, and it would have to be treated accordingly. I, therefore, gave a tremendous jerk, which threw the whale way over the treetops and got my line entangled in the branches of a maple tree about twelve feet from the ground. At the same time Lewis had a bite and wanted to be wise and profit by my disaster. He was too lenient and had the pleasure of seeing his fish roll from the bank and into the river again. Our blood was now up; we saw that we had a supply to draw from, but it was up to us to regulate our jerks so that we would reap some fruit from our labor, and further-more it was up to me to get my line disentangled from that maple tree. How we got it down I don't remember, but when we got to work again a fine string of bullheads was the reward of a couple hours of fishing.

We counted our fish and decided that we had enough for breakfast. The owls commenced to hoot, and we beat a hasty retreat for home. Upon looking back we could see the glim-mer of our fire among the trees. This in combination with the mournful cadences and wailings of the owls had its effect on our fertile imaginations, and the result was that there was no end to the speed we wished to attain. This rate of traveling soon brought us home, and we deposited our trophy at Fa-ther's feet with an air of triumph and told him to hop to it. After some jesting, we relieved him of the rash promise he had made but upon the condition that he should clean the fish and have them ready for Mother to fix for breakfast. This request was complied with and a splendid breakfast was at our disposal, and was disposed of, the next morning.

This was by no means our last fishing trip. In those days the Skunk River had hidden beneath its effervescent bosom a liberal supply of bass, pike, and pickerel but would yield them up only to patient and proficient anglers. Our piscatorial effi-ciency had not as yet reached this stage, hence we had to content ourselves for the time being by simply listening to what such men as Joren Boyd, Osmund Helgeland, and Anfin

Rindo had accomplished along this line and wait. But more about this later. I must come back to the prairie.

The next victim for the prairie watch was Kittel Grov. The first morning he started out he seemed to be in high spirits but not so in the evening when he returned. Kittel had a vocabulary that was a wonder of the age. I had pictured life on the prairie in no glowing terms. But in listening to this mastermind of description you would have thought I had attended a wedding while he had attended a funeral. The comparison would have been just as great. The bulls had terrorized him even beyond his ability of description. He had even now a lordly looking crew with him in the herd, but he said this was only a small fraction of what he had to contend with out there. These were pets and playthings compared to the rest of them. I tried to console him by saying that he had only one day to my three of this work.

The third co-sufferer on this cooperative deal was Baara Erik. But he came mounted on an Indian pony that his father had bought for him from some Indian while out here on one of their semiannual hunting excursions. Erik was a stout, well-built fellow, and as he sat astride his Indian pony the look of defiance seemed to be stamped all over him. Kittel had poured his tale of woe into him without reserve, but judging from the outward appearance of Erik he seemed to be ready to face the music. In addition to the pony he was rigged out with a regular cowboy whip. Woe betide the bull, man, or bird that would run up against this outfit.

The monotony of the prairie did not seem to affect him like it did his predecessors, at least he had no complaints to offer. He chided Kittel and me not a little for being afraid of nothing, for he was a natural-born tease. To this rebuff Kittel promptly answered: "Me sko vara vaala kara me og vist me hadde naage te ria paa" (We would be brave lads, too, if we had something to ride on). Kittel had a dog by the name of Watch; old man Grov pronounced it Vas. The coming week he declared he would take him along and show those pesky bulls a thing or two.

In the order of routine laid out, Kittel's Ola came next. He was the youngest of the Knutson family or, in other words, if he will pardon me for using the common phrase, the baby of the family. Taking this into consideration and furthermore the fact that he was rather undersized for his age, it was rather a hard proposition for him to face the grim reality of being exiled to the prairie for the full length of a day. Especially so, since he had been forced to digest both my version and Kittel's nightmare description of the undertaking. We can therefore fully excuse him for getting down on his knees and imploring his sister Bella to go with him. In this he was successful, and in her excellent company he survived the day without any serious mishap. But you would not have to go any farther than to him to get corroborative evidence of what Kittel and I had lived through.

Bella had her sewing along and Ole his never-failing pen knife. He was an inveterate whittler. You would never chance upon Ole without that knife in first-class shape. All the figures he would design and whittle out were a caution. He could hardly refrain during school hours. If we wanted to find him all we had to do would be to follow up the fresh shavings, and we would invariably hit upon the subject of our search. Along the path leading from the Knutson place to the schoolhouse and other paths frequented by him his designs were very much in evidence. It was even told that creations from this untiring whittler were found under the old schoolhouse at the time of its removal. Considering the fact that Ole was a nephew of the world-renowned wood carver and sculptor Ole Glosemot, it is little wonder that our friend was thus gifted.

I am unable to remember who the fifth member of this prairie crew was, but I am inclined to believe that it was Andrew Knutson, Julia's brother. Andrew was quite musical; and, since he had no musical instrument upon which he could give expression to his feelings, he had to resort to the means at his command and give expression to his pent-up feelings in some way; this then came out in the shape of whistling. There was no mistaking Andrew when he came along the road or anywhere else, whether in the daytime or after dark.

This art was detested by some of the old people; some of them actually believed that whistling belonged to no other region than the nether one, and he would necessarily have to be tutored by the Devil himself. I believe that, if it had not been for the prejudice against the art, Andrew would have become quite renowned. And he had such a neat way of doing it. It was not necessary for him to draw his lips to a point in order to whistle; he did not even have to change the expression of his face to produce the desired tones and effects. He could laugh and whistle the most difficult strains at the same time. He was a very rapid talker; one could hardly avoid the impression that he had acquired this habit from the fact that he had no time to spend away from his whistling.

If Andrew was the fifth member of the herding crew, I know that his time was well spent. He was a very generous hearted fellow and, like his father, was loved by all in spite of all the whistling. My vacation, to my great sorrow, for the first week had come to an end. If I only had a pony at my command like Erik everything would be different. An idea now struck me and struck home with terrific force. I had noticed that Sampson and Frank Wier, who had always been in the habit of walking when bringing the cows home from the prairie, had one season been allowed the luxury of riding horseback. And the way they could account for it was that they had a mare that had nothing else to do that season but to raise a colt, and if they would be careful and live strictly up to the rules laid down by their father they might use her for fetching home the cattle. This year our Fly bade fair to become in like condition; what would be the matter with my riding her? That was the question I was going to put to Father. Mr. Wier was a very strict man; now if his boys could be granted such liberties I certainly ought to stand a reasonably good chance. The first time I accosted Father on the subject I was rewarded with a half-hearted answer in the affirmative. At any rate I took it as an encouragement.

Since our old friend Mr. Wier's name has been mentioned I think it proper to give a little of his biography. He ran away from his home in New Hampshire at the age of seventeen and went to sea, where he made voyages that brought him into all of the most important parts of the globe. After getting tired of this, he landed and came west. He walked through what later became Chicago. He carried a reserve pair of boots on his shoulder. For this pair of boots and ten dollars, he was offered a lot the regulation size, right by the wall of old

Ft. Dearborn. But he shook his head and trudged on. His aim was Iowa, where he arrived at Clinton County in the year 1836. There he settled down to hunting and trapping and kept this up for eighteen years. When game became scarce, he tried the wilds of Wisconsin for one season. From there he came to what later became our community in the year 1855.

He was an interesting character and when pressed hard enough had many interesting anecdotes both from land and sea to relate. He was brought up in the strict old school, and the same measure though slightly modified was brought to bear on his own boys. His word was just as good as gold. No squirming from the truth with him. Absolutely no shirking from duties around Wier. I remember the day after our sister was born; he could wait no longer; he had to come up and see her. I can remember just how he looked as he stood leaning on his ironwood cane and said, "By Jiminy I just prayed that you should get a dishwasher."

As before stated, my vacation had come to an end. The next Monday morning found me trudging along, Chip in hand again, bound for the prairie. At the crossroad I was met by Kallavaag and *gamle* Gjert; they had come to a mutual agreement that I must not herd the cattle on the quarters. Kallavaag said there was no grass. *Gamle* Gjert chimed in and said that the milk flow was scant and the milk pails looked *hol oigde* (hollow eyed) the evening and morning following my herding on the quarters. I must take them to the open prairie. If the truth must out, I had planned on another day's company with my friend Julia. But this pressed the bottom out of my whole plan, and I felt rather hard against my employers. Still, at the bottom of my heart I knew they were right, for those tracts were being continually cropped close by Knut Phillops' cattle, Christian Logan's, Knut Baker's and Syre Wier's as well, yes even Niklas and Ysten Sevold furnished a few cows. Turn how I please, there was nothing for me this morning but the prairie proper. I had to bow, though very reluctantly, to the inevitable.

Chip and I trudged on, and the monotonous rattle of hoofs did not cease before we had reached the summit of Taalige Lars Hauen. Here the cattle started out in various directions seeking for tufts of grass that would suit their individual tastes, and I dropped down on a boulder to review the past and dream of the future. I found great consolation in caressing Chip and had long talks with him on the burning questions of the day. After some time I lifted my eyes to scan the horizon for familiar objects. My eyes finally got focused on the hills east of Long Dick where again appeared the herd Nehemias and I had seen the week before. This at least gave me something tangible upon which my thoughts could dwell for the time being. What did the manager of the outfit look like? Would he be a congenial companion? Was he big or small, young or old? And what about his dog and horse?

After deliberating thoroughly upon the different questions, my mind was fully made up on one thing, and that was, let him be white or black or even green, I must have someone to speak to or go crazy. I should at least meet him halfway. I accordingly moved my herd eastward; at the same time I thought I could detect a westward move among his cattle. When my herd had come within about a half a mile of the creek, his herd was about the same distance east of the creek. Now what next? I was not left long in doubt, for out of the thick of the herd emerged an object on horseback followed by a dog.

Chip got on his nettle as quick as he saw there was a dog in the outfit. I noticed even at the distance of about a mile that he was laboring hard with his arms and legs, evidently for the purpose of making up speed, but all this energy might have been reserved for something else, for labor how he pleased, the dog was able to keep up without having to change his gait even into a dog trot. There were long intervals when he disappeared from view, as the intervening space was made up of gullies and ridges, but when he finally reached the summit of the last ridge something burst upon my vision that would have tickled Darwin more than it tickled me because this must certainly be the much sought-after missing link.

At first I was undecided whether or not I should run or stand my ground. Chip commenced to bark and tug furiously at the twine, but I soon decided that even though I was clumsy, I could outrun this outfit, barring the dog. Talk about a rag-a-muffin; here it was in all its majesty. And that horse, just as blind as a bat, and he looked as though every muscle on his body had been atrophied for the last two decades. The saddle I can't begin to describe. I shall begin with what ought to have been the hat. There was nothing left of it but the crown, and that had assumed the shape of a cone, tufts of hair stuck out through it at different places, and it gave the appearance of having grown there and being a part of the structure. He had one shirt on, but that was not encumbered by any such thing as buttons. His pants were held somewhat in place by one suspender fastened to its respective place by one ten-penny cut nail and a shingle nail. This description of the clothing will have to suffice because there was nothing more to describe.

When this scarecrow halted a few paces in front of me, I could do nothing else but stare. He returned the compliment by staring at me. I couldn't get it over my lips to speak because I thought this apparition could hardly be connected up in any way with the human family, and then again I did not know what language, if any, to use. Or he might even be one of those deaf and dumb fellows that I had heard some talk about. I looked at his dog, the only redeeming feature in the whole picture. He edged up towards Chip, and the hair along his back started to bristle. It began to look to me as though there would be a dog fight then and there, as Chip showed no signs whatever of backing up. Upon seeing this my visitor called out Fido! sharp and clear; this immediately put a stop to the onslaught. From this moment the ice was broken. I saw now that he was at least an honest attempt at humanity, and I fell in love with him at once. Outward appearance cut no figure with me at all, just so I had someone to speak to.

He now dismounted, and his steed was allowed to shift for himself. I tried to find out where he came from and his family connections, but in this I was not successful. I then was forced to come to the conclusion that he "just grew" like Topsy. I asked him what his name might be, to this he answered John, but most people called him Patta (sucking) John. I then asked him why he had this prefix to his name, and he answered that it was because he was just lately weaned.

Now that we fully understood each other, conversation drifted in other directions. Upon his advice Chip was liberated from the twine and was allowed to romp and play with Fido, who bade fair to become a good tutor. I can recall very little of what we talked about that day, except that he knew where some people had planted turnips and watermelons, a knowledge which was destined to bring us grief later on in the season, and that the next day we would let our cattle mix together and that we could separate them easily when it was time to drive them home.

I remember when we had our dinner I gave Chip a piece of potato cake. Fido, being by far the oldest, thought he had a right to claim it. This was the first time that Chip showed me that he had a principle and that he would die in his tracks fighting for it. He did not desist till he had thoroughly licked Fido and the potato cake remained in his possession without any further dispute.

John offered to let me ride his horse, but this well-meant treat I blankly refused. After some time, he started upon the laborious journey back to his herd, but not before we had made arrangements to meet again the next day. I can't say that I was overly proud over this acquisition of mine, but it meant that the terrible loneliness that I dreaded so much was done away with.

That evening when the time came for me to gather up my cattle and start them home, I was surprised to notice that Chip on his own accord ran around the herd and gathered them up just exactly the way he had seen me do it. If they did not care to move, he would just touch their heels with his nose, and, if that wouldn't start them, he would touch them up a little with his teeth. This would naturally cause some of them to kick; but, to avoid being hit he dropped flat on the ground, and the kick passed over him. Pride because of being the owner of such a dog took possession of me right then and there.

The following two days passed without any notable events taking place. When Kittel's day came around, I took care not to tell him anything about Patta John. On his return in the evening, however, he could tell me that he had seen a "*skrubba skremsla*" (scarecrow designed to frighten wolves) out on the prairie. I knew at once that he had reference to my friend

Patta John. He then proceeded at once to give a graphic description of him. I wish I could have remembered at least part of it; it would certainly have been worthy of record.

As before stated, I was highly elated over my dog's actions the last day on the prairie. I have often wished that I had had a picture of this noble animal. After he got to be fully developed he would compare in size with a large Scotch collie with the difference of his being black where many of them have an orange color. His breast was just as white as snow.

I remember on one occasion that Chip and I, though unknowingly, played quite a trick on Mother. It was one evening just as she was preparing supper that I came driving home from the field, and I had Chip with me seated at my side in the spring seat. Upon seeing this Mother hurried to tell Martha Oespever, the hired girl, to put an extra plate on the table for there was swell company coming home with Peder. In those days a man with a white bosom shirt on wasn't seen every day. Mother didn't hear the last of this for many a day.

Chip had quite a heavy coat of hair, which I suppose had much to do with his great fighting ability. Many or few opponents made no difference to him; he was never known to be the underdog. Nothing was allowed to fight in his presence. He wouldn't even allow us boys to scuffle or wrestle nor permit strangers to pitch onto us. He just could not bear to see anything overdone. For instance, if people drove by someplace too fast to suit him, he would see to it that they would slow down to a reasonable gait.

He had it especially in for Taalige Lars Christian, who always was in the habit of driving faster than the regulation gait laid down by Chip. Christian tried to thwart him and used the whip on both him and his horses, but next time when he came along at the usual breakneck speed wielding the hateful whip, Chip stood ready by the roadside and jumped right into his wagon, walked up to his seat, and gave him a look that was sufficient to bring the desired result. The horses were stopped at once; Chip got out, sat down by the roadside, and gave him a look as if saying, "You can go on, but keep to the speed limit." Christian told me this himself so that I know it to be a fact.

Another thing that he absolutely would not stand for was

that anybody should drive or ride past us while on the road, that is if our speed was what he considered to be reasonable. I remember one Sunday on our way to church, Pete Egland came riding horseback at a breakneck speed; this was too much for Chip, and he stopped him before he had covered a stretch of twenty rods. The queerest part of it all was that Pete could not figure out why his horse behaved so strangely, for no sooner had he urged his horse into a run than he started to kick and jump in such a furious manner that Pete had to allow him, as he thought, to select his own gait, little dreaming that it was Chip that was managing the whole business.

The only time I ever saw Chip outdone was once when he tried to stop Baara Erick. He was riding a young spirited horse which was considered one of the champion racehorses of our community. Chip did his level best, but he could never come any closer than within about three rods of his heels.

At another time when we together with many others in a long procession of lumber wagons on the way home from church at Story City, old man Osmund Riveland was riding his old steady family horse. He was of a very loving nature and wished to move along the line for the purpose of greeting everybody. He naturally had to urge his horse into a trot in order to reach the foremost ones, but Chip was at his heels at once, and the old horse started to kick and plunge. Chip showed no partiality but treated them all alike, whether it was our old friend Riveland bent on a worthy mission or a sport out for a lark. It made no difference to him. His rules would have to be respected. Of course we did not sanction this and tried to break him of the habit, but it was impossible.

Chip showed in many ways that his intelligence was way above that of the average dog. It happened one day that our cattle broke down a panel of Henry Henderson's fence and got into his cornfield. It was shortly after the roasting-ear season, when it is considered very dangerous for cattle to indulge freely. Father was very uneasy over our cattle and for our good neighbor's cornfield as well, so I called Chip and got to the opening in the fence in short order. He seemed to understand that there was something wrong without ever having seen anything like this before. He grasped the situation at once, plunged right into the cornfield, and let out a few furious barks to let everybody concerned know that he was in dead earnest. This was enough to bring nearly all of them back to the opening. The remaining stragglers he brought out one by one. Father was now fully converted and confessed freely and of his own accord that a dog like that was worth having.

Poor Chip was always uneasy when any one of us happened to be away from home, especially so if we stayed away overnight. He absolutely refused to taste food before the delinquents had returned. He acted as though he was responsible for everything that belonged on the Follinglo Farm.

There was one thing that Chip absolutely refused to have anything to do with, and that was skunks. He also kept entirely aloof from shotguns or any kind of firearms. He had an inborn antipathy against anything that savored of explosions. Thunder and lightning drove him home even from his duty. It would never do to take Chip along if we wanted to go swimming. He would not allow us to jump into the river, and, if we did so in his presence, he would jump in after us, grab ahold wherever he could, and haul us out. If we tied him on the bank, the poor fellow would howl and whimper so pitifully that we had to desist from our sport, and the way he would lick our hands and show his happiness in getting us all out safe and sound would have made quite a study for an artist.

Many things could be related about this dog friend of mine, but we must go back to other doings. This was a very busy season on the Follinglo Farm. The house must be finished before the cold weather set in, farm work must not be neglected, and all material such as lime, brick, paint, and oil had to be hauled from Nevada. A clear head was very essential because it simply would not do in those days to forget anything considering the distance that had to be covered in order to get them. Mother had her share of work that season; the carpenters, Ola Sandness and *gamle* (old) Mattis, the mason and plasterer Ola Mathison, the painter Nels Meland, and later on another painter, Ola Ros, together with the teacher Lewis Anderson and Mother's own brood demanded three square meals a day.

I believe this summer will always be remembered by Henry,

and for the reason that *gamle* Mattis could not eat pie or cake. The kind old man must have taken a special liking to Henry, because he would always say, "Kom hit Henrik aa faa paien min" (Come here Henry and get my pie), an invitation which was always accepted. The rest of us, and especially Nehemias who also liked pie, threw wistful glances at old Mattis's pie, but it never came our way. It is held by some authorities that pastry will make people fat. Who knows but what his over-indulgence accounts for the extra avoirdupois that was added to Henry's frame?

Lewis thought he had his share of work to perform this season. Most of the fieldwork was left to him, and then he had his lessons to learn and recite to the minister once a week. Of course I had the worst job of them all. Fly's colt was not three weeks old, and I was promised that I might ride her the next day. The next morning found me mounted as proud as you please on Fly's back. Her colt and Chip brought up the rear. I was supposed to live up to the following orders. First, not to ride too fast. Second, to dismount as soon as the herd had settled down to grazing and allow Fly to eat grass. Third, to water her at noon.

To dismount was easy enough, but to get mounted again out on the prairie where there was nothing any higher than the ground itself to get on top of was a proposition that I had never thought of before I was brought face to face with the grim situation. Fly was quite tall, and I was just the opposite, and fat and clumsy at that. I tried to figure out some feasible plan, and the result was that I grabbed her mane and tried to worm up along one of her forelegs. I tried to get one foot on each side of the knee joint, and, being barefooted, I could do this without worrying Fly too much. My first attempt was a failure. I tried it again but noticed that Fly's ears commenced to turn my way. This was a gentle hint that she was getting tired of this business. I, therefore, immediately let go my hold and came down to earth as quickly as possible. I then fell to petting and caressing her in a vigorous manner until I thought in this way that she could be made to forget all about it.

The third and last attempt might have brought about a victory if it had not been for the colt that just at the crucial moment when I had brought my toes over the backbone all of a sudden felt the pangs of hunger and came up to nurse. This brought the ears down and out of sight at the very same time that her teeth brought up against the most prominent and outstanding part of my anatomy. This made me forget again what I was trying to accomplish and down to earth I came again with a thud. I felt now that I was down and out and not only up against it but down against it and I was almost as far, if not farther, away from reaching my goal as ever. The question was not what should I do, but what could I do next?

As I lay there nursing my wound I made up my mind fully on one thing, and that was, if in some way I should get on top of that mare, I would, regardless of all rules and regulations, stay until I reached home. In one of my former trips on the prairie I had occasion to witness one of the Eide girls in a similar plight, but she had formulated a plan that had helped her out of the predicament! I laughed at the time, little dreaming that I should be called upon to resort to the same method myself. This is the way she did it. She watched her chance when the horse had his head down in the act of nibbling grass and then she flung her foot over the horse's neck. After getting somewhat balanced, she gave the horse a gentle tap on the nose with her foot, and up she went just like being lifted by a hoisting drum. After the horse's head was up, it was an easy matter to slide headfirst down his back, turn completely around, and acquire the position desired. This she did and was off like the wind a good deal quicker than can be told. Now it was up to me to perform the same stunt or be reduced to the humiliating condition of walking home. This would never do, for hadn't I begged and implored and even made mild threats in order to gain what I was now in possession of? And then to be outdone? No, that would never do.

I studied and pondered and thought perhaps some other avenue might open because I dreaded the performance very very much. But study how I might, no idea would suggest itself. There was nothing for it now but to imitate Miss Eide. Bent upon not being outdone this time I walked bravely over to Fly's neck. I could not help but notice, however, that her ears had an inclination of a downward trend, but by much stroking and petting I brought them back to a somewhat normal position. After they had gained what I considered a permanent equilibrium, I made a desperate plunge and flung my leg over her neck, clutched fiercely at the mane, and the show was on.

Fly did not wait for the gentle tap; I was flung up just like an arrow from a spent bow, and my nose started to plow along her vertebrae at the rate of twenty miles an hour. In spite of all the friction I was able to create by clutching with my hands and rigidness on the part of my legs, the force from the sudden impact was not broken before my nose had just about reached the base of the tail. The turning around process would have been comparatively easy if Fly had not worked herself up into a swinging trot that threatened to dislodge me as I was, let alone trying to turn around. It would never do to allow myself to be outwitted. Therefore, under great stress, attended by some bodily pain, I made a desperate effort that brought me in position just as Fly broke into a gallop. During this acrobatic feat the idea came to me that Fly should be left at home and stay there as far as I was concerned. Owing to the excruciating pain brought on by having to hang on Fly's back so long, I started my cattle for home earlier that evening than usual.

It was a warm, sultry evening. I remember just as I got home that Anderson came home from the schoolhouse with very rapid strides. When he got close enough so that he was able to reach us with his voice he said: "Boys go and dig some angleworms this evening; we must go fishing. The weather is just right for a record-breaking bullhead catch." The bad effect of all the trials and tribulations I had lived through during the day was immediately swept away upon hearing this.

After an early supper we set out. Now since we had Anderson with us, we could honestly and truthfully quote the old song and say, "We are not brought up in the woods to be scared by the screech of an owl." Nothing either real or imaginary was allowed this evening to distract our attention from what we set out to do. After our fire had been made to our liking, fishing was on in real earnest. As Anderson had foretold it was, and ever afterward remained with us, a record-breaking bullhead catch.

As we sat on the riverbank tugging away at our bullheads, Anderson would tell us stories from the wilds of Dakota. He had, by the way, been back there during the hunting and fishing season the year before. Among other things he told us about a bear hunt, and after the story was told he showed us the bear claws that had belonged to the very bear in question.

It became necessary once in a while to gather driftwood. I for one showed some signs of uneasiness because I had a mortal dread that I might run up against some kind of snake, and what we dreaded the most was the rattlesnake. Anderson noticed this and told us that he did not believe that there was any danger as he had never seen a rattler anywhere along the Skunk. After we got quieted down again, he pulled an envelope out of his pocket and asked us if we could guess what it contained. We tried everything but failed. He hauled out a monster bullhead, rebaited his hook, and then told us that it contained a tail of the biggest rattlesnake that he had ever seen. He asked us to count the rattlers, and there were fourteen of them. He then proceeded to tell us that he had shot him while walking through a prairie dog village while on one of his hunting excursions in the Dakotas the previous fall.

This led up to many questions and answers touching upon the habits of that cute animal, the prairie dog, and their great scourge, the rattlesnake. This evening stands forth as one of the prominent milestones in my recollections. Lewis Anderson showed in many ways his love for nature and natural things and took pains to impart his superior knowledge to his scholars.

It happened during one of his spring terms of school at the old Sheldall schoolhouse that a large band of Sacs and Foxes from the Liscomb reservations pitched their tents about half a mile southwest of the schoolhouse. It struck Anderson that this would be a good chance for his scholars to study the real Indian. They were a motley collection of Indian hunters and squaws and a very liberal sprinkling of papooses. He put the question to the school if they wished to visit the Indian camp, and hands went up.

This was a great day for all the children who were fortunate enough to attend school that day. There they could see the young bucks practicing with their bows and arrows, the squaws preparing the meals of soft-shelled turtles, wood squirrels, and other quadrupeds, the papooses rolling around on the ground, and an old warrior that had outlived his usefulness, covered with smallpox scars, leaning up against a tree smoking his pipe. Everything seemed to be accompanied by the musical Indian laugh except the old warrior who was just as sober as the sphinx, evidently nursing a grudge against his white brothers.

At another time during the same term Anderson surprised us by asking us how it would be to spend a couple of hours by the river for the purpose of taking lessons in swimming. He was an expert swimmer and could not have suggested anything that would have suited our fancy any better than this. He provided a place for the girls to play right at the edge of the woods, but we boys marched right by with a superior air bound for the river. The river was flooded way above its banks. This made it necessary for Anderson to locate someplace where the water was shallow enough for us to play in. The place he selected was right by the old ford where the water flowed over a level stretch, making a uniform depth of about three feet. Here he spent some time with us going through the first rudiments of swimming. Then he left us to ourselves and told us to practice diligently and cautioned us over and over again not to venture too near to the river channel proper. He was now in for some sport on his own hook and accordingly plunged right into the swift-flowing current. He got so completely absorbed in the sport that he did not keep his eagle eye on us as closely as he had intended.

No sooner had he been spirited out of hailing distance on the bosom of the noble Skunk than Kittel's Ola and I ventured too close to the bank. I shudder yet when I think of what might have happened. Ola promptly slipped into the current, let out a hoarse, strangled yell, and immediately disappeared. He seemed to have the presence of mind, however, to reach up one of his hands, and for a wonder my slow mind telegraphed my right hand out as quick as a shot and clutched his hand. The grip he gave me I can never forget, nor can I forget the tug of war that ensued. This was a life or death question to both of us. People that have been fortunate enough to never have felt the grip of a drowning person do not know what it means. There were times when I thought I had him, and then again I thought he had me. Once I felt the deep water under one foot and I thought we were both going, but for some unaccountable reason we happened to balance the right way and I was saved. There was no more playing in the water for Ola and me that day, but we were determined on one thing; that we must master the art of swimming.

Anderson will always be remembered by the pupils who had the good fortune of attending his school. He was a strict disciplinarian but always on hand when it came to good, wholesome sport. He took special pains to teach us the value of keeping as close to nature as possible, hence, those expeditions to the woods.

Shortly after he married our Aunt Martha, they moved out into what was then known as the wilds of Nebraska. There, while on a hunting expedition one day in the early spring, while the ice cakes were still floating down the Missouri River, he shot a big white goose, and it happened that this goose fell onto a little island, midstream in the treacherous Missouri. Anderson, who had his little boat with him, thought it would be a small matter to row out there and get his goose. After getting there, he pulled his boat up a little ways on the sand and went to pick up his game.

He was aware of the deceitful tricks of Old Muddy, but that day it must have been in one of its surliest moods, for no sooner had he turned his back on the boat before that part of the island was washed away, and the boat went merrily downstream. He soon found that the little island would not last very many minutes. He therefore strapped his rifle and goose on his back, jumped into the ice-cold current, and swam ashore. The distance he covered was at least half a mile. I am exceedingly sorry to have to chronicle that this was his last hunting expedition. That ice water was too much even for his rigid constitution. He took sick and died shortly afterwards. The news came back to our school district and surrounding country as a sad blow. It was no easy matter to get familiar with the grim reality that our dear old teacher was no more here on earth.

During the season that I was herding cattle two new squatters settled right in our entrance to the prairie. One of them was a big Dane by the name of Johnson. He always wore a full beard on the Tolstoi order. His boon companion was a big black dog, a cross between a mongrel and an Irish setter. This dog was not of a mild nature, hence he was a menace to our movements. Chip decided early that this dog's nature would have to be subdued, and he could not count on anybody else but himself to do it either. The other squatter was Tonnes Tonneson.

Everything went well with our new neighbors until the time that the haying season started. When my cattle saw haycocks galore spring up like mushrooms right on their own free range it was too much for them. Right here they saw a chance for some sport, and all of them, yes even Plomrei, saw it at once. Horns and tails were immediately set at the proper angle, a charge was made, and the haycocks were tossed in all directions before I could even hand in my protest, much less try to prevent it.

While speeding on towards this scene of wild action, I caught a glimpse of a black streak that shot by. This was nothing more nor less than the Dane's dog coming to rescue the haycocks. Now or never thought Chip and was after him in a jiffy. So absorbed was I in watching what was going on ahead that I did not notice what was being brought up in the rear. Just as Chip took the last tail end of pride out of that black dog, thus proclaiming himself king over all dogdom east of the Skunk River, I turned around and beheld the huge Dane with the Tolstoi whiskers and Tonneson coming at full tilt, each armed to the teeth with pitchforks. This was no place to stop to think or reason; my legs would do nothing else but run. There was no question then as to a speed limit; they immediately got into this peculiar string halt action known to, and indulged in, only by nightmare patients. I take no pride in saying it, but it is true nevertheless, that I was carried clear home in this fashion before a halt was even considered.

I immediately poured out my story, but it did not affect Mother the way I had expected; I could plainly detect a humorous twinkle in her eye, which gradually grew into a smile and finally developed into a good laugh at my expense. This had no exhilarating effect on me, and I blankly refused to go back and gather up my herd alone. I cannot recollect at this time who went with me, but it must have been one of the shareholders in that herd. We had a talk with Johnson and

Tonneson, and an agreement was entered into which was to the effect that I should herd the cattle on the quarters the next day so as to give them time to gather in their hay. I rather looked forward to the next day's work because Julia said the evening before that she might spend the day with me out on the prairie. And not only that but it was not necessary for me to provide for dinner as I was expected to take dinner with her folks. The privilege of being able to count on our old friend Syvert as my host was indeed something worth looking forward to.

That morning when Julia let down the bars for their cattle I couldn't help but notice that she was excited about something. As soon as I got within hailing distance she reported that she had seen a terrible big snake right south of Springa Hauen the day before. She further stated that she had told her father and her big brother Albert and even Andrew about it, but they simply laughed at her and said it was just her imagination that was getting the best of her. Andrew wouldn't even stop his whistling long enough to listen to her.

I was the fourth party to whom she made an earnest appeal to go and look for that huge snake. The description of him as he lay coiled up was enough to make the blood run cold through the veins of a braver person than I, let alone to go and search for him. I tried to get out of going to search for him by saying that he would likely be miles away from the place he was seen yesterday and that it would only be wasting precious time that ought to be put into our favorite game of monka. She simply refused to listen to my weak or cowardly excuse but commanded me to come. I must admit that I did not embark on this hunting expedition with any zest worth mentioning. By the way, have you ever tried to search for something that you wished at the bottom of your heart that you would never find? That was the kind of a hunt I was engaged in at this particular time.

Julia led the way to where she had last seen the monster. As we neared the spot, my legs started to give some plain signs that they were ready at any given moment for another demonstration of the string halt action. "Right over there by that tuft of grass, on the other side of that Indian compass is where I saw him yesterday," was what I heard next, and "there he is now!" Julia screamed and grabbed hold of my arm, which by this time hung limp by my side. A snake like this one I had never seen before, nor have I ever seen one since. I believe to this day that he was at least one rod long and in perfect health. The markings were the same as an ordinary bull snake or rattlesnake, but in place of dark gray spots it sported red spots.

We were both of us riveted to the spot, as it were, for a while, but, when we got started to run, it easily put to shame my sprinting of the previous day. When we got settled down to where we were able to talk, we agreed on this that it would simply be tempting fate to try to kill that huge monster. The rest of the day was spent as far as we could get away from the tract of prairie occupied by that snake. Ever since that time I have never ceased to wonder at what kind of a snake that could have been.

The next morning found Chip and me meandering along the lane bound for the big prairie again. This morning I made up my mind on joining forces with Patta John if I could find him. Yes, sure enough, as soon as I reached the prairie where the cattle trails wound off in different directions, I could see Patta John's herd, and I thought I could discern a slight drifting in my direction. I must own that I felt some concern before I had passed Tolstoi's hayfield, but I soon learned that he had lived up to his part of the contract and had moved the hay home, for there right close to his dugout stood a fresh haystack and leaning up against the same stood the Dane fully equipped, ready to wage war against me and my cows should we venture too close, and the big black dog was sitting up on his haunches ready to join in the melee if occasion should arise where his assistance was needed. About twenty rods farther east, leaning up against another stack, stood another sentinel in the shape of Tonneson. I had to run the gauntlet between these two forces as my trail led right in between their respective dugouts. I tried to whistle, but it was all a lie on the face of it, for I had all I could do to keep from stampeding as on the former occasion. Chip's patience was taxed almost to the breaking point because he wanted to get at that black dog once more. Well, I am happy to report that we got through without bloodshed.

Chip

The very first thing Patta John called my attention to that morning was that according to his reckoning of time, weather conditions, and all symptoms of nature, and if dame nature had not deviated from her natural evolution of things and had performed her functions not contrary to old established traditions, the turnip seeds he had seen sowed into the rich soil on Jens Flatebo's farm ought by this time to be developed into good-sized turnips. And further that he considered it up to us to make such investigations on said premises as would leave us no longer in doubt as to the maturity and even flavor of the same. This idea appealed to me very strongly, and without any further consideration or red tape we immediately set out.

This turnip patch was in an isolated place; hence we took no special precautions in trying to sneak off unobserved. And in our eagerness to find out what mother earth held in trust for our special benefit we paid not the slightest attention to Helge Lund, who farmed the land and who lived scarcely a half-dozen stone's throws away from our starting point. If we had but just craned our necks in his direction we could not have avoided noticing Late Jens sitting on the sunny side of their shack with all the time in the world at his disposal, calmly figuring out our maneuvers, and at the same time laying plans to get even with us, with the least exertion to himself. He could have stopped us by just raising his voice, but that was out of the question because it would take more energy than he saw fit to spend.

We found the turnip patch, helped ourselves, and returned satisfied that we had not overdone anything, when to our great surprise we beheld Late Jens coming shambling along in a direction which plainly indicated that if he did not swerve we would be right in his road. This looked rather threatening to us, and the first impulse was to run, but upon second thought we considered this as below our dignity and stood our ground with fear and trembling. A guilty conscience will generally tremble, if not steeped too long in crime, when brought face to face with the proper authorities. Now since this was our first offense we had the full benefit of our consciences.

Not until I saw the fiery gleam in Late Jen's eye did I fully realize the magnitude of our offense. I somehow got the impression that all of this lazy fellow's unused energy had been stored up for this special occasion. As soon as he got close enough he droned out the following questions and with more emphasis then I had ever thought him capable of. "Who gave you fellows a permit to raid our turnip patch?" He did not even give us time to answer before he gave poor Patta John the first broadside. I was next in order, but Chip would not submit to anything of the kind, and he plainly showed Late Jens that he had a hand in this game, and this he did by jumping right in front of me, puckering up his nose, thus bringing to view red gums and white fangs enough to take all the grit out of poor Late Jens. And this ended the whole affair.

A few words here about the Lund family would perhaps not be out of place. There were the father and mother, four boys, and just one girl of whom Jens was the next to the oldest. Humanity in its depraved condition is prone to make outright fun of fellow beings who are unfortunate enough to be burdened with peculiar traits in their general makeup and their way of moving among their fellow men, that is, if they move at all. Now this was the fault with our friend Late Jens; he did not stir unless he had to, hence, this appellation of Late Jens (lazy Jens).

We oftentimes to our great chagrin find that we have misjudged and misinterpreted those peculiarities, and this discovery in nearly every instance is made too late. Later on, when doctors got to be numerous enough so they would reach around, it was found that poor Jens had all those years been suffering from tuberculosis, and not only he, but the entire family, with the exception of their mother, who came to an untimely death by being hit by lightning. She had a mortal dread of thundershowers and would as a rule go down into the cellar while the elements were ripping and tearing outside. After one of these showers she was found dead on the cellar floor. All the rest of the family died as it seemed at regular intervals inside of a few years from the dreaded white plague. Henry, the youngest, my confirmation classmate, lingered the longest. I wish to this day that I had let those turnips alone.

During this season Mother had a girl by the name of Anna Espe to help her with her work. She was of about Lewis's age and our Aunt Julia's, who also stayed with us that season for the purpose of preparing herself for confirmation the following fall in the same class with Lewis. Julia was a bright girl and full of life. She was about one year older than I. Lewis and Anna looked down upon us as a pair of youngsters with little or no experience compared to theirs. Julia, who was of the resourceful kind, always contrived to lay plans and schemes that might in some way outdo our wise rivals. Sometimes we would win out and then again not. I can remember in particular one afternoon Julia came tripping over the lawn brimming over with something. When she got near enough, she called to me and said, "I've got it!"

"Got what?"

"A scheme."

I promptly answered, "I'm game; out with it."

This is what she unfolded. We should challenge them on a fishing contest, and nothing but game fish should be considered. The ones that made the smallest catch must submit to a forfeit of some kind. She felt so confident in winning out that she said in almost the same breath that we would let them off if they would simply acknowledge defeat. I saw in this some wholesome sport and agreed on the spot. Lewis and Anna were sought out at once and just as promptly took the challenge. Julia was now on her mettle and turned to me and said: "Why not cause this to come to a focus right now? Why not make an onslaught on those pickerels this very afternoon? When can we ever expect a more ideal day for fishing?"

These arguments were so convincing that it took a stronger nature than mine to withstand them. Mother was next consulted. We laid before her the whole plan, and since she possessed the blessed nature of seeing and feeling anything that savored of humor, it was entirely unnecessary for us to enter into details. She grasped the situation at once and urged us to get started, the sooner the better. I accordingly set out posthaste to unearth some angleworms. Among our collection of weapons could be seen a huge fishhook from which we intended to dangle a long, limp frog right in the face of the poor pickerel. This was considered by some fishermen to be the best bait. In this particular case the best was not any too good. At the last moment a small minnow hook was added to our outfit; this was intended only for the purpose of luring out dainty morsels in the form and shape of minnows who in turn should lure the pickerel if the frog should for any reason fail us. Little did we dream what remarkable caprice this miniature hook was to play before we got through that day.

When we got to the river we selected the most picturesque place we could find, thinking that this in itself ought to have its effect on our game fish. Right in a bend of the river a big soft maple tree had been undermined by the current and had fallen outward directly across the stream so that its top nearly reached the other bank. It rested squarely on a big branch, which was embedded firmly in about midstream. We were almost tempted to think that the elements had arranged this fairy bridge for our express benefit, and we fancied we could already see some predestined monster pike dangling on our line. We walked trustingly up that log, selected each our respective perch, and dumped in our frog.

We expected all those pickerels out there to show due appreciation at once, but alas not so. Our frog did not seem to cause the least bit of excitement. All the most wonderful actions and gymnastics stunts we witnessed that afternoon would have made an interesting chapter on fish lore if someone interested in gathering material for natural history had just been present. But we were there for no such purpose. In vain we stirred our frog around, moved him from one place to another, but still nothing doing. One pickerel had the audacity to stick his snout out of the water and snap at our line. Right under our log they were gamboling and playing so vigorously that they lashed the water into spray, but our dead frog lived through it all. Joren Boyd, the oracle on fishing, baited his hook with live frogs, but this our nature revolted against. We just simply couldn't do it; we would rather pay the forfeit.

Julia grew frantic over this grand display of fish and nary a one could we lay our hands on and claim as our own. She suggested discarding the frog and baiting our hook with a common, ordinary angleworm. This was done in a very generous way, and no sooner had this new bait disappeared below the surface than we were rewarded by a ferocious bite, but that was all the good it did us. No fish, no bait. We put on a

Chip

new bait, but the result was the same. We kept this up for quite a while with no change whatever; the result was ever and always the same.

By this time Julia got so desperate that she said: "I am tired of dealing out honest worms to this thankless multitude. Tear some hair out of my scalp and tie those measly worms on that hook so they won't come off by being merely sniffed at." This was done, and now ensued a grand tussle with that hook which would under ordinary conditions have insured a catch, and it did in this case also. But all we got for our work, worms, hair, and all was a tiny bullhead about the size of my thumb. Julia was now gradually growing despondent. It was now my turn to try to offer some plausible remedy. I made a hit and miss guess at something and suggested that we must try to secure a minnow for bait. Julia brightened up a little and re-marked we must hurry and get one: it was nearly sundown now, and you know we promised to be home about that time.

This last remark made me hustle. I got my minnow hook baited in a hurry, but where should I go to get my minnow? Our big maple tree evidently brought down by the last flood had stood guarding a narrow isthmus about six rods wide. On the other side of this neck of land the current was much swifter than on our side. I fancied this would be a good place to throw in my tiny hook. As I stood there I could not help but speculate with that huge maple out of the way, how long it would take before the water would cut right through this isthmus.

As I stood there thus speculating I was all of a sudden most rudely interrupted by something terrible at the end of my line. I yelled at Julia and said, "I've got him. Come quick and help get him out!" She needed no second call. She was at my side at once, and together we worked and fought with that record breaker out there, whatever it might be. We had a new strong line, but that minnow hook, how could we expect it to bear the strain? We had to put an end to this suspense. I therefore leaned back and lifted with all my might. The big fellow came out but dropped off the hook so close to the bank that we thought we had lost him for sure. I got between him and the water and started to kick and push as best I could. Not before we had gotten him about halfway between the two channels did we feel justified in saying he was ours. The next thing was judging his weight. Julia declared him to be a fifteen pounder, but I thought twelve pounds would have to be enough.

We lingered no longer at the river that day but picked up our fish and partly dragged and partly carried him home. We laid our catch at Lewis's and Anna's feet and said, "Duplicate this if you can." They frankly confessed that they never expected to be able to catch a fish that would even approach this one in size; so the game was called off, and we decided to go fishing, all of us together, the next fine day. This was our first start on game fish, and a good start it was. I never saw a fish as big as this one taken out of Skunk River either before or since that time. We had no scale in those days, hence we could not accurately determine his weight, but there were twelve in the family to feed, and those twelve did their level best but could not get away with more than half of our pickerel. Julia and I got a fair taste of being worshiped as heroes. To me those fishing excursions were a great balm. I verily do believe that if it had not been for some such delightful variety that prairie job would have been too much for my brain.

There is still one incident from my life on the prairie that summer that is very outstanding among my recollections. It was sometime during the last days of August, or to make it still plainer, it was during the watermelon period, if you please. Watermelons were then, as they are now, much coveted by the boys, and especially so by boys sitting around on the prairie in the scorching sun and denied even a drink of water. I must admit that it sounds kind of fishy, but the fact of the matter was that this particular season was so dry that we were frequently ordered away from some people's wells while in the act of trying to secure a drink. On this particular morning I had Nehemias along, and upon passing by the last house before entering out upon the hot and dry prairie we mustered up courage enough to ask for a drink of water, but the answer came promptly, "De faar injke vatn her" (No water here this morning).

On this part of the prairie there were no natural springs, but there was a splendid watermelon patch not a thousand miles away, and if we could fall in with Patta John that patch would have to be looked into and possibly be made to yield up some of its superabundance in moisture. Sure enough, when we had scaled the summit of Taalige Lars Hauen, Patta John and his dog, Fido, were not over a mile to the east of us. He had left his herd and his blind horse on the other side of Long Dick and came on a forced march to meet us. We found in this case as in so many others the great truth in the old proverb which says, "Great minds run in the same channel." He did not even have to speak. We could plainly see watermelon depicted on his good-natured oval countenance. I was not the one with a heart to discourage such an undertaking.

'Tis true I had not yet forgotten that Late Jens deal, but this had nothing in common with that deal whatever, and we needed some moisture. It was impossible to get Nehemias enthusiastic about this deal. He said that he liked watermelon but could not reconcile himself to the idea of having to steal them. Patta John and I owned up to the same honest feeling, but we added this prefix that, if we should ever get a watermelon treat, we must go openly and honestly right ahead and steal them. Nehemias finally gave a reluctant and half-hearted consent to lend a hand to the venture. I want to say right here that we would have been far better off as far as feeling was concerned both inside and out if we had listened to and heeded some of his arguments.

This much adored watermelon patch belonged to Taalige Lars Christian and Theodore Jacobson. Taalige Lars Christian was the sole proprietor and owner, but since Theodore was known among the toughs both as the light- and heavyweight champion and also known as a fellow who had never been overburdened with what is ordinarily known as feeling, he was let in as an equal partner with Christian. First, because he would claim as big a share as he saw fit of that patch whether he was made an honorary member of the firm or not. Second, he was supposed to act as Lord High Executioner on such miscreants as might accidentally stray into said watermelon patch. Let it be said right here that this job was religiously looked after by Theodore, we and many others found to our great sorrow.

This magnificent watermelon patch was located west and a few degrees south from the summit of Taalige Lars Hauen. The above-mentioned summit was at the present time our point of vantage. From this our outlook we could see the Taa-lige Lars home. We could see Lars Anna strike out with her knitting dangling in front of her and imagined we could see her deft fingers making the unceasing rows around those am-ple stocking legs, while she herself was speeding along at a rate that would be considered utterly impossible by her grand- and great-granddaughters, or any other daughters — let alone knitting a modern, up-to-date stocking for every twenty lin-eal miles traveled. This was an art, or let us call it a feat, that would leave our present-day acrobatic women in perfect awe. In vain we strained our eyes for the well-known form of Taalige Lars Christian. Neither could we discover the pugi-listic form of Theodore Jacobson, the watermelon patrol, anywhere. Now, if they had no subofficer unbeknown to us, right now would be the opportune time to snatch our melons. Therefore, after another spell of careful deliberation, we set out, cherishing the fondest hope as to the outcome of this our effort.

Right close to the melon patch lived an honest squatter by the name of Ola Nordlening. He lived in a dugout and sod house combined. As we neared the patch, we noticed two urchins on top of the sod roof but paid little or no attention to them. Our business now was to select our melons, and in as short a time as possible, all of which we did. In looking over our spoils we found that Nehemias had one, Patta John had two, and I had two. It was our business now to be back to our hill as soon as possible and watch developments. We found to our great consternation that things were developing a good deal quicker than we had bargained for. Back on the sod house we saw a woman frantically waving a red flag. So much for the two children.

Well take it all in all, those signs augured nothing but ill to a guilty conscience. To tell the truth the watermelon appetite was not quite as keen now as when we started out. But we were in the game and must see it through. As soon as we had gained the summit of Taalige Lars Hauen we squatted down, ripped open some of our melons, and fell to with a gusto. We got so thoroughly absorbed in our attention to the whims of the inner man that we came very nearly forgetting what was rapidly developing on the outside. By chance I happened to look up, and what I saw came very nearly freezing the blood in my veins, the last mouthful of watermelon fell with a splash on the ground. Away in the southeast, just rounding the corner of the Rev. Rasmusson farm, came the mounted police at a breakneck speed, lashing their horses if possible into still more speed, thus giving poor me the impression that every gulp of watermelon we were allowed to swallow would be an irretrievable loss to them.

I immediately called Patta John's attention to this oncoming wave of justice. He just as promptly said, "Let not their coming interfere with this our splendid repast. Eat, drink, and be merry for tomorrow we may die." He was used to being cuffed and banged around so that a couple wallopings more or less made little or no difference to him. He further reasoned, "It's no use to try to run over this endless prairie; they can run us down with their horses in little or almost no time. And there is no place to hide, and even if there was they would get us after coming out of our hiding place. So I say again, let us stay right where we are and eat while we may."

Nehemias, being of a nervous temperament, began to show many signs of uneasiness. In order to try to soothe him I said that as long as Chip and I are alive they won't touch you. But this was far from having a soothing effect. On the contrary, it made it only too plain to him that bloodshed was unavoidable. Patta John, true to his principle, did not let up on those melons before Theodore and Taalige Lars Christian stood right before him demanding an explanation. As no explanation was forthcoming they commenced to apply their remedy. They had all they could do to keep our Patta John from eating watermelon while the operation was on. Theodore, the great big ruffian he was, kept raining blows on his poor carcass until Taalige Lars Christian finally said the words, "Think it's enough."

I was the next in order, but Chip did not think so. Christian had rubbed up against Chip before so there was very little ginger to start with as far as he was concerned. Christian started for his horse almost right away. Theodore, on the contrary, would have to be taught a lesson. All the lesson he needed was that Chip showed him a faultless set of teeth set in the same red gums that had created such a sensation on

Late Jens. Theodore felt somewhat beat and made haste to get mounted for the purpose of getting away as soon as possible, but this was against Chip's principles. He had to ride away from the scene of action rather too meekly to suit his bull nature.

These scenes or settings from the prairie of central Iowa, or you may even call them little dramas, had sooner or later to come to an end. The squatters were rapidly decorating the hillsides with their thatched roofs, sod houses, and even frame houses. This spelled only too plainly that this would be the last season on the prairie for the milk cows belonging to the settlers along the Skunk River. I, for my part, must say that I had had enough of it and would hail with enthusiasm any change that might suggest itself. Although looking at the different aspects in connection with this passing of the prairie in this garden spot of the world, it couldn't help but leave pleasant memories and recollections even on a mind like mine so thoroughly set against this prairie solitude. I believe the true definition of the word prairie is solitude, or a place to make people crazy. But in spite of all this I am glad that I was one of the pioneer boys, that I am one of the privileged few who have been granted the opportunity of seeing this grand country in its wild prairie state with its semiannual prairie fires and other accouterments peculiar to a new country.

Among the pleasant recollections are those of acquaintances made among the prairie folk that grew into friendships which were well nigh unbreakable. And good reason why, because it grew, as it were, right out of the virgin soil and was cemented together with deeds and actions, synonymous of love. Such actions, for instance, as caring for each other in case of sickness and death. Even contagious diseases made no difference to those splendid pioneers. Acts of kindness were grafted into other noble acts, this resulting into a healthy growth of goodwill towards all. Fungus growths, such as petty jealousies, were not even allowed to germinate. Yes, recollections of this nature which had to do with the very vitals of life have been garnered and stored away in memory's treasure-house to stay, and undisputed at that by any other interests of a more recent date that might clamor for a like place in the treasure-house. Who, for instance, can forget or who would want to forget instances like the following which resulted in new acquaintances and in due time developed into a friendship that has stood the test ever since?

About one mile and a half northwest from Taalige Lars Hauen, or about one mile north and about three-quarters of a mile east from Springa Hauen, was a new cabin into which moved a widow and her four boys, John, Carl, Hartwick, and Ole. They had come from the ice-clad regions of Norway, the region best known as the land of the midnight sun. We soon learned from one of their near neighbors, one Lars Mathison by name, that their name was Sparboe. I thought this a very musical name and laid plans to meet the boys and get acquainted with them as soon as possible. One evening in bringing my cattle home I switched them into the cow trail of the so-called northern division. This well-defined cattle trail led me and my charges right close to Mrs. Sparboe's house and equally close to Ole Mathison's house on the opposite side of the trail.

I started to look, but in vain, for the boys from the land of the midnight sun. I very naturally thought that they must be of a different type from us American-born fellows. I was not left very long in suspense pondering this question, however, for right by the side of the cattle trail, scattering my cattle to the right and left and everywhere, emerged a figure out of a hole in the ground. This figure rapidly assumed the shape of a well-developed boy of about my own size, complexion of the Caucasian type. In fact, there was nothing abnormal whatever about him. The only remarkable thing about it all was that he came out of this hole in the ground. By the twinkle of his eye I could see that this was just one act out of many that he was sort of dramatizing out there on the prairie.

After having stared at each other the reasonable length of time, I put the question to him. What was he doing in that hole? To this he answered that just now he was imitating a bear, and, on seeing my cattle, he was tempted to try what effect, if any, a real bear would have on a drove of common ordinary homebred prairie cows. I then asked him if he had tried it on people. To this he answered no, but that he might try. He then started to laugh, and our acquaintance was already established. This was Hartwick, as anybody might guess that ever had the privilege of being one of his acquaintances.

Later, during the same season, I learned to know the rest of the boys, and we have stayed acquainted ever since. Now just to illustrate what this grand old prairie has been capable of doing for these raw recruits and many others like them I will tell something about this family. It would possibly surprise people who saw them at the before-mentioned crude stage to learn what they have accomplished since that time. John and Carl own a big portion of the prairie that surrounded them at that time. John has also served our county as supervisor for a term of four years. Carl ranks among the upper crust as a shorthorn breeder of our state. Hartwick started out as a successful teacher in our township, later as a teacher in a business college, and still later he was mayor of our county seat. Ole was a highly gifted young man, but I regret very much to have to chronicle that he died before his ambitions could be realized. So much for the boys from the frozen north. And likewise so much for the Iowa prairie that took them into her confidence and showed them some possibilities.

The season was now drawing to a close, and as has already been mentioned all signs of the times indicated that this would be the last season out on the open prairie for the cows of our vicinity. The question then naturally arose, how can we solve the cattle question next season? Father for one must have this settled before the cold weather set in because if he could not arrive at some plan in the fall as to how to care for the stock the following spring he must in some way dispose of the largest portion of them. While this question was being thus duly pondered, who should come along but one Torgrim Rotem, who lived way out on the prairie and held out the liberal offer that he would herd and look after our stock and furnish the salt from the first of April till the first of October for the small sum of one dollar per head, providing he could gather up as many as five hundred head or more. All he would ask of us was to mark the cattle and then in the fall come and get them, after paying up the price agreed upon per head.

Now then, this was all good and well as far as the young stock was concerned, but what about the milk cows? There was a rumor afloat that Mr. Boyd, a hardware dealer at Ames, had a wire called barbed wire that could be fastened to any ordinary wooden post with a staple. This was something that would have to be investigated as soon as possible. If this proved a success and if the price was not prohibitive, the cattle problem would soon be settled. The young stock would be consigned to Torgrim Rotem, and the fawn-footed Salrei and her subordinates would be confined to a twenty-acre lot, quite a change indeed to this roaming tribe.

I can remember it was one of the last days of September that Chip and I started out for the last time with the cattle. Their aim now was not so much the open prairie as the poorly fenced cornfields. Come to think of it I believe Nehemias was with me that day. This proved to be another ill-fated day. Our cattle had a craving for a change of diet, and this brought them into Knut Baker's cornfield, where they did some damage. This Knut Baker had an enormous bulldog, which looked to me as though he could swallow an ordinary man alive. We heard his braying in the cornfield and dared not venture near enough to be of any assistance to poor Knut to get the cattle out. Chip could have done the work in a hurry, but we dared not trust him near that bulldog. But be this all as it may, I had to take ten bushels of corn down to Knut Baker after corn picking that fall, and that bulldog with that peculiar hitch to his upper lip sat and looked at me all the while I carried the corn into the crib. That dog looked as though he had never seen anything funny as long as he had lived, and he was no spring chicken either.

Well, this was the "finale" of my prairie work. The next and last act was to collect my wages from *gamle* Gjert and Kalla-vaag. This feat was soon accomplished, and it amounted to exactly enough to buy Lewis his confirmation suit. This, I believe, ended the common, everyday events of that season.

The following winter was like the rest of the early winters, blizzards that lasted as a rule three days or more, protracted sieges of this kind of weather nearly every week, thus making the care of the stock a gruesome test of human endurance, especially so when the wells gave out right in the midst of such a siege and when the haystacks (stuck around as close to the stable as possible) were completely covered with solid drifts so they would have to be entered into from the top instead of from the end. You of the younger generation imagine if you can the thankless task of shoveling this snow. Something like coping with the smoke out of a huge chimney. Always some new smoke crowding in on you, with the vast difference, however, that the more you shovel the bigger hole you get and the greater chance for the new drifting snow to pile in on you. You can hear the cattle bellowing for this hay that is so slow in coming forth and the water that ought to have been in the well but is not. I dare say that even you, the resourceful youth of the present, would have become crestfallen, discouraged, and even blue. Instances like the following were not uncommon in those days.

During those terrible snow winters it was not unusual for the cattle sheds to be entirely snowed under, cows, calves, and all. Now in such a shed precautions like the following were sometimes resorted to. Fence posts were stuck into the snow that had drifted fully as high as the roof of the shed. On these posts were fastened some old-fashioned black wire. This would turn away ordinary stock, even horses, but there was one occasion in my memory that this improvised fence had to be regarded as a complete failure.

Mental telepathy was a word unknown to science in those days, but the same laws of nature which governed the same forces made it possible to set the same powers in action in spite of the absence of the word, then as well as now. A message of this nature must have found its way out of an entirely submerged cow shed, and it must have set some unknown wave in motion, which in turn must have struck some subconscious sixth or seventh sense of some bull, thus causing a vibration sufficiently strong to loosen him from his moorings, plunge him into the snow, in quest of something to which he was involuntarily drawn in a cow shed fenced as heretofore described. He completely ignored the fence, however, and soon found himself on top of the cow shed. I flatly refuse to give any more testimony in the case but will leave it to my readers to figure out the fate of this particular bull walking on top of that thatched roof built with little else in view than economy.

The next spring opened up as usual. Torgrim Rotem made his round among the neighbors and said that he would be here to gather up the cattle that should go into his herd the 15th day of April, and it would be up to us to mark them in the fall. The plan Father adopted was a small wooden block about the shape of a bell. Into this block he burned the letters O.A.L. This block was fastened to a stout rope which encircled the neck of each individual steer or heifer.

After this had been accomplished steps had to be taken to get the proposed fence, one hundred and sixty rods long, set across the farm for the twenty-acre pasture for the milk cows. One hundred and sixty willow posts were cut and set. The intention was that these posts should grow. They all promptly died, however, except one which grew to an enormous size. The branches of this tree actually spread out two rods on all sides of the main stem, thus forming a cone that measured four rods through. The stem measured three feet in diameter. Thus we see that if they had all grown we would have been up against a proposition when the time came that we would want them removed.

After the posts were set, Father went to Ames and brought home the first barbed wire I ever saw. This wire cost fifteen cents per pound. It seemed to be effective and turned the cattle in those days, but our modern cow would just turn up her nose and walk right through it. After that time there were no more rail fences built on Follinglo Farm.

After our cattle had been in Rorem's care about two months, a messenger arrived saying that during a stampede the previous night three of our cattle had been killed. They were easily identified by the peculiar mark around the neck, and he would very much like that Father would come and view the remains and see for himself that they had been properly killed. To this Father answered that the loss was great enough as it was without his having to spend a good day out of the corn-plowing season.

The messenger then went to work to give a graphic description of the stampede. Torgrim Rorem had brought a whole lot of this new-fangled barbed wire out on the prairie and had erected a yard six wires high for the purpose of driving the cattle into every evening. The evening in question was one of those sultry evenings dark as pitch owing to an overabundance of humidity in the air. Cattle always seem to be restless in this kind of weather, and it takes little or nothing to start them out on a stampede. It so happened that one of the leaders came in from the prairie very late that evening and, riding up to the pen, either the man or the horse blew his nose. This was enough to start the cattle off on a glorious stampede, which resulted in the killing of quite a number of the cattle.

Several days after this drama had been played out on the prairie we had a very heavy rain. Father suggested that we had better go out on the prairie and see about the remaining cattle, if any, we had in that herd. It was too wet to plow corn. Now the question was whether or not Long Dick, Bear Creek, and other drains were swelled to such an extent that it would be dangerous to venture across the prairie. There were bridges across the channels proper of Long Dick and Bear Creek, but there were no approaches up to the bridges, hence to us boys it looked as if Father was taking chances on crossing those streams. Our horses went in so deep at places that we just saw their necks and backs above water. If I should say that we were not scared, I would be uttering a falsehood. If we had had just an ordinary wagon, the box would have floated out of the bolsters, but we had what in those days was called a two-seated buggy. (Now it would be called a road wagon.)

The next season Ole Rorem, a son of Torgrim, herded our cattle. His stamping grounds were just about where the town of Radcliffe is now located. He came around early in the spring with a big branding iron. The mark he burned into their hips was a huge figure 7, which I verily believe could be discerned at a distance of at least eight rods. Those cattle carried this mark to their dying day.

During these two seasons and the ensuing one, settlers kept coming in at such a rapid rate that it became necessary to move the herd clear up into Wright County. Hans Jetar (Hans the herder), mounted on a spotted pony, took charge of the cattle after they had been routed out of Hamilton and Hardin Counties. Hans kept this up for quite a number of years and made himself independently rich from the venture. I can truthfully say that I did not begrudge Hans the money he made by this kind of work. Stacks of greenbacks would have been very weak bait as far as I was concerned. I had had my share of this kind of work. When Kallavaag and Gjert paid me, I made a sacred vow that never again should filthy lucre tempt me into spending another season on the desolate prairie.

Our next teacher was Christ Thorsen. He boarded with us, and like Lewis Anderson he was a chronic angler. Many a bullhead came to an untimely end through the skillful manipulation of his hook and line. I would hardly have time to go into a detailed description of any of our fishing excursions in company with this expert, especially since it would be largely a repetition of similar excursions heretofore chronicled.

There is one incident in connection with Christ Thorsen's stay with us that I can never forget. It was on the morning of July 2, 1877, that he woke us boys up rather early and commenced plying us with the question of how many brothers we had. We did not answer, partly because we were drowsy and partly because we regarded it as a practical joke that he was about to play on us. He fired the question at us again and again, until we finally answered in unison that we were four brothers. To this unanimous declaration he promptly answered that we were mistaken and told us to guess again. We then gave him the names of all of us, but he still insisted that we were mistaken. After he had tormented us in this manner long enough to suit his taste, he told us that there was a new brother downstairs awaiting the privilege of shaking hands with us. This piece of news caused us to jump out of bed at once, and inside of an incredibly short time we had formed a circle around our new brother and bade him welcome to Follinglo. This was Martin Olai.

The seasons came and went and ever since the raid of the horse thieves, nothing but blessings seemed to have been dealt out to our community. Of course we were troubled more or less with the pioneer sickness ague, and among the cattle the dreaded black leg would occasionally cause a calf to keel over. As long as we knew of nothing worse, we thought this was bad enough. About the time that our latest brother was some over two years old we were destined to see a change, a change that made us very willing to admit that so far we had been a much favored set. Diphtheria, the most dreaded of all diseases, without any warning whatever pounced down upon us and struck the apple of our eye, our only sister. When she was taken sick we had no way of diagnosing the case, hence we were left in ignorance as to the nature of the sickness.

Our friend Kathrina Meltvedt came to see her as soon as she heard that she was sick. She gave us no encouragement but told us to send for the doctor at once. Father did not have to be told twice but started out posthaste to consult Dr. B. F. Allen. The old doctor happened to be sober that day and, upon hearing some of the symptoms, put on a very serious look and said that it did not sound very good to him, and he wanted to see her at once. Father and the doctor started out on horseback, and you might know that it did not take them long to reach our home, as the people in those days knew how to ride. The old doctor hurried into the house, where he found Mother holding our sister on her lap. Dr. Allen, in spite of his great fault, was very kind and considerate. After having seen the patient, he shook his head and said, "I am extremely sorry to have to say that this is a case of diphtheria, and my best judgment tells me that she cannot last over twelve hours."

Those who have lived through a similar experience can tell how we felt. I am not in the least ashamed to own up to the fact that we all broke completely down. She had almost completely lost her power of speech, but that wonderful girl looked at us all and smiled. After the excitement had subsided she started with Father and Mother and then struggled through all our names. After this trying ordeal on her part, she added with another smile that she expected to meet us all in heaven wearing beautiful white clothes.

This was the last we heard her say. Her mission on earth was completed, and I dare say that her short sojourn with us here below was a godsend. How can any of us go wrong when we recall how painfully she struggled through all our names and wound up by saying that she would meet us all in heaven and lovingly smiled her adieu before closing her eyes to this earth. This was a hard blow that none of us can forget, nor do we want to forget this beautiful memory. Her coming and going can be likened unto a beautiful butterfly that flutters a little while and is then snuffed out of existence, but not before those beautiful colors of her gentle character have been indelibly stamped upon our memory. Let us thank God that such had been our privilege.

In those days when the dreaded diphtheria struck a home where there were many children there was usually not very much hope entertained as to the recovery of anyone affected. And since there was no such thing as a disinfectant it was considered almost a miracle when anybody in a family escaped the disease. As soon as our sister was buried, the telltale symptoms asserted themselves in my throat and almost as promptly were Lewis and Nehemias affected.

This looked very discouraging, indeed, especially since our doctor knew of nothing to prescribe. The only remedy he used was whiskey. This he lavished very freely both outside and inside our miserable throats. Of course this did nothing but harm. Poor old Dr. Allen stood helpless. There were no textbooks on the subject; the usual way was to take it and succumb without a murmur. But in our case this good old rule was ignored. Father invented a remedy of his own and immediately put it into practice. He took alum and laid it on the stove and melted it and then let it burn dry. After this was done he pulverized it thoroughly. The next move was to fill a long goose quill (which was put together in sections so as to make a good long one) with this pulverized alum, open our mouths, and blow it with all the force he could muster up straight down our throats. This drastic remedy did the business. There are some remedies that are said either to kill or cure, but the way I remember this treatment was that it killed first and then cured afterwards. Well suffice to say, I honestly believe father's remedy saved our lives.

In those days there was no quarantine law; the good old neighbors came and helped us whenever help was needed and that was nearly all the time, but none of them got sick. In a family about six miles away from our home, three children got sick and died from the dreaded disease. The next season four girls out of five in the Branjord family took sick and died, the oldest one being thirteen years old. The sympathy of the whole surrounding country went out in full measure towards this family, for this was the second time those people had been thus stricken. The first time they had three children, all of whom took sick and died.

The winter our sister died we had three teachers boarding with us, Richard Pierce, B. F. Merrickle, and James Blake. They had all been brought up in the same community and appreciated very much the privilege of being able to stay at the same place. Pierce and Blake were good singers, and during the winter evenings, especially after our great loss, this came in good stead. Merrickle had a great bass voice, but the trouble was that his ear was so defective that it was impossible to use him. In spite of the earnest protests from Pierce and Blake, he would sometimes join in. His voice could be likened unto the roaring of a lion. If by a mere chance he happened to strike the right chord, it was such a surprise to the other singers that they would have to break down laughing. Even though we shall have to admit that Merrickle fell down as a flat failure when it came to singing, he had other qualifications which brought him on a par with the best ones. At least we thought so because he was our teacher, while Blake taught the Phillops School and Pierce the Branjord School.

Right here I find that in my overzealousness of narrating history I have jumped over a space which must be filled in in preference to anything else. Hence it becomes necessary to turn back several years. I have not yet mentioned Wiester, our own Obediah McCowen Wiester. He was a small Pennsylvanian Dutchman weighing at the most one hundred and ten pounds. The first time I can remember seeing him he came to our place riding a mule, and the mission he was bent upon was to put in an application for our school. Father was a little bit afraid that he was not quite heavy enough to hold down the position, but Wiester was not of the kind to give up. After he made several laborious trips on that mule, a contract was finally signed, and I want to say without reserve that I believe this transaction meant more to the young hopefuls of our school district than we were capable of realizing for many years to come.

Wiester was born and raised in Westmoreland County, Pennsylvania. He must have received a thorough Christian training because his every action was a reflection of true religious principles. This man was never down in the mouth but always jolly. Swimming was his favorite recreation. He had a way of his own in swimming which gave even Chip a hard chase to keep up with him. He was also a great ballplayer. He introduced the vicious game called sack ball. The halt and maimed were very much in evidence as long as this game was in vogue. It became a very popular and fascinating game. Wiester got his share of the sack balls slammed against his shins; it was all taken and given with the best kind of brotherly feeling. Our poor legs were nothing but blotches and blue spots as long as this siege was on. After George got hurt so that he had to consult an M.D., this game was condemned never to be introduced again. Wiester had a great voice, but not of the kind that could successfully be used in music, because his ear was very defective. I once heard him make an attempt at singing "Hold the Fort for I Am Coming," but before there was a letup I sincerely wished he would hold his tongue instead of the fort.

No, his stronghold was elocution and penmanship, not music. Southwest from our house about ten rods stood a big oak bar post. After school hours we would often find Wiester perched on top of this post, and as he put it, exercising his lungs. He had a voice that was very penetrating and far-reaching. In testimony whereof our neighbors would have born me out if they were still among the living. "Oh, you hard hearts, you cruel men of Rome!!" was the exercise that reverberated through the air usually at twilight when the sound waves could go undisturbed to each individual eardrum.

Wiester was a very strict disciplinarian. When he played he played; but when he worked, he worked. This system he tried hard to infuse into our natures and, if possible, make it a habit. Wiester made it a rule that nothing but the English language should be used in and around the schoolhouse. Although he himself tried hard to acquire the Norwegian language, and in fact mastered it before he left our community, he said this branch would have to be left to Augestad, but while we were attending English school this rule must without fail be respected. He further stated that the first as well as the last offense would be punished with a willow switch fresh out of Mr. Sheldall's hedge, and it made no difference who the offenders might be, big or small, boy or girl, the punishment would be meted out as here set forth. We could not quite get familiar with the idea that this kind, good-natured, jolly teacher would or could live up to this rigid rule, so we came to a mutual understanding that we would openly violate this rule and see what he would do with the whole mob.

We did not have to wait very long before we found out. We were called into the schoolhouse and ordered to take our seats. He then said very solemnly: "All those who have broken the rule just laid down, raise your hand; now be honest about it, no squirming from the truth." All hands went up. He then appointed a committee of two to go and get the switches (and they had to be according to specification). Immediately upon the report of the committee, Wiester took the switches and applied them to every back in that schoolroom. After that time we never doubted his word.

Wiester was a real artist when it came to penmanship, and I suppose some of the most pleasant memories we have of that time were the thirty minutes' instruction in penmanship which lasted from three-thirty to four in the afternoon of each day. No shirking was tolerated during this period and absolutely no whispering. Wiester had right under his desk a pair of fur mittens. If he noticed anyone engaged in whispering he would put a cat to shame in picking up one of those mittens and throwing it so that it would fall just exactly on top of the seat right in front of the offender with a thud. This would always have the same effect on everybody concerned. The colloquy would be cut painfully short never to be resumed, and this thud was always accompanied by a stern command: "Bring that mitten here!" The poor miscreant was on his feet before he knew a thing, and little wonder because that voice belied the size of the man a dozen times.

Another interesting feature about that first winter term of school taught by Wiester was the lessons in fancy reading or, to use a more learned term, lessons in elocution. Wiester would first go through the painful ordeal of reading the different stanzas as they should be read and acted; then it was turned over to us to do likewise. Some of us had the imitative ability and might have mimicked ourselves through those difficult passages, but we lacked the cheek and gall somehow, hence we would never make good along those lines. I can distinctly remember one lesson that went something like this: "Come back! Come back! he cried in grief across the stormy water, and I'll forgive your highland chief. My daughter, oh, my daughter!"

We were drilled thoroughly on this lesson. "Come back! Come back!" and "Oh, my daughter!" echoed and re-echoed back and forth between the old schoolhouse and the Skunk River woods many and many a time, and it looked for a long while as though all this energy had been thrown to the four winds, but not so. One day Ole Knutson appeared on the stage all wrought up over this elopement case, imagining himself as the heartbroken father of this Scottish lassie, and bawled out some heartrending comebacks across this stormy water and gesticulated so fiercely that we thought for a while that the sorrow had been too much for him, that it had actually gone to his brain. After this grand display of talent, the whole school started to cheer and roar. Wiester declared himself outdone both in volume and gymnastics and announced that the next lesson in elocution would be about all those cannons that rolled and thundered.

Early that spring shortly after Wiester had closed his first term of school in the old Sheldall schoolhouse, Augestad started his Norwegian school in the same building. Wiester decided that he wanted to attend that term of school and learn to master the Norwegian language. He made the necessary arrangements with Augestad and forthwith joined in with the rest of the young upstarts of the community with his dinner pail and A.B.C. book headed for the institution of learning. But be it understood that the responsibility of discipline and good order through this term of school did not rest with Wiester but with Augestad, something that was soon felt by the rigid Norwegian disciplinarian. This man Augestad was just the opposite of Wiester when it came to size. He must have been at least six-feet-three. Anyone viewing the pair together on the road could not help but think of the stork and the house wren.

Augestad lived out on the prairie and had about two miles and a half to walk every morning. Sometimes he had to wade across creeks and runs, thus causing his lower extremities to

Chip

get pretty thoroughly soaked through. He generally carried a reserve pair or two of genuine newcomer stockings with him. When he pulled them off, and when they were set so that they clung pretty well to the skin, they looked to be about a rod long before they and the feet parted company. He would always hang them up in the southeast window so that they would have the full benefit of the rays of the forenoon's sun.

As they hung suspended in this fashion it was more then a temperament like Wiester's could stand up under without asserting itself in some way. Well, the upshot of it was that one day when Augestad should take them and put them on he found them tacked to the window sill and about a bushel of coal inside of them. This operation had the tendency of adding another foot or two to the length of what we considered normal in the stocking. It is needless to say that this caused quite a twitter among the pupils and some hard figuring on the part of Augestad as to where he should lay the blame. He must have mistrusted who was at the bottom of the trick because there were never any questions asked. He emptied out the coal, turned them wrong side out, and put them on.

By the way, have you ever seen a newcomer put on a pair of stockings? This is an acrobatic stunt where the native-born American with all his ingenuity is compelled to stand back and honestly admit that he could not do it. For how can it be figured out by natural or unnatural laws, mathematically or by methods known to civil engineering, how those abnormal dimensions in the shape of stockings could be placed where they belonged without first having to remove the outer garment? Still I venture to make the statement that this feat was performed very successfully time and again in the presence of Wiester and all the rest of us by Augestad.

The newcomers in those days wore britches made out of homespun. They were made very roomy, each pant leg at least as wide as the modern hobble skirt. This made it possible for Augestad to roll up his pants not less than four feet, thus giving some room to work when it came to putting on the stockings. These he would take and roll into a wad, which would very much resemble a huge doughnut. He would then place them on the floor, step into the holes of the doughnut, and start to roll them up and, in this manner, finally envelope the enormous legs which to us looked like pictures we had seen of the Colossus of Rhodes. But don't think for a minute that this completed the job. He had yet to wrap about a rod of garter string around each leg. These garters were very artistically made, being woven out of woolen threads that were dyed so as to represent all the colors of the rainbow and strong enough to tether a bull with if necessary. This completed the operation. Through the whole ordeal nothing but sober faces were supposed to be tolerated, but this mirth-provoking tableaux was entirely too much for anything human, and Wiester was no exception to the rule.

It was always a difficult matter to get down to sober study after these episodes. The foregoing is a faint portrait of Augestad's outer appearance. A picture of his real nature would be considered by those who knew him to be vastly more difficult to put into words. I at least will not attempt it but will let it go by simply saying that he was more interested in the cause that he was working for than he was in the meager pay that was forthcoming and that we have many things even at this day to thank him for. During this term of school Wiester mastered the Norwegian language to the extent that he could read and write quite fluently. Very soon he had to assume the grave responsibility of disciplining the crowd who had been his schoolmates during the Augestad school, but he was equal to the occasion.

We have no means by which to measure the valuable work performed by this most excellent teacher to a certainty, but I feel safe in saying, and I know that my old schoolmates will bear me out in the statement, that Wiester did everything in his power both in his way of teaching and his faultless example to encourage us to keep in the right path. One of his main concerns was how we would fare spiritually. Let us all hope that when the great day comes he may not be disappointed in any of us. There would be many things to relate about this our true friend, but I must leave that to someone else better qualified than I am.

The 10th of May in the year 1881 was another great day for the inmates of the house of Follinglo, for on that day our second sister was born. We decided at once that her name should be the same that our first sister had. It is needless to say that this new acquisition made everything just right in this world as far as we were concerned. Even old Chip performed some stunts in order to show due appreciation.

We will now make a jump of a year or two (this is, by the way, the time that Lewis was studying law at Iowa City), leave our new sister together with all the rest of the family in the care of old Chip, and strike out on a prairie chicken hunt. It was in the fall of the year of 1882 that Martin Henderson and I conceived the idea that we should hitch up to our road wagon our Fanny and their Flora (the two champion trotters of that age in and around our community) and start out for what we imagined to be the woolly West in quest of prairie chickens. We were to meet Lewis at Webster City, where he was continuing his law studies with Judge Chase, and from thence proceed on until we reached Grandpa Anderson Follinglo. This was to be our first stopping place. Here we were to add a fourth member to our force, namely Uncle Anders.

When we arrived at Grandpa's place, we found them in the midst of haying. This made it necessary for us to join our forces with theirs and finish haying before we could proceed any farther. This took us about two days, but we lived high and had a very enjoyable time. It could not be otherwise in the presence of Grandpa and Grandma because they seemed able to divine just exactly what would tickle our palates the most, the first meal as well as the fifth on every consecutive day.

The place where we had planned our onslaught on the prairie chickens was out on the prairie in Calhoun County not very far west from where Callender is now located. The station at that time bore the name of Catio (Caesho). It is said that this name had the following origin. When the station was yet in its infancy and the first train came through the conductor stuck his head in through the one car door and started to yell Callender, the name of the station. He got the first letter C and wound up with a horrible sneeze which clung for many years.

We finally got started for the hunting grounds, but now our main concern was where to find a bird dog. Uncle Anders knew where there was one at a certain farm place which belonged to a friend of his at Lehigh. We made for this place and made known our errand in as gentlemanly a manner as was possible, but the proprietor refused in a very curt manner; in fact it was all done in such a mean way that our dander was aroused very nearly to a boiling point. We told him now in no pleasant tone that we would see the owner of that dog and possibly call again. This made it necessary for us to call on another man by the name of Los Porter, who had a bird dog, but we found later to our great chagrin that he was a hunter dog in name only, and in place of doing us any good, he was the cause of a whole lot of trouble and grief.

After having hobbled and tethered Porter's dog in our wagon, we considered ourselves fully equipped. We gave our speedy horses to understand that we were anxious to reach our destination so as to get a chance to exercise our ability on those prairie chickens as soon as possible. We had traversed nearly half the distance to Lehigh, had come by Andrias Monkajor's dugout in a steep hillside, had also passed by Sebjon Kristen's establishment down in that deep Brushy Creek bottom, had passed over the Devil's washboard, and were just entering into the Devil's kitchen, where the scenery with its shelves and niches was so suggestive that I give the originator of those names no credit whatever for hitting upon them. And so thoroughly engrossed were we with the devilish scenery and a pheasant that thundered by us, immediately followed up with a volley from our guns which echoed back and forth alongside us, that we did not notice before we were partly surrounded by a trio who seemed to be right in their native element. They had an infernal gleam in their eyes demanding of us whether we knew anything about the murder committed right there on the hillside, pointing with their thumbs towards a house which we had but recently passed. One of them had the audacity to step up and make the remark: "I see you have Los Porter's dog tied up in your wagon. How can you account for that?"

This was too much for Anders. He promptly answered: "Yes sir, and what of it?"

This had a somewhat cooling effect. Then the question was put to us: "Are you officers of the law hunting for the murderer?" "No sir! We know nothing about the whole affair."

And with this last remark Martin switched up the horses, and we pulled out of the kitchen.

After we came out on the main thoroughfare, we hastened along as fast as we dared, but we had not proceeded far before we were halted again. This time the obstruction in our way was a sane man seemingly with an even temperament. He took us to be officers on the track of the murderer and volunteered information as to the appearance of the fellow. He had a mask on, had a long black beard, a slough hat, long rubber coat, and rubber boots. He was last seen by the daughter of the house where the murder was committed. In fact she emptied the chambers of a six-shooter after him.

The following is the story of the ghastly affair as related by him: The man whose wife was murdered was township treasurer (I cannot recollect any names). He had at the time about twenty-four hundred dollars in the house. Now this money was wanted and wanted badly by this ruffian, and he timed his call so as to avoid meeting the treasurer; in fact he did not care to meet anybody, but circumstances willed it so that the lady of the house and her grown-up daughter were the only ones in the house when he chanced to make his call. He walked right up to the house with a cocked revolver pointed at the woman and demanded the money at once. The poor woman said: "Don't shoot and I shall find it for you." She then walked right up to the bureau where the money was concealed and acted as though she would live up to her promise. Instead of the money she pulled out a six-shooter and had it almost leveled at the rascal, but he was too quick for her; he fired first, and the bullet struck her dead almost instantly. This same bullet went through a partition wall and was picked up from the floor of an adjoining room. This poor woman's daughter, who must have been of the brave kind, took the revolver out of her dying mother's hand and emptied the whole business in the direction of the fleeing rascal. She claimed that one of the bullets struck him just as he was climbing over the fence, but it was never proved, as time, money, and litigation never brought anything to light.

After this sad story had been related to us, we felt as though our trip was half spoiled. It made us sick at heart, but the spirit of adventure had such a decided upper hand over us that we had shaken ourselves out of the gloomy lethargy and had recuperated so that we were decidedly ourselves by the time we drove into Lehigh. The first man we sought out was the owner of the dog before mentioned. His name was Grant. He told us that on our way back home we could take the dog as he could never make any use of him because he refused to stay in town with him. We promised him and especially ourselves faithfully that we would.

After having fed our horses and rested a while at Lehigh, we again resumed our journey. Our destination was Thrond Throndson, an old Valdres living out on the prairie a little ways from Catio. That trip over hills and valleys, following an old prairie road, dodging the ponds and swamps along the route, was an interesting one. It was right in the midst of the prairie chicken season, too early for the mallards but just right for mud hens and shypokes. The prairie chickens were safe while we were on our way out there, unless it might have been just a select few right in our path. We had to make Throndson's that evening or stay out on the prairie, and it did look very much like rain, hence we had little or no time for chickens, but the shypokes along the route had a hard time of it. All you have got to do is just to point your gun at a shypoke and he turns up his toes. They always gave me the impression that they would just as soon die as do anything else; the least little friction along their hobbly path or the slightest nervous shock would snuff them out of existence.

But be this shypoke philosophy as it may, before we reached Throndson's night had overtaken us, and it turned just as dark as pitch, and not only that but it started to rain. Anders had to get out of the wagon and strike matches in order to make sure we were still on the right path. The first match he struck nearly upset our horses, not to mention our road wagon, which stood on edge just long enough so as not to make us quite crazy. There came a hysterical yell in unison from the wagon intended to enlighten Anders along the line of self-preservation, and it went something like this: "Quit striking those matches, or you will be classed with the shypokes and treated accordingly."

Just as this maneuver was taking place, sheet lightning revealed to us that we were just outside of Throndson's stable yard on the grade through a pond. We soon got righted and passed safely through a bar, and our horses stopped right by the stable door. At first sight who could blame us for considering ourselves very fortunate for hitting upon an abode of humans just at the crucial moment when it started to rain in a darkness so dense that you could almost cut it with a knife? I want to confess right here that upon second thought, after we had been made wise to the real situation, I for one would gladly have sacrificed my supper and my shelter and braved the oncoming storm rather than to seek shelter and break my fast at such a place.

And why, might someone ask? Because it was a private lunatic asylum out on the prairie. The first inmate out of the institution that accosted us was a bearded fellow by the name of Knut. He was a pleasant-looking sort of a fellow, but the faraway look that was stamped on his countenance showed only too plainly the weakness that he was heir to. He bade us welcome and helped us unhitch and feed our tired horses. When this had been attended to, we were invited into the house, but Knut took great pains in telling us that we must hide our guns and ammunition securely, because there were some crazy girls in the house that might assume the role of Lord High Executioners and kill us during the night.

This last piece of information had a wonderful effect on us. Intermittent chills kept chasing each other up and down our backbones and threatened to raise our hair on end. Just think of it, girls crazy enough to murder us during the night, and here we were deliberately walking right into their stronghold. Here was where we figured on getting our supper, but this lofty idea was promptly dismissed. And indeed what good would a supper do us? Our appetites vanished with the first intimation that murder was possibly lurking behind the walls that we were just about to enter. We were pulled as it were by unseen wires into that house in the wake of our guide Knut.

The first one we met was the lady of the house, a kind old lady. She appeared to be in possession of all her faculties, but long suffering had made her a cripple of a peculiar sort. When she walked she assumed the shape of a correct angle, but whenever occasion demanded it she seemed to be able at a moment's notice to shoot up and assume a perpendicular shape as straight as a die. These actions brought us involuntarily, all in unison, to think of the shypokes and that this was probably the ghost of all the shypokes that we had wantonly murdered on our way out here, and in this way punishment was justly being meted out to us. The next individual we saw was a young lady, in the first stages of insanity, huddled up in bed.

I thought if we do not see something very soon in the nature of a radical contrast we shall all go crazy. In this we were gratified for the time being, because old Thrond himself arrived on the scene, and a greater contrast you never saw. He was a typical old Valdres and the picture of health — a very distinguished looking gentleman. His hair was white and hung in long curls reaching clear down to his massive shoulders. He looked to me like the picture I had seen of some of our heroes from the colonial times, and still more so the next morning when we saw him mounted on one of his steeds out on the prairie rounding up his cattle. He bade us welcome to his home, such as it was, and expressed his great sorrow that we should be brought into such surroundings but thought probably that we should stand it a little while when he had to stand it all the time.

As we stood thus talking to this venerable old gentleman by the flickering light of an old grease lamp (kerosene lamps were prohibited on account of all the crazy people) the old lady took steps toward preparing a supper for us. She went into a lean-to and started a roaring fire. We could see through the door that was left ajar that the same rule was all the rage in that department also, namely that she had no lamp but as a substitute she carried around in her hand a stick dipped in some kind of fat. This, after having come in contact with fire, answered as a torch. It was soon made plain to us that fried eggs were what we were in for, and the way she attacked a case of eggs for our special benefit was something worthwhile remembering. And then the different positions she assumed alternating between the correct angle and perpendicular viewed by the aid of the uncertain light from that torch made her look like a specter that might and might not be of a tangible sort. This was the way she did it. She put a skillet on the stove, and after it was sizzling hot, she extinguished the torch and went for the eggs with a vengeance. The breaking of shells was plainly audible, good ones and bad ones went in together, all for our commonweal. After this was done, she again lit her torch and, jabbing it into the stove, singed the wings of several dozen flies hovering above our prospective supper and soon pronounced the job finished.

The above was viewed by a corner of our eye only. The eye proper was focused on something of an entirely different nature. Right in the corner of the room and right close to where I was sitting was a rude stairway in the form of a ladder leading up through a hole in the ceiling. I had just figured out that up there was likely the place where we would be consigned to bed, and I had further figured out that it might be possible to close that opening against anybody that might be on murder bent. But that theory was completely shattered by the demon-like laugh that reverberated down through that hole in the ceiling and took such hold on all nerve centers of my miserable body that I was for the time being paralyzed. Immediately following this awful laugh a phantom in the shape of a young woman descended just as noiselessly as a cat from one tread to another. She was but vaguely discernible on account of the poor light in the room. Every time she struck a new tread in coming down she halted long enough to give us a nerve-racking giggle.

Let me say right here that the sizzling of those eggs and that infernal laugh made me think of regions not of this earth. After she had worked herself down so that she was very nearly on a level with me sitting on a chair, she perched like a bird on one of those treads and, resting her chin in the palm of her hands, looked me square in the eye and said, "I mor-en sal jeg skyte dig" (I'll shoot you in the morning). This she kept on repeating until it jarred so on my nerves that I got panic stricken; and before I was aware of anything, I up and bolted for the only exit there was. When I got into the shanty, I grabbed for what I thought was my hat lying on the floor, but instead of a hat I plunged my arms nearly up to my elbows down into a slop pail. At my discomfiture and spasmodic movements the other boys laughed really more than their health would permit.

What's the use to dwell any longer on this sad and gruesome picture of life? In fact, I refuse to chronicle any more of it. It's sufficient to add that we had our supper, such as it was, slept in the barn, had our breakfast, such as it wasn't, and started out for the hunting grounds.

It was impossible on nearly empty stomachs and after such nerve-racking experiences as we had but recently lived through to put very much soul into our work; hence, the prairie chickens were none the worse on account of our presence among them. The burning question now was where to get our dinner. Anders finally ventured the suggestion that we go to Ole Throndson's, a son of Thrond Throndson, for dinner. The rest of us very reluctantly gave our consent to this proposition, because we thought we had had just about enough of the Throndsons. Anders assured us, however, that Ole was in possession of all his faculties, that he was township clerk, and that he had been over to the Old Country and had but recently returned with a young wife. After this powwow on the all-absorbing dinner question, we jumped into our wagon, clucked to our horses, and started out with much fear and trembling for our next eating place. We told each other that this time there must be something doing in the line of edibles or we couldn't vouch for results.

Well, we found Ole at home and his wife as well. They were a fine couple indeed. There was no augury of evil this time. We had timed our call just exactly so that our host and hostess, that is if they wanted to be honest about it, could not possibly misinterpret the real cause of our call. We wanted to be early enough so that Mrs. Ole should be spared the inconvenience of first planning a dinner for two when, as it was, circumstances had placed four more at her door who might just as well be included in the same plan. And yet not so early that they might possibly allow themselves the liberty of thinking that we might want to continue our chicken hunt yet a while before dinner.

We were not kept in suspense very long, however; our hungry stares must have had their effect, because in an incredible short time the good woman had potatoes boiling and a splendid specimen of a trout simmering in a skillet. To our ears this was the sweetest of music. And then add to this the splen-

Chip

did harmonious effect of the rattling of dishes, knives, and forks, and the exquisite cadence performed on the coffee mill, which betokened that the finale would soon be reached, made life to us indeed worth living. Little did we dream as we sat there thus enjoying this splendid repast in our mind's eye, gulping an abnormal flow of saliva, that something entirely unheard of should at the last moment so distort and demolish our splendid dinner that we were again left in penury and want.

This is what happened. When the trout was ready to be served and was placed on a platter, which was then set on a small table close to the stove, our dog, that miserable cur, that worse than nothing of a whelp, dashed into the room, snatched our trout, and made for the prairie. The flow of saliva abated, and we sat there staring at each other with low-hanging jaws and parched lips. Mrs. Ole was on the point of crying, but Ole came to the rescue and started to laugh at the ludicrous affair. We considered it far from a laughing matter, but finally joined in, though very reluctantly. In order to make the poor woman feel good we vied with each other in telling her the most genuine lies, namely that we would cheerfully take up with what the dog had left us and wound up with the basest of all lies, that we were not hungry.

Immediately after dinner Anders called us aside and with a quivering voice said: "Now boys, it's root hog or die. This is getting to be a plain case of starving to death, and we must get out of here before we get so weak that we are unable to move." We all agreed that this was no lie. He further argued, and with some force, that we hitch up at once, get a dozen prairie chickens, clean them, and then hit the pike for home and get them fried, and the sooner this was accomplished the better. We all agreed to this too, but by this time we had also learned not to count chickens before they are hatched. Under the most favorable circumstances we could not reach home before midnight, and then there was the case of the would-be dog owner of Sport, Grant's dog, that would have to be looked into. To hook up our team, hog-tie Porter's dog under the seat, and to bid our kind host and hostess good-bye and offer thanks for our dinner consumed but very little time.

Anders now took it upon himself to pilot us to a stretch

of open prairie where he thought prairie chickens would be abundant. We reached this place shortly before sunset, and sure enough, no sooner had we entered in among the golden-rods, rosin weeds, and tufts of blue joint before our dog under the seat began to show signs of uneasiness, which we inter-preted into a dog lingo that bespoke chickens. We turned our team, drove up to the nearest line fence in sight, tied them, looked after our priming, untied our dog, and got ready for operations.

While Anders untied the dog we noticed that he had a very earnest talk with him. I don't remember just what he said to him, but I presume that he admonished him in various ways, probably he might have administered some mild reproof. I seem to have some vague remembrance of seeing him pat him on the head and remark, "Now be a good dog." But, as I say, I could not hear testimony of this to a certainty. But I do remember that when he dropped him on the ground he told him with a rising inflection in his voice: "Now you son of a bitch let us see if you can redeem yourself." But he didn't. No sooner had he touched the ground before he was off at a lightning speed that would puzzle any coyote, scattering prairie chickens to the right and to the left. Both dog and chickens were way out of range for our guns. I can't soon forget the striking figure that Anders cut standing between me and the setting sun, a long lank figure leaning on his gun viewing the destruction going on around him with a look on his countenance plainly indicating that his heart had forsaken its proper recess and had descended into his boots.

His first move was a voluntary vomiting contortion which expelled his tobacco cud. The first expression that followed was something like this — I am too hungry to chew tobacco, and then pointing in the wake of that dog, where a fresh covey of prairie chickens had been scattered to the four winds, he said, "There goes our midnight supper." And still holding the same rigid pointing attitude he drew our attention to the dog saying: "Look at him! Look at him! Look at the — son of a bitch." After having finished this elocutionary outburst, he flung down his gun and started out in wild pursuit after the dog. Intermingled with something inaudible as he went swish-ing through the prairie grass we heard him say, "We must get him or he will work our complete ruin yet." The comical picture that this receding figure made in the twilight coupled with the terrific yells that came at regular intervals brought to Martin, who was highly gifted along that line, resounding peals of laughter. Lewis and I soon caught the spirit, and in our weakened condition we soon found ourselves all in a heap, indulging in a hysterical laugh. Each one of us felt that if we heard one more of those high tenor yells we were done for.

Little by little the laughing subsided, and the true situation soon brought us to our feet to join in the general melee. I am unable to recall details of that mad chase, but Anders finally got the dog by the collar, and he was hauled up to the wagon and tied and then tied again to the axle. After this operation, Anders, though very short of breath, managed to wheeze out, "Now it will be your turn to yell and howl." And I might as well add that he had done it with a gusto that can never be equaled outside of the bird dog family.

That we must have some of those chickens was a simultaneous determination of all of us. We accordingly set out in an opposite direction from the one the dog had so thoroughly traversed and very soon ran into a goodly bunch of them. We fired seven shots but did not get seven birds. This started the dog under the wagon on a new curse of howls and yelps. We kept it up, however, and soon had about a dozen chickens. It was now fast growing dark, and we were yet about twenty miles away from Grandpa's place. We had the satisfaction, if nothing else, of having made more noise on that prairie than had ever been heard there before or would likely be heard hereafter, barring the possibility that in the earlier days it might have been the scene of an Indian battle. On going home we made rapid progress, reaching Lehigh by about eight o'clock. By ten we had reached the place where Sport was kept, the dog that was a dog.

Oh how different our trip might have been if we had had him in place of this worthless Porter dog. Out in the still and silent night in reviewing and recounting what troubles might have been averted if this man had not been so mean we worked ourselves up until we got so hardened and reckless we felt that we could storm a battery if need be. Anders felt, however, that he had to impart to us some truths before we hazarded the undertaking of abducting this dog. It was namely this, that Sport was a great watchdog, and he might not allow us to lay hands on him, especially at this time of day. And furthermore there was a giant of a white bulldog that might and might not break some of our legs. But he added further that he was not saying this to discourage this honest deal and said, "I am game for one. Who will be the other?" Lewis promptly spoke up. Martin had charge of the team, and Anders turned to me and said, "You keep that worthless cur quiet, and if he tries to make the slightest noise, choke him."

Lewis and Anders at once made for the barn, where it seemed that everything had been made ready for them, for right in the middle of the aisle curled up on a bunch of hay lay Sport and the white bulldog, and a lantern hung on a beam right above them. Anders picked up Sport so quick and so smoothly that the bulldog did not even wake up. It sounds somewhat incredible, but knowing Sport as we learned to know him later it has always remained a puzzle to us how he would allow himself to be handled the way we handled him that night. But be that as it may, we had him.

When they got up to the wagon I blundered out a question, but Anders promptly cut me short by saying, "Shut up," and then added that we must do some driving. My dog started to make some noise, but I had my hand on his windpipe, and I shut him off just as effectually as Anders shut me off. Now Martin's good horsemanship came in good stead and likewise Flora and Fanny's trotting ability. They were called upon to give their best licks for a good cause, and they seemed to do it cheerfully. There were not many words exchanged between us before we got about three miles away from that white bull-dog. The spirit of exultation that had lent us wings and had infused temporary courage into our collapsed systems from our successful abduction of Sport suddenly left us to be followed by a miserable creeping sensation of fear.

We were now up to where we had to pass through the Devil's kitchen. If it is within your power to imagine a place that would rightly suggest such a name and then further imagine that you were thrust into the same in the middle of the night with questionable property in our wagon, and then add to all this the hideous murder that had been committed in its

Chip

close proximity just a couple of days previous, I know that you would not put us down as cowards on account of our admitted weakness. Anders made an attempt at strengthening us as well as himself by forcing this remark, "I wonder if old Harry (the Devil) has any leftovers from supper?" But it came in such a shaky manner and his voice had such a sepulchral twang to it, accompanied by a clattering of teeth, necessitated by the relaxing of the tense muscles of his jaw, that I am sorry to say that as a bit of humor it was a complete failure. Meanwhile Martin guided our horses through the kitchen and just made ready for the hazardous drive over the Devil's washboard. Here we halted because somewhere around here was the home of Porter's dog. We trusted that he was sufficiently well acquainted to find his way home and, therefore, dumped him out with the assurance that we would never need his services again.

We cleared the washboard and soon got onto the prairie road and by twelve o'clock we drove into Grandpa's yard. He, being a renowned joker, got up and told us to move on; this was no harbor for fellows of our type. Meanwhile Grandma and Aunt Julia got up and seemed to divine what we so sorely needed. We had long ago given up the idea of waiting for our prairie chickens to be prepared. What we needed now were short-order accommodations. Grandpa looked at us after we had cleared the table after several helpings and, with a humorous twinkle in his eye, remarked on our voracious appetites. The next day, after having glutted ourselves on prairie chickens and numerous other good things, we left Grandfather's place and drove home.

This is the way then that Follinglo Farm became part owner of that wonderful bird dog Sport. Martin Henderson kept him because we knew that old Chip would never take up with a new dog as long as he lived. After we got Sport settled in his new home, we sent his former keeper a card telling him of his transition. Time and space will not allow me to recount any of the glorious hunts we had with this splendid dog, but I want to venture the staggering assertion that our Sport was the greatest dog of his kind that ever barked in or near the Skunk River woods. Long will he be remembered.

It was about this time that we organized the River Side

Orchestra, which was followed a few years later by the River Side Cornet Band. At the meetings of the first-named organization, old Chip and Sport had occasion to meet and get acquainted, but their interests were so far different that there was no chance for rivalry, in short they ignored each other entirely. Chip was nothing but a nervous heap in the presence of a gun, while Sport was seemingly elevated into the seventh heaven by getting a sniff at powder.

It was during this interesting period when imaginary music strains were being borne in upon us by what we imagined could be the future possibilities of our string band and during the incumbency of Nellie Richardson, a very successful teacher and highly gifted musician, at the old Sheldall school-house, that our household was again stirred by the advent of the eighth and last of the Follinglo progeny. This happened on the 18th day of May in the year of our Lord 1884. He was after due consideration given the name of Gustav Adolph. Since we were so taken up with our musical instruments, and further, since he demanded perfect silence so that practicing would have to be suspended for the time being, we at first regarded him as an intruder, but he gradually wormed himself into our affections and was very soon one of us. The next spring, on the 11th day of June, Lewis was married.

History was now being made so fast both in our little musical world and by other interesting events vying with each other for attention that I consider myself up against an insurmountable barrier which I must leave to abler minds to overcome. I shall, therefore after this, confine myself more strictly to the biography of the Follinglo dogs. I shall, however, allow myself some digressions wherever I feel called upon to do so.

Chip was now growing old and feeble. He had frequent attacks of epileptic fits. He still felt responsible for everything that was going on on the farm. There was no dainty morsel of his bill of fare that could tempt him to eat when any one of us was away from home. Those occurrences grew to be more and more frequent as we advanced in years. He would take occasional strolls to Story City and see to it that Lewis was all right. He gradually grew accustomed, however, to the fact that Lewis had established a home of his own and lost no meals on that account.

Chip

The grim reality dawned upon us now that it would be only a question of time before duty would demand of us to put poor old Chip out of misery. He lived to exceed the age commonly alloted to dogs, namely twelve years. Then we had to let him die. I feel sure that a dog like Chip cannot help but leave his good influence on a family of children. I have looked and looked, but in vain, for a dog like Chip ever since. We shall always remember him.

Carlo

Out on a remnant of the south prairie lived a squatter by the name of Endre Bjerkeland. He had kind of a checkered career. He emigrated to this country from Norway just in time to go into the army and serve through the Civil War. After the war he went back to the Old Country, took unto himself a wife, raised a large family, and, after many years, came to this country again as a full-fledged newcomer again, with a plain brass ring suspended from each ear, believed at that time to be an effective antidote against weak eyes. This man and his family squatted on the above-named patch of prairie to take up the cudgels against the wolf that was persistently clamoring at his door. To this man's humble cottage we were directed in our search for a new dog. Sure enough, there was an innumerable litter, a squirming, wriggling mass of dog where one could detect characteristics of more than a half score of prominent dog breeds and an intermittent blending of colors that would put Chinese fireworks in the shade.

Out of this conglomeration of whelps and hounds and curs of low degree we were given the privilege of taking our choice for one dollar, with the exception of one that he expected to reserve for the propagation of the breed. The lot finally fell on one that resembled our departed Tige, a brindle. He was as yet too fresh to be moved. Mr. Bjerkland intimated, however, that we might leave the dollar, which we did. Two weeks later Martin was given the important mission of bringing him home. We gave him the name Carlo.

We were so many of us now, and each one had his own way of training dogs that poor Carlo did not develop any special traits. The cattle business on the prairie was now a thing of the past, hence his development as a shepherd dog was sorely neglected. But where he shone was when it came to playing with the children. His nature seemed to be a fondness for sport. Nothing serious concerned him, no assuming of responsibilities like our pioneer dogs. I wonder if he had already scented the coming spirit that is bothering some of our present-day boys and girls, namely the lack of seriousness?

But hold on, I am not going to preach. We shall leave this to someone who can handle this important subject better than I can. Poor Carlo, unlike his predecessor, did not stay with us very long. His untimely end came together with what might have culminated in a tragedy that would have changed history as far as we were concerned on the Follinglo Farm. It was on a Sunday during one of the summer months. We had company and had just indulged in a company dinner. The younger children, together with Carlo, were out in the road playing. The rest of us were in the house listening to one of Luther's sermons read to us by Father, a custom strictly adhered to by the old pioneers, especially on Sundays when we had no services in the church.

As we sat thus, we were suddenly startled by a rifle shot out in the road followed by a cry of the children and a piteous yelping of the dog. There was a spontaneous rush for the door. Father made for the road to ascertain if all was well with the children, while Henry and I ran to the stable and mounted Hagen and Fanny and soon found ourselves in wild pursuit after the ruffians. There were four of them in a two-seated buggy. Behind the buggy they had tied a road cart. As soon as they perceived that we were after them, they cut the rope that held the cart, lashed up their horses, and worked themselves up to a speed that bade fair to bring them to the woods before we could reach them.

I rode Hagen, and he was rather nervous and strong-minded. Everything went well, and I was gaining on them to my entire satisfaction, when all of a sudden Hagen wheeled up to Old Wierson's closed gate and stopped all of a sudden. This put me on the other side of the gate. While I was in the act of picking myself up, I noticed Henry flying past like a rocket, mounted on our spirited Fanny. He likewise flew past the place where the pursued party had turned into the woods.

After I got mounted again, Hagen did his level best to catch up with Fanny. When I got nearly up to the edge of the timber, I slowed down some and watched the ground as I thought it might be possible that they would turn out of the road and try to hide among the thick underbrush as quickly as opportunity afforded. This surmise I found to be correct. I saw their track and urged Hagen in after them, but where was Henry? Likely half a mile farther down the road, and here I was alone up against four desperadoes. But there was no turning back now. I was so riled up over their action that I felt as though nothing could stop me.

I was soon ordered to stop by one of the party, who pointed a rifle at me, but I, like a fool, rode right up against them. Two of them were engaged in unhitching their horses and told me that if I had not disappeared by the time they had tied their horses they would lick me within an inch of my life. I told them I would go when I got good and ready and furthermore that all I would need to do would be to whistle and I would have help enough to lift them into kingdom come before they would have time to say Jack Robinson. I also stated that it was not my intention to jump onto them single-handed. All I wanted was to see what they looked like so that I might be able to report them to the proper authorities and, if they didn't like my way, just let me know and I would blow my whistle. This sounded brave; but, if the truth had been spoken, I was just anything but brave. Or, in other words, if you seem to be able to draw from the above that this young man was fearless, let me assure you right here that you are presuming entirely too much.

The only thing that kept up my courage was that I was mounted on Hagen. All I would have to do was to touch his ribs and the speed limit was instantaneous, and woe betide the object that was too close to his heels. My bluff worked, however, and their threatened onslaught came to naught. I got away from them without any further trouble. When I got into the road proper I was again joined by Henry, who came back from his wild goose chase. Looking up the road we saw the whole immediate neighborhood, men, women, and children, en route to the woods, seemingly on the warpath. Quite a distance in advance was Father. He was bareheaded and had covered the whole distance of about a mile as fast as he could run.

This exciting chase right after a heavy meal, coupled with the fear that Henry and I might get killed in the fray, was too much for Father. He took sick in the form of a violent case of Cholera Morbus. To us who had never seen him sick before the world looked gloomy indeed. Doctor Emmet came and went many a time before he could truthfully say that there was some hope for his recovery.

All our kind neighbors took turns to watch over him and to help me. When he finally got over the danger period and the doctor prescribed fresh fish for him to eat, that venerable and dear old man Osmund Weltha happened to be with him. His hair and beard were just as white as snow, his figure was bent, but he got up from his chair by Father's bedside with alacrity that could hardly be credited to a man of his years and said: "Thanks be to the Lord, I have received a mission." His bright black humorous eyes twinkled as he hastened through the door. That same evening just before supper he returned wet to the knees, his shoes full of water, carrying a pail which contained two live pickerels. As he handed them to Mother he said: "I prayed God to send them to me, and He heard my prayer." Such a man was old man Weltha, and may we never forget him and the good influence he brought to bear on the community in which he was a prime mover.

Well, I left the aggregation down the road rather abruptly. When we got back home, we found poor Carlo quite dead under the grainary. The evildoers made for another state the next day in order to avoid being prosecuted. I am happy to be able to chronicle, however, that they afterward felt very sorry for their action and that we can now reckon them among our friends.

Carlo the Second

Follinglo Farm was again dogless. Bjerkeland was again called upon to display his wares. As he was the only dog vender within our reach, there was no alternative. Sure enough, there was a man by the name of Torekaaven way out in the prairie on the other side of Radcliffe who was also in the dog business, but the distance was too great, hence the idea of seeing him was abandoned. And then Bjerkeland had this hungry look about him that suggested true appreciation of the price of a pup. Martin was elected to shoulder the responsibility of selecting and bringing home the new dog. This time the lot fell on a spotted one, black and white. We called him Carlo after his half brother. He developed into a very handsome dog; his nature was nothing but sheer goodness, and, like his brother, he was a great fellow for sport.

The following winter an epidemic that got the name of La Grippe swept over the country. It affected human beings, dogs, and cats alike. We were all sick from it. The cats got it, commenced to sneeze, and in due order kicked up their toes, with the exception of one. After a while, Carlo commenced to show signs of being affected. It went to his brain, and he had spells in which he was completely crazed. During one of these attacks, he showed signs of desperation, and we got alarmed to such an extent that we had to call in Old Knutson with his gun put to an end to his misery. So there went our second Carlo.

Carlo the Third

By this time Father got to be a little bit skeptical in regard to this dog industry. He said the idea of having to go through the ordeal of bringing up a pup every season was taxing his nervous system beyond endurance, and we must cut it out. We listened to this discouraging harangue but considered it by no means final. We knew too well that Father liked dogs and that he enjoyed having them around if for no other reason than to get a chance to tease them. Therefore, with an undercurrent of hope, since we were so thoroughly acquainted with Father's nature, negotiations were slyly going on with Endre Bjerkeland. He reported that he had now on hand a fresh supply of choice pups that would be disposed of at the ridiculous low price of a dollar a piece, always respecting the old adage, first come, first served. This in itself, of course, contained the not entirely obscure meaning that, if we wanted the first choice, we must not delay. Accordingly, Martin was dispatched with all respectful speed to close the deal which made Bjerkeland the cheerful recipient of another dollar and we another pup. Father's countenance fell way down below zero when he saw him, "naa ein hond ig jen" (not a dog again) was all he could get beyond his lips. His eyes, however, bespoke the language of a martyr.

This was a black one. He developed into a big dog with no special aim in life. He resembled no special breed. There were prominent characteristics of a half-dozen breeds sticking out all over him. His ears were those of a dachshundt, his long-drawn bark and howl was that of some kind of a hound, his tail had the wiggling ability of the bird dog. He had also something in common with the Irish setter, but the crowning effect of the whole being was that there was no individuality whatever. Poor fellow, he was a living example of a Jack of all Trades and Master of None. I tried to coax him into what seemed to him a lost art of hunting prairie chickens. He seemed to have a vague smattering of gifts along this line, but come to simmer it down there was nothing doing but the tail. The rest of the body was entirely out of harmony with the job.

Father imagined by putting two and two together that he could trace some not entirely dormant ability as a cattle dog hidden somewhere in his anatomy. He made several appeals to this hidden spark, but it refused to ignite. Positively the last chance he gave him to redeem himself as a cattle dog came about as follows: It was towards evening, and there was lots of ice on the ground. It was one of those misty days, one might almost call it a heavy fog. At any rate, together with the gathering dusk, one couldn't see but a very short distance. Father was standing on a smooth stretch of ice, bracing himself on a pitchfork which he had jabbed into the ice. It occurred to him that now or never he needed the services of that worthless dog. He started to call him in a modest and subdued tone, but, as the dog did not show up, the tone grew in volume until it reached a high falsetto that could be heard to the remotest corner of the farm. He started to pronounce clearly, ""Here Carlo, here Carlo," but, as the call was not heeded and as the volume increased, little attention was given to pronunciation and annunciation. Towards the climax it came "Ho Colo, ho Colo, ho Colo" — and the climax did come with a crash, for the dog had heard and made speed that would have done credit to his remote hound ancestors.

True to the call, he made straight for Father, who was unable to see him through the mist. When he came up to the ice, the impetus was so great that he had no means at his command by which to stop, hence the inevitable followed. With unerring aim and force of a cannonball, he struck Father's legs and fairly lifted him from the ice. When he came to after the stunning episode the dog was licking him in the face. His first impulse was to grab the fork and deal the poor dog the death blow, but the same force which had sent him sprawling had also lent wings to the fork, so that he had to put in some diligent searching before it was recovered. By this time the feeling of revenge had subsided and was replaced by a feeling of thankfulness that there were no bones broken.

Among the comical scenes of which there are many that could be related which occurred on the farm, this one has always stood out prominently as number one. One day Martin and Bertha as they were playing with Carlo noticed that there was some slight inflammation in one of his eyes. They reasoned that it might prove serious and something must be done. All of a sudden an idea struck Martin. "I've got it," he yelled. "Let's put earrings in his ears. That's what Andre Bjerkeland put in his own ears for weak eyes, so why not apply it to the dog?"

Martin immediately secured some hog rings and the necessary tong. The dog took the treatment without flinching in the least, but not so when they had to be removed again, for no sooner had Mother witnessed the transformation before she ordered them taken out again posthaste. Here Martin found himself up against a proposition that was way above him, a slight irritation had already set in, and those rings could not be touched without causing a pain. He would under no condition submit to this second operation. We all took turns at it and finally succeeded after having made a special trip to town for a sharp file to get them removed.

This dog was highly gifted in one direction, and that was he seemed to be able to divine where we were going. After we had hitched up a horse or team as the case might be, he would line up just so many paces in the lead and hold his own, never swerving, but trudging right on until the goal was reached. If we tied him, he had enough of the bird dog instinct left in his system to take up the scent and follow us up.

Never was this made as plain to me as one day when I hitched Clark up to my brand new road cart for the actual purpose of going to see a girl who I imagined I was interested in. In those days a road cart was all the rage. How would a young man feel at this present age seated in a road cart bent on seeing his best girl? Well, at any rate, I was seated in the road cart, and the dog stood ready to lead the van. This was to be my very first call. Nobody knew where I was going; thus it became doubly aggravating that this dog seemingly should know all about it. He trotted right ahead of me whirling that tail until I got dizzy looking at him. Sometimes it struck me as a bad omen. Supposing this girl's heart was just as changeable as this dog's tail was wiggly and other ridiculous thoughts kept chasing each other through my distracted mind, which was fast becoming loony, all because I had my eyes riveted on that windmill right in front of me. I reached my goal, but the dog got there first. I pounded at the door, but the dog had already looked in through the window before I reached the porch. This trip sealed that dog's fate. I promised him that he would never accompany me on a similar trip again, and he didn't.

Chip the Second

None of us dared broach the dog question now, nor the next month, in fact it was not considered safe for quite a while. The episode on the ice lingered long in Father's memory. Even if, according to the natural evolution of things, his memory could have been dulled on the provoking subject, some evil spirit seemed to be ever ready to pour fresh oil on the dying embers in shape of a reminder. And there was also my humiliating experience that for some reason or other had leaked out, and it behooved me only too well to lie low on the all-absorbing dog question. For wasn't it I who had signed the death warrant of our last dog? And why? No, the question must be laid on the table and await some self-made adjustment. On account of the above contingencies, the burden of making the coast clear for the installing of a new dog was laid upon the shoulders of the younger children of the family with the rest of us as silent partners. Martin, who was supposed to be the leader of the enterprise, had heard through one of his playmates that Stone Charlson was in a position to satisfy our wants. No more Bjerkeland stock for us.

Stone Charlson was one of the old pioneers. He had been a sailor on the Great Lakes way back in the fifties, had cast his lot among the woodchoppers along the Mississippi down through the southern states, supplying wood for all the steamboats plying between New Orleans and Memphis, had skipped from those states just in time to avoid being made a Confederate soldier. He then went to Wisconsin, where he wielded his ax among the pines during the frightful period of the Civil War. Shortly after the war he came to Iowa, where he bought a beautiful farm adjoining the Skunk River woods, married one of the girls of the community, and raised a large family of boys and girls, twelve in number.

It was one of these boys who could report to Martin that they had a litter of pups that would fairly make a fellow's eyes stick out to see and that he could have one just for the asking.

This naturally brought the dog fever out in all its fury. Ways and means were eagerly discussed. Father was being stormed by arguments from all directions. Mother in her quiet, diplomatic way and with a twinkle in her eye, which we interpreted as sympathy for the cause, advised us to lie low and matters might adjust themselves. To us this meant a victory because in her sweet and gentle way, superior statesmanship had oftentimes been shown, and with discredit to no one. From a man like Stone Charlson we had every reason to believe that we would get a good, intelligent, and fearless dog. He was a man that tolerated no inferior stuff or humbug on his place. He was a close observer of things, made nature one of his deep studies, and I dare say that I believe a good many of our horticultural professors could have studied to good advantage under Stone Charlson. His nature was an unassuming one but allowed no dictation; he attended strictly to his own business and feared nothing which the following story will illustrate.

As has already been stated, Nevada was at one time our nearest railroad station. Stone like the rest of the early settlers had to make his quarterly or semiquarterly trips to Nevada. Right across the river lived another settler by the name of Joren Boyd. This man had served through the war and with some Iowa regiment. Whether there or elsewhere, he had contracted a great liking for whiskey, and, as a rule, he kept a generous supply of this beverage on hand because in those days whiskey was cheap, only twenty-five cents a gallon. Now it came to pass that while Stone was on one of his trips to Nevada, Joren had just gulped his last drop of whiskey, and the problem he had to solve was when, how, and where was he to get his next drink? The nearest supply station was Nevada, and that was twenty-one miles away. Suddenly he bethought himself of the fact that Stone that very day had driven to Nevada and, if he mistook not, he had an empty gallon jug in his wagon. In some manner he must get this jug out of Stone's wagon when he came back.

In order to realize his aim, he laid the following plan. He knew that Stone could now be expected back before near midnight and that he would have to pass through a narrow road hemmed in by a thick growth of trees. While passing through this place, he intended to accost him wearing the garb of an imaginary ghost, stop his team, scare Stone out of his wits, and grab the jug. Stone came, the apparition appeared right in front of the team, and the result was that the horses stopped with a snort. Stone stepped out of the wagon, deliberately picked up a pole about the size of a fence rail, and made for the ghost, addressing him thus: "Now if you are human speak, or I will smash your noodle." The ghost spoke, and the jug was rescued. A dread for supernatural things seems to be bred into the human race, but Stone wouldn't scare worth a cent. Joren had to go without his whiskey and thank his lucky stars that he wasn't tongue-tied.

This kind of man we thought could speak with some authority when it came to the question of dogs. The fact that we were negotiating with just such a man had its good effect on Father, who at last gave his consent, though very reluctantly, Chip came, made rapid growth, and soon showed signs of superior intelligence. It wasn't long before Chip and Father had sworn allegiance to each other.

Chip was a cross between something and a rat terrier. He was a small fellow though about twice the size of an ordinary terrier, very plump and muscular. He was decorated with the most wonderful tail I ever saw. When he felt real trim and in the best of humor this tail was curled up and resembled very much a bologna with about three coils to it and rigid enough so that, if he should happen to sit down on it, it would act as a spring cushion. But, on the contrary, when he was downcast or the world in general seemed to go awry, the tail relaxed and seemed to be a burden to him. His color was brindle with exception of his breast, which was white. He had also a white streak in his forehead which culminated in a white nose. Fear was something entirely foreign to him. He would just as soon fight a Bengal tiger as anything else. He kept the place clear of vermin of all kinds. The slickest job I ever saw performed on a skunk was done by him. One of those formidable creatures had worked his way into our implement shed. Chip knew he was there, but the doors were closed so he could gain no entrance. He came running with his tail coiled up to a solid wad and let us understand that he needed help. By this time we had learned to respect his signals and wasted no time in giving him the necessary aid. All we had to do was to open the door; he bounded in and killed the skunk so quick that the poor fellow did not even get time to be on the defensive; thus we were even spared the unpleasant aroma.

Another instance I can recall when he showed a marked degree of intelligence was one dark night, it must have been about seven o'clock, we heard his bark furiously at something out in the grove. Since he could not arouse our interest out there, he came up to the porch, stood on his short hind legs, looked in through the window, and barked at us. This brought us to our feet, and Martin and I took a lantern and the rifle and followed the dog. He led us up to a tree and let us understand that the object he was after was up among its branches. On looking up, we saw two bright eyes gleaming down at us. One of us held the lantern so as to reflect on the gun barrel while the other one was to hazard a random shot at the bright eyes. We took a careful aim and fired and, sure enough, the creature came down and hit the ground with a thud. It was a polecat, one of Chip's arch enemies.

While Chip was yet young and before he grew too corpulent, he even was a partial success as a cattle dog. He would as a rule notify us when there was anything wrong around the stables and cattle yards, but he would not always take part when it came to driving them. At such times his tail would get flabby, and he would slink away and by his actions say nearly as plain as words that this was really outside of his profession. At one time it happened that he notified us that the cattle had broken into the stockyard and were maltreating the haystacks. We ran out there and kept playing hide and seek with those cattle among the haystacks for quite a while. Chip could have helped us out wonderfully, but he refused. Henry got out of patience with him and picked him up and threw him like a ball up against the side of a steer. This made him feel so cheap that he looked more as though he would have a fainting spell than anything else when he hit the ground. His tail got just as limp as a rag, and it took a long time before he could muster up enough courage to appear before us with a normal tail.

About this time our country was all of a sudden overrun with wolves. It was considered somewhat phenomenal. Ever since the first settlers had come nothing of the kind had been seen. It was not at all unusual to see as many as three or four in a pack. One man stated that he had seen a pack of twelve one day, but I wouldn't vouch for its truthfulness. If we should be allowed to draw any conclusions from the howls and yelps that we heard some nights one might be tempted to believe that there were millions of them. This was a source of great annoyance to our Chip. He would go out single-handed and fight them, but of course he would always get the worse of it. One night we lay in our beds and listened to their demonlike yells, which seemed to come out of a nearby corn-field. The next morning we found poor Chip almost killed. We nursed him back to life, but his tail wouldn't curl worth a cent for a long time.

One morning we found that the wolves had killed twenty-four of Mother's turkeys. By this time it had become a serious question. One of our neighbors shipped in a big staghound and two greyhounds for the purpose of exterminating the wolves, but the wire fences had become so numerous that the poor hounds knocked themselves silly running up against them while on the chase, while the wolves bounded on look-ing back over their shoulders at the poor yelping hounds on the other side of the wire fence. We had heard that a Newfoundland dog with just enough sprinkling of greyhound blood to lend him speed would make a good wolf dog. Just such a pup could be had from one Nels Jepson at Story City. We reasoned that such a dog, if joined by Chip, would make a team that would be invulnerable. Father readily consented to this deal, and we, in turn, made the deal with Mr. Jepson. When we brought home the pup, we also brought a huge gro-cery box that we made over for a dog kennel. Now then we had two dogs. The new one we named Hector.

Chip & Hector

One night during this wolf siege I was called upon to stay up with a sick neighbor. He had an unusually hard time of it that night so that by the time I was relieved, about one o'clock the following morning, my nerves were entirely unstrung. I was told that I could go to bed and try to snatch some sleep, but I preferred to go home a distance of just half a mile. I had barely gotten out into the road when a pack of wolves started to howl. In my nervous condition this acted like an electric shock on my system. I had all I could do to go out into the darkness as it was, and I felt as if I was walking on air. This was all it took to touch me off. I started to run and, before I was aware of my own action, another hellish chorus in response to the first one from another direction put me into a speed that would have puzzled a racehorse. I have often wondered if the roar of a lion could have put such uncanny terror into me. If the distance had been three miles or ten miles, I couldn't have stopped unless I had been laid low from sheer exhaustion. What's the use to dwell upon it? It almost makes my gray hair stand on end now to think about it.

Hector was fast developing into a big dog. He was assuming huge proportions in some respects. We flattered ourselves in thinking that we would soon have an outfit that would work havoc among the wolves. When he was full grown he was a rather queer-looking dog. As before stated, he had a sprinkling of greyhound blood, I think about one-sixteenth. This seemed all to go to his legs and nose, the balance was Newfoundland dog. The sum and substance of it all was a Newfoundland dog mounted on greyhound legs. His color was jet black; he had a fine coat of curly hair. His pace, before he broke into a run, was that of a pacing horse. How this combination would distinguish itself out among the wolves remained to be seen. Chip was the boss, and if there had ever existed any doubt about it, it had long since been removed. We hoped against hope that Chip would instill some of his grit into him after they should get out into the field. But in this hope we were doomed to become grossly disappointed. He had the means of locomotion, and he used it to its utmost capacity, but always in the wrong direction.

The first trial test he was put through was one fine spring morning. I was up on the north eighty seeding oats, and Chip and Hector, of course, went with me. After getting up there, I noticed a big wolf lying down within easy range of a rifle, basking in the sunshine, in what was at that time a part of our pasture. Of course the rifle was at home, which was invariably the case when an easy shot presented itself. Chip soon got the scent of the wolf and made for him; but when he got close up to him, he hesitated, seemingly because he did not know whether or not he could count on Hector if it should come to the worst. Hector was at a safe distance in the rear taking a rather dubious view of the situation. After a while he grew a little bit braver and soon commenced to lift up his voice in long-drawn barks, which got to be more and more staccato as the excitement grew.

They kept running around the wolf in a circle the best part of the forenoon, barking with no letup. Chip plainly made several efforts to urge Hector on for an attack, but his best efforts availed him nothing. Finally Chip got disgusted with the big coward and hazarded an attack single-handed. This brought the wolf to his feet with a bound. Bounding by Chip as though he never knew that he existed, he made for Hector, who in turn started to howl and to make the greatest effort of his life to follow his pointed nose across lots for home and protection. I doubt very much if any living thing in those parts had ever cleaved the atmosphere at that rate before or since. The wolf followed him clear up to the barnyard, a distance of 160 rods. From my place of vantage I could discern Chip doing his level best on his short legs to follow in the wake of the black and gray streak. He was bound to kill that wolf or die in the attempt, but he did neither. After the wolf had chased Hector home, he made in a northwesterly direction for the woods. Chip rolled through the grass and labored after him, while Hector lay panting inside of the grocery box made over expressly for him.

The queer action of this particular wolf was accounted for

a few days later. He had killed one of Martin Phillops' lambs that morning and had gorged himself to such an extent that he wouldn't stir until he had rested just so long. This demonstration and others that soon followed made it plain to us that Hector had missed his calling and that we must hit upon some nice plan by which we could dispose of him. Just at this stage of the proceedings Lewis and family moved to Decorah, where Henry was at the time attending Luther College. The thought then suggested itself. Why not donate him to Lewis's boy, Clarence? Hector was indeed an excellent playmate and a very handsome dog, in spite of the fact that he was far from true to type. This proposition met with general approval, and, accordingly, Hector went to Decorah where he, at a lucky moment, redeemed himself and made himself worthy of standing out prominently as number one among the Follinglo dogs.

It came about in this manner. Clarence and Hector were out playing, and as a standing rule of all children, of whom Clarence was by no means an exception, Clarence was to select the most dangerous spot within reach to spend his leisure moments. This time it was on the banks of the Upper Iowa River, where Clarence promptly plumped into the water and would surely have drowned if it had not been for Hector, who just as promptly jumped in, grabbed him, and successfully towed him ashore. Now then who will dare say that Hector was a failure? And, furthermore, he was a great source of amusement to Henry, Gynter Magelssen, Nick Ylvisaker, and Erling Bothne, who conceived the idea of erecting a tent in Lewis's yard and imagining that they were way out in the woolly West. This camp they called Bear Growl Camp, and Hector was an imaginary bear, which gave the clue to many a make-believe story culminating in ever so many hairbreadth escapes.

Chip & Kate

This year of Bear Growl Camp undoubtedly stands out prominently in Henry's memory. That year instead of coming home to spend his summer vacation, he stayed right on at Decorah and played baritone in the Northern Iowa Band. This, in my opinion, was the time when the foundation was laid upon which was built the present Luther College band. I believe that Bear Growl Camp had much to do with the future success of this grand organization.

It was while playing in the Northern Iowa band that Henry got acquainted with Harry Hitchcock, the soloist in the saxophone section and also a dog fancier of the highest order. This young man had a bull terrier bitch by the name of Kate, which was the apple of his eye. Young Hitchcock took sick, and it was made apparent to him as well as his friends that he could not live many days. Henry went to see him as soon as he learned that there was no hope for his recovery. Harry knew that Henry had looked with coveting eyes on his beautiful dog. He therefore told Henry that when he was gone he should take Kate and be good to her. This then is how this grand representative of her breed, Kate, came to Follinglo Farm.

She was snow white with the exception of one ear and one side of her face which was brown. I cannot describe her so as to do her justice as far as her general makeup was concerned. Look at the dog listening to his "master's voice" in front of the Victor phonograph. When I say that his beautiful picture doesn't flatter Kate you can begin to figure out that there was some class to her. She had a very quiet disposition. Her principal vocation or pastime was to carry a stick in her mouth and wiggle her tail, but she wiggled it differently from other dogs. The whole body worked in sympathy with the tail, and there were times when this wiggling motion worked up to a momentum that seemingly threatened to break her off in the middle. Poor Chip felt very much out of place in the presence of this artistic lady, and it took him quite a while before he could get accustomed to the situation. There is very little that can be recorded about Kate. During her sojourn among us she took part in no stunts worth mentioning. Her strength lay principally in her fine appearance and splendid behavior. Her line of business was that of coach dog, and she would undoubtedly have been a credit to her breed along those lines, but her life on the farm gave her very little chance of developing those traits.

We had one laughable experience with her, however, which I can't so soon forget. There are certain periods during the fiscal year that dogs like Kate must be consigned to seclusion, that is, if one figures on getting a decent night's sleep. This very necessary precaution had for some reason or other been neglected one evening. Towards midnight of a crisp November night the moon was at his best; the stars even were so bright that if the moon had not outdone them they would have been capable of causing shadows. Father came and pounded at our door and told us that something was tearing down our house and that we must get up at once. He furthermore stated that the yard was full of dogs and wound up by saying something that I can't remember, but I can recollect that he laid great stress and emphasis on the word bitch, so that before we got up we had a pretty clear conception of what was the cause of the rumpus outside.

Henry and I got up and worked our way cautiously up to the window facing the south porch. There we saw Kate sitting on a bench in the middle of the porch surrounded by dogs of all descriptions. The most aggressive ones sat right on the porch; others occupied the yard, seemingly satisfied just to get a glimpse of the white beauty. When we opened the door, they scattered just like chaff in a gale. The biggest one, a long-legged yellow fellow, was in such a furious haste that he jumped right over the picket fence which was just a trifle too high for him. This got him into a terrible predicament because his hind legs fit right in between the pickets and got wedged fast. There he hung yelling for dear life until we helped him out. Talk about making tracks! That is just exactly what he did when he hit the ground. After he was liberated, Henry went and picked up Kate and carried her under his arm in the direction of the old granary. I stood by the gate holding it open for him to pass through. By this time the dogs understood that we harbored no ill feeling towards them and meant them no harm; therefore, they joined in the procession one by one and marched single file behind Henry to the granary. If I had been given the talent of sketching, I believe I should have made myself world famous right then and there.

When we came up to the porch again we found another subject which I fear would have been a study that would have baffled even Michelangelo; for there sat the homeliest representative of the whole dog creation. He was blind in one eye with a tangle of hair enveloping his whole face. As he sat there giving us occasional side glances with his one eye, he presented such a comical picture that a hysterical laugh set in which came very nearly being too much for our health. Poor fellow, he was more than satisfied to be allowed the privilege of sitting, even though for a brief moment, on the spot where Kate had last been seen.

The next winter, after having finished his work at Luther College, Henry went to Roland and took up the work of giving private music lessons on wind instruments and organized the Roland band. He then took Kate with him, and since he had become interested in St. Bernard dogs, he gave Kate to a friend who was in the butcher business. There she lived on the fat of the land and reached a ripe old age.

Noble, Sheppo, & Chip

While at Roland Henry got acquainted with Theo. Hermanson, a dog fancier of the highest order. This man had a St.
Bernard bitch of considerable value. She had been sent to him
by a friend from the state of California, who had parted with
the sum of $200.00 in order to get her. He found, however,
that the climate of California was not adapted to St. Bernard
dogs, so he sent her to Iowa. She had taken several prizes at
shows, and she had a full brother who had taken first honors
at the International Show. Mr. Hermanson made the following proposition to Henry. Since Sheppo will have pups in the
spring and since he was afraid she might hurt some inquisitive
kid if he kept her in town through the time of the big event,
he would give Henry the choice of two pups out of the litter
if he would take her to Follinglo and look after her until the
pups were old enough to dispose of. There were four of them
that had already been spoken for long before they were born
at the rate of twenty-five dollars each.

Henry gladly entered in upon this agreement. Sheppo was
brought to the farm and in due order of things brought a litter
of nine pups. According to agreement, we picked out our two,
a beautiful pair indeed. We called them Noble and Sheppo.
It was interesting to watch them grow and develop. After
one year Noble tipped the scale at one hundred and eighty-
five pounds, a magnificent type of the St. Bernard breed both
in markings and size. Young Sheppo was equally as good
but could not come up to Noble in size and weight. The next
fall Henry took up his band work at Roland again and took
Sheppo with him. She became the mother of a few elegant
pups, some of which were sold for twenty-five dollars a piece.
Poor Sheppo, after she had successfully raised her family, was
killed. A coarse brute of a man who really belonged inside a
penitentiary shot her dead from a window in the hotel where
he was staying.

All the affection we could spare for dogs now had to be centered on Noble and old Chip. The latter was by now getting old and grouchy and was fast becoming a nuisance. In the summertime he would go through the screen doors whether they were open or shut. In the wintertime he would insist on staying in the house. If he couldn't get out just when he felt like it, he would promptly start gnawing at the door, and if he was unable to get in he would resort to the same means. Father said that if we insisted on keeping this dog we would have to install a doorkeeper. Chip's fate was hanging in the balance for quite a while, but one Sunday when we were all of us away to church he committed such a havoc in the house that it was made plain to all of us that Chip was no longer for this world. He had in some way sneaked into the house, and when we left we had locked the doors on him. When we returned we found him on top of the organ gnawing away at the window frame. He had left his mark on the mouldings adjacent to all exits, demolished lace curtains and other curtains, and showed in ways innumerable that we just had to dispose of him. His hide made a splendid pair of driving mittens, but I find it rather against the grain to make use of the fur that once enveloped the gritty, nervy, and intelligent Chip.

I cannot enter into a detailed description of Noble. A dog of his grand makeup would have to be seen in order to be appreciated fully. The only way I could show him off and do him justice would be to show his picture of which we have several. Should therefore anyone come to Follinglo Farm for the purpose of wanting to see a dog that was a dog, all they would have to do would be to intimate a desire to see Noble's picture. He was a great playmate for the children, and what made it doubly interesting to me was that it was now my own children that were being entertained by him, and woe to any man, bird, or beast that would interfere with the little ones whom he imagined were under his special charge. He was a great scourge and menace to tramps and peddlers. They would usually walk by our place just as though they were on a forced march. The tramp gait was a lost art for the time being. If they slackened their pace, two short barks way below the ledger lines of the music staff, causing the earth to shake beneath them, usually gave them a fresh start. His voice was so strong that when he stood on the porch and let out a bark the dishes would rattle in the pantry.

The only approach to trouble we had with Noble was when he went to see his little sweetheart. This was a little yellow bitch owned by Mrs. Throndson. This dog was so small that a man could put her in his pocket. If this tiny creature happened to be on the opposite side of a gate, it mattered nothing even if the gate was built strong enough to turn a bull. Noble would tear it down and go through. Thus one day this little flirt kept playing hide and seek with him so long that he completely demolished four gates for two of our neighbors. The ludicrous picture this out-of-all proportion pair presented brought a laugh that broke down all pretense at seriousness on the part of the complainants. Thus we learned that Lincoln was right when he said: "If you can keep a man laughing, he will seldom hurt you."

Noble stayed with us for many years, but finally rheumatism got the best of him. He died a natural death, a distinction which is shown very few dogs. The look he gave me the last time I patted his head was to me very touching. His hide adorns the floor of our music room as a rug, but, as for me, I generally walk around it.

Chip the Third

The present dog incumbent on Follinglo Farm is a purebred Scotch collie. His name is Chip. So far he has been one long continuous question mark as to what he will really amount to. The pioneer dog was surrounded by an entirely different environment than those of his fellows of the present age. Then he had his herd of cattle to look after, while now he has the automobiles to look after, morning, noon, and night. Then there was an occasional wolf to help harden a fellow, now the biggest game going is a measly cottontail. Under those conditions it is extremely difficult to become a dog worth comparing with the pioneers. Chip's interest seems to be just about equally divided between the rabbits and the automobiles. He has been run over twice, but that only seems to enhance his interest in the dreaded machines. No matter how good his intentions may be in trying to sober down to business that really belongs to his calling, whenever one of those automobiles comes along they must have his undivided attention. Well, such is life in this ever changing world of ours. It had its effect on dogs and man as well.

With this I must close my narrative and hand my well-worn pencil back to Alfred, hoping that some day he will pick up the thread and carry it on farther. I am sorry to have to confess, however, that I have completely worn down the rubber (eraser), but it is to be hoped that when he takes up the work he will be above making as many mistakes as I have made, hence the matter of the rubber does not matter so much after all.

Epilogue
Of Transition, Calamity, & Continuity

PETER TJERNAGEL HARSTAD

From the Civil War to the present, five generations of Tjernagel farmers have witnessed and weathered the business cycles of the American economy, including the farm depressions of the 1890s, 1920s, 1930s, and 1980s. Coming as it did in the wake of the unprecedented prosperity of the World War I era, the agricultural depression of the 1920s was the most difficult for the Tjernagels. Many urbanites experienced good times during the "Roaring Twenties"; most farmers did not. In November 1921 United States Secretary of Agriculture Henry C. Wallace of Iowa warned that unless the price of corn rose above the current twenty cents a bushel, farmers would be burning corn as fuel. Farm prices did not rise significantly during the decade.[1] Despite hard times, the Tjernagels joined with two neighboring families in the mid 1920s to bring electrical power lines from Story City to their farms. A photograph of the "Follinglo Orchestra" in a book published in 1925 to celebrate the centennial of the first substantial Norwegian migration to America shows the Tjernagel family in their music room, illuminated by electricity.[2]

It pained Peder Gustav that it was difficult for his children to establish themselves independently. With the added problem of drought, the 1930s were no better than the 1920s. The persistent farm depression and Peder Gustav's death in 1932 took a heavy toll on Jennie.[3] Two of her most promising sons, Herman and Erling, tried to strike out on their own, remained single, and never achieved the independence they sought beyond Follinglo Farm. Such was the price of two decades of agricultural depression.

In 1936, on the occasion of the centennial of Ole Andreas' birth, his oldest son, Lewis, commissioned the printing of a family tree. It listed fifty living descendants of his parents. Eight people then resided at Follinglo Farm, including Jennie, six unmarried sons, and Unko. The document recorded no children born on the farm since 1916. Nor would there be any resident children until 1948. Thus a full generation, thirty-two years, passed without producing a potential farmer.

A high percentage of the nonresident members of the family plus their spouses and children could be counted upon to visit the farm annually. Through the years the ranks of the extended family grew through marriages and births. Providing hospitality was integral to the Tjernagel tradition. Jennie, joined by Tante in 1940, played hostess to all comers. This put a strain upon them, but neither allowed it to show.

During the early years of my life, our family visited Follinglo Farm nearly every summer, usually at grain-threshing time. The spacious, orderly farmhouse seemed to accommodate any number of people. Some years I came ahead of the family or stayed longer than the rest. I was particularly pleased when my visits coincided with those of first cousins of my approximate age. Playing with them and my siblings in the barn, shocking grain, drinking cold water from the artesian well, feeding pigs and shorthorn calves, learning to make a milk stool, and "helping" our cheerful uncles were unforgettable experiences for city boys and girls.

Grain threshing involved all available hands. During the period of my memory, Follinglo Farm owned its own threshing machine. Mounted on lugged wheels, an ancient Oliver tractor inched into position. The giant belt connecting it to the threshing machine was given one twist, then tightened. Supplying belt power was the only function that prevented the Oliver from becoming scrap metal to aid the Allied cause during World War II. Belts, pulleys, wheels, and chains began to whirl. Where there was undue friction Martin applied lubricant. Men fed bundles of grain from hay wagons into the pulsating beast; out of the stack on the opposite end came straw and chaff. Golden grain (whether oats, wheat, rye, or flax) poured out of a side hopper and ran like liquid into a tight wagon box or was bagged. To supplement the labor force my uncles sometimes hired a hermit who lived in an abandoned school bus down by the Skunk River. Known only as "Gullixson," he usually drove a team of borrowed horses. One year my father, the preacher, lent a hand. It surprised everyone that he set a brisk pace and kept it up all day. He even joined in the banter and told of following the grain harvest in Minnesota and the Dakotas when he was a seminary student twenty years earlier.

Wit, wisdom, and humor might crop up at any turn. Such was the case one July day as Uncle Alfred and I approached the threshing machine with a wagonload of oats bundles, pulled by a team of grays, the last draft horses at Follinglo Farm. The occasion gave rise to an aphorism that Alfred insisted came off better in the Norwegian language: "A farting horse never tires, and the man who farts is the one to hire." One did not learn such lessons in a parsonage in the capitol city of Wisconsin.

There were somber times, too. The lives of God's creatures, great and small, even those of chickens for the Sunday dinner table, were to be respected. One morning while I was at the farm, one member of the team of grays tangled a hind leg in a barbed wire fence while rolling on its back in the pasture. During efforts to break free, the horse nearly severed its hoof below the pastern. There was no chance for recovery, and the animal had to be destroyed. As was the custom at Follinglo Farm, a neighbor came in for such duty. Banished to the house, I sobbed when the shot rang out. When I returned to the scene there were tears in my uncles' eyes. That ended the era of horsepower at Follinglo Farm. The other member of the team lived on in retirement.

On 4 January 1943 Unko wrote Olaf, then stationed at Chanute Field, Rantoul, Illinois: "Last Monday morning I found Old Riley forever asleep in his stall. No more will he push eagerly against the gate and seek to wedge through as I swing it open barely saving my life in the act." Sensitive Unko repented for roughness "when I had to pull his unwilling head around at the end of the furrow." In the same letter he speculated about whether "God's creatures will rise again," briefed his nephew Olaf on the current crop of visitors, and reported that the shorthorn bull, Follinglo Progress, sold for $270. "Things run along quite smoothly," he concluded. After two long decades of depression, prosperity was at last returning to Follinglo Farm.

Stories abounded when Lewis, Martin, and Gus came to Follinglo Farm with their families on Sundays to mingle with the houseguests. Their arrival was the signal for a quorum of my bachelor uncles (Herman, Erling, Peder, and Olaf) to gather with their uncles under a shade tree by the smokehouse while the women headed for the house. Although not excluded from these male gatherings, I was frequently frustrated because both generations usually delivered their punch lines in Norwegian. If delivered by Martin, they also came between aromatic puffs of smoke from his pipe.

One of the stories that was told and retold involved Mother's youngest brother, Sigurd. It dated from the late 1920s and involved the then incumbent canine and the Lutheran minister. This particular dog had the aggravating habit of scratching at the porch door until someone let it in. One Sunday afternoon the minister came calling while Sigurd napped on a horsehair couch in the living room. Sigurd heard what he thought was the dog at the door and told it to go away. The tapping persisted and he shouted, "Go away you son of a bitch!" But it was the minister, not the dog, and he was out to court Sigurd's sister Martha. The courtship withstood this temporary setback and resulted in the fifty-seven-year marriage of my parents.

Conversations around the dinner table were more restrained than those outdoors by the smokehouse. The presence of Grandmother, Tante, and Unko ensured decorum. To my young mind it seemed that these three had been associated with Follinglo Farm from time immemorial and would be forever.

I was present at Follinglo Farm in August 1945 when the United States dropped the two atomic bombs on Japan, followed by the emperor's announcement of surrender on 14 August. This news brought jubilation to Follinglo Farm. It was now unlikely that Uncle Olaf, the fighter plane propeller mechanic on the western front, would be transferred to hazardous duty in the Far East. Uncle Peder's way of celebrating was to get the shotgun and fire several rounds into the air between the house and the cow barn — to the cheers of his assembled nieces and nephews.

While spending time at Follinglo Farm during the 1940s and early 1950s, it dawned on me that I, Peter Tjernagel Harstad, am part of a greater whole, and that, in certain settings, my status as an individual is subordinate to my place in the lineage. Nevertheless, my Tjernagel ties strengthen rather than diminish me. I am a link in an unbroken chain of generations going back on the Tjernagel side through my mother, Martha Karina, to my grandparents Peder Gustav and Jennie, to my great-grandparents Ole Andreas and Martha Karina, the founders of Follinglo Farm. They were of the generation of Store Per, and, like him, had come to this country from Norway.

Reading Ole Rolvaag in high school only strengthened what I already knew. There once were "Giants in the Earth," who transformed the native prairies of the American heartland into the most productive farms on earth. To me, later generations are equally interesting but for different reasons. A rich, diverse, and layered heritage, greater than the sum of its parts, is available for me to draw upon and to pass on to the next generation.

Sensitive yet practical people, my Tjernagel forebears strove to live at least a portion of their existence in a zone between the spiritual realm and the world of unrelenting daily toil — a place where beauty and utility go hand in hand. That is part of what Nehemias had in mind when he concluded, "Unless there be music and poetry in a man's soul, there will be no loveliness about his yards or buildings." Grandfather attended to the more structural applications of this principle and Grandmother to the adornments. Long after they were gone, their successes remained evident in the values and character of their progeny and in the appearance of their farmstead.

Buster, a faithful black mongrel, sniffed the air and greeted the bright, crisp morning of Monday 9 December 1968.[4] Under his watchful eye were seven Tjernagel residents of Follinglo Farm, the fields, livestock, rodents and reptiles native to central Iowa, farm machinery, and a century's accumulation of farm buildings. The latter ranged in size from a small concrete smokehouse to an enormous wooden horse barn, both long ago relegated to adaptive uses. Since the publication of an edition of *The Follinglo Dog Book* for the family in 1966, Interstate 35 had nicked the farmstead. This constituted a serious affront to Buster, but the consequences could have been worse. While in the design phase, the right-of-way for I-35 aimed, dead center, at the farm buildings. Were it not for their antiquity and uniqueness, they would have been demolished in 1967. Foursquare highway engineers lost that battle largely because Follinglo was a Century Farm. I-35 veered ever so slightly to the west to avoid the Tjernagel's buildings, including the gem that crowned the highpoint of the farmyard.

This was the seed house, or *stabbur*, Peder Gustav's 1916 masterpiece. In Norway a *stabbur* is an unheated wooden farm building where grain is stored high and dry above the snow-drifts and away from the threat of fire. A *stabbur* looks like it is built on stilts. The prime storage area is on the second floor, which overhangs the first. Peder Gustav designed his to look like its Norwegian counterparts. However, he used concrete for the support columns as well as for other parts of the structure. Classic *stabburs* feature ferocious gargoyles on the low ends of the bargeboards near the eves. Every good Viking knew that they frightened off evil spirits. A *gabelspir*, or wooden pike, attached to the ridgepole at the front of the building impaled any bold enough to attack from above. Peder Gustav replicated such features for his *stabbur*. He and his brother Martin used the building for drying, storing, and testing seed corn prior to the availability of commercial hybrids in the 1930s. When Uncle Peder Julius married in 1947, he converted the *stabbur* into an attractive residence for his bride, Marie. Because it was small, the couple referred to their home as the birdhouse. The year 1948 was eventful; after a thirty-two-year hiatus a child, Michael Peter, was born to resident Tjernagels of Follinglo Farm.

In 1968 the *stabbur* butted up against the northbound lanes of I-35. By this time, however, Jennie and Nehemias of the older generation were deceased. Peder Julius, Marie, and their four children lived in the century-old farmhouse.

Buster had higher aspirations than watching traffic on the interstate highway. A born optimist, he aspired to control the air space above Follinglo Farm. He eyed birds and airplanes suspiciously and regretted that he was not licensed to fend them off. Earthbound, he went about his responsibilities that clear December day in 1968. A large combine sat idle in the farmyard, its work done for the season. The unique concrete corncrib, constructed by Peder Gustav and his brothers in 1914, brimmed with 10,000 bushels of corn and soybeans. By the late 1960s, many Iowa farms had no livestock. The Tjernagels, however, continued to fatten swine with some of their corn. In fact, Buster had several broods of piglets to protect. The shorthorns were gone.

Buster's owners, like all families, rural and urban, had their vexations. Rheumatoid arthritis required the farm manager, Peder Julius, to use a wheelchair. His twenty-year-old son, Michael, a college student, had just been drafted and was spending his last days at home before reporting for military duty. The Lyndon Johnson administration needed men to fight in Vietnam. Strapping Martin, age eighteen, had a draft number, too.

Throughout its history, Follinglo Farm has been blessed with a succession of capable women: first Martha Karina, next Jennie, then Tante, who never married and who returned to her girlhood home to help her widowed sister-in-law. At age eighty-seven in 1968, Tante was hospitalized for tuberculosis at Oakdale. Marie, Peder Julius's wife, followed in the best tradition of Follinglo Farm women. She soon needed every ounce of her strength and capability to hold together both her family and the farm.

The humdrum of daily life continued into the late afternoon of 9 December 1968. Buster watched for the school bus and when it arrived greeted the two Tjernagel girls. Sigrid, age fifteen, began preparing dinner while her mother took a bath. A few minutes after 6:00 P.M. the youngest Tjernagel, twelve-year-old Ingeborg, fed Buster and tied him up for the night near the smokehouse where he had access to his comfortable dog house. Peder's older brother Herman, a bachelor who lived with the family, was in the habit of watching the evening news — important to a farm family with commodities to market and males of military age. Ingeborg joined him. While Martin tended swine in the barn, Michael went to the bedroom to bring his father into the living room, part of Ole Andreas and Martha Karina's original 1864 home.

Off the living room to the south was the newest part of the rambling home — a spacious music room with a parquet floor of black walnut and maple laid down by Peder Gustav. Here Herman and Peder Julius had played in the family orchestra years earlier. Handmade "music chairs," likewise the products of Peder Gustav's craftsmanship, lined the walls. Their graceful lines mimicked stringed instruments and caught the eye of all who entered the room. On the floor lay a colorful, all-wool, yarn rug ten feet in diameter, handmade by Jennie and Tante. The focal point of the room, however, was a solid black-walnut music cabinet six feet high and wide and two feet deep, with a dozen drawers. Peder Gustav had painstakingly inlayed wood on the drawers to spell out the names of major composers — Bach, Beethoven, Dvorak, Greig, Mozart, and on through the alphabet. A special drawer contained opera scores. The one labeled "Miscellaneous" mystified me as a child.

At 6:15 Marie entered the kitchen with curlers in her hair while Sigrid looked into the oven. Then it happened. An eerie piercing sound heralded an ear-shattering, earthshaking BOOM! "The windows in the house blew in," explained Marie, "the telephone came flying across the kitchen, wood beams, plaster and chaos filled the whole house. Thick dust was everywhere. A huge red ball of fire came through the broken paneless window, rolling slowly between Sigrid and me."

Wet and in curlers, Marie's hair singed but did not burn. Flames scorched her hand, and flying glass lacerated Sigrid's back. As suddenly as it had come, the fireball receded long enough for decisive action. "We have to go out the south music room door," shouted mild-mannered Herman. Michael picked up his father, and they all fell in line and evacuated the house in the only direction that could have saved them. By then, the kitchen was ablaze. Soon, the floor, rug, chairs and music cabinet of Peder Gustav and Jennie's music room fueled a final crescendo. Out in the yard the Tjernagels saw their house, outbuildings, treetops, and patches of grass on fire. They had no idea what had caused the holocaust.

When Martin opened the barn door to come to dinner the explosion sent him sprawling forty feet back inside. He quickly recovered and headed for the house, but flames engulfed the kitchen door where he usually entered. He scrambled through a broken dining-room window in time to see the family fleeing, grabbed his father's wheelchair, and joined the rest away from the spreading flames. Debris blocked traffic on I-35, and flames leaped over all four lanes to start a grass fire on the other side. Miraculously, all seven Tjernagels were alive, but Peder was in severe shock, Sigrid's back and arm needed stitches, and Marie's hand was burned.

Michael asked, "Where should I put Dad?" Martin ran to get the family car, but when he drove up he was sitting on broken glass and the back of the vehicle was on fire. "We can't put Dad in there," exclaimed Marie. Just then a neighbor drove up and rushed Marie, Peder Julius, and the two girls to the Story City hospital. Emergency vehicles and more neighbors arrived, but they could do little other than watch the buildings of Follinglo Farm burn.

News spread quickly that an Iowa Air National Guard F89 Scorpion jet fighter with a crew of two had crashed at 6:15 while on a mission from Des Moines to Mason City. Flying inverted and at a high rate of speed on that clear December evening, pilot John H. Rooks may have mistaken mercury vapor lights on the ground for stars in the sky. He went into a dive (rather than a climb) and slammed into the ground under full power at a speed in excess of 600 miles per hour. Residents of Story City felt tremors four miles away. Fortunately, the sturdy workmanship of Peder Gustav's concrete corncrib shielded the house from an instantly lethal deluge of burning aircraft fuel. The corn and soybeans ignited, and the fire could not be extinguished. Captain Rooks' body lay eerily near a crater thirty feet deep and fifty feet wide. That of his radar observer, Larry L. Thomas, was found a half mile away. The combine, parked near the point of impact, was thrown fifty feet and destroyed along with three cars, two tractors, and nearly all of the other farm machinery. An Air Force investigator summed up the damage when he reported that the farmstead looked like a Vietnam village after an air attack.

Among the precious items that went up in flames were the clock that had ticked out the chapters of Tjernagel lives since the reign of Fido the Second (and the presidency of Ulysses S. Grant), decades of Tante's diaries, and, very likely, the manuscript of *The Follinglo Dog Book*. Although firefighters prevented the *stabbur* and some of the other buildings from burning to the ground, all of the structures sustained catastrophic damage and were razed. The Follinglo farmstead familiar to four generations existed no more.

And what of Buster, the faithful, black mongrel that had harbored a suspicion of airplanes? Severely burned, he was mercifully dispatched by one of the law-enforcement officers on the scene.

"Mom, let me borrow your comb," requested Sigrid from her hospital bed after doctors had stitched her up and attended to the immediate medical needs of her parents. Then the enormity of the situation struck Marie. She had no comb. Nor did she have a purse, a driver's license, a car, a house, or clothes; in fact, she was still in her bathrobe.

Relatives, friends, and neighbors extended help generously, as rural and small-town Iowans do when there is need. "We were reminded again that all things material are perishable," wrote Marie in a card of thanks published in the local newspaper. "We are truly grateful to Almighty God for miraculously sparing our lives."

But things had not yet bottomed out. Peder Julius died fifty-two days after the crash. Marie debated whether she should ask the draft board to allow her oldest son, Michael, to stay home to help sort through the chaos. After prayerful consideration she rejected this idea, certain that her second son, Martin, "a farmer since he was two years old," would then be drafted immediately.

On 11 March 1969 Tante died, the last of her generation, and Marie had Tante's affairs to settle also. The next month Michael went into the army. After training and three months of military service in Vietnam he contracted infectious hepatitis and came home with a 100 percent disability.

Nor was this the end of the problems. The Friday after the crash Adjutant General Joseph May of the Iowa National Guard showed up at Marie's temporary dwelling in Story City in full military attire. He came to the point quickly: "Who are you going to sue?" After she gained her composure Marie asked: "Sue? Sue?" He replied, "You'll have to sue the State of Iowa or the federal government."

The United States Air Force locked into the position that

the Iowa National Guard was responsible for the crash and the damage, and therefore the State of Iowa should settle the claim. The State of Iowa countered that the two crew members were federal employees and the plane was on a federal mission, and therefore the United States government must pay the Tjernagels.

Months dragged into years, but the Tjernagels received no settlement other than an initial $5,000 emergency payment. The story of federal/state wrangling over the claim deserves to be told in full, but not here. Iowa Governor Robert D. Ray finally cut the Gordian knot 22 April 1972 when he ordered that no aircraft or vehicle assigned to the Iowa National Guard "shall be moved or be used in any manner" until he received assurance that the federal government would pay the Tjernagel claim. Assurance soon came, and a check for $101,330.70 arrived four years lacking one day after the crash.

Marie wrote of the ordeal, "God does not give us more trials than we can bear, but at times I felt He overestimated my ability!"

Determined to farm, Martin did not wait for legal resolution. He needed money for machinery and supplies. The spring after the crash local bankers took heart and got the eighteen-year-old started. He plowed around the ugly crater that had been the farmstead, past the few singed and sickly Norway pines that survived the fire, and out into the rich Iowa soil that had lured his forbears to southern Hamilton County a century earlier. The land obliged and yielded bumper crops of corn and soybeans. Martin fed hogs and raised turkeys. He also pulled a house trailer to the farmstead and took up residence with his bride, Diane, and they started a family. In due course they built an attractive dwelling on the site of the original 1864 home.

When Michael came home, sick and broken, he was told he might never be able to work again. This did not deter the brothers from talking and planning. Five legal entities had interests in the farm: the Jennie Tjernagel Estate, Bertha (Tante) Tjernagel Estate, Peder Tjernagel Estate, H&P Tjernagel interest, and Herman Tjernagel interest. When the brothers Michael and Martin decided to buy the ancestral lands their credit was good, and the moneylenders again obliged.

Martin worked at least as hard as did his Norwegian-born great-grandfather, Ole Andreas, who broke the prairie sod during the 1860s. Michael pitched in when he could and gained strength steadily. After three surgeries and rehabilitation he could work hard and farm alongside his brother. Marie, her two daughters, and her sons' wives gave love and unstinting support in the tradition of the women of Follinglo Farm.

At the end of the twentieth century the two brothers, grandsons of Peder Gustav, own the farm, which consists of 110 tillable acres. They raise grain which they feed to calves and pigs.

In 1996 a family genealogist identified 550 progeny, living and dead, of the founders of Follinglo Farm, representing twenty-five countries. Christian missionary work has been the main reason for the diaspora beyond the United States.[5]

Other than the land itself, few physical vestiges remain from the era of *The Follinglo Dog Book*. Some native prairie plants survive along the fence lines, as do a few concrete corner fence posts as sturdy as Peder Gustav Tjernagel, who designed and poured them.

NOTES

1. Peter T. Harstad and Bonnie Lindemann, *Gilbert N. Haugen: Norwegian-American Farm Politician* (Iowa City and Des Moines, 1992), p. 151.

2. Olaf M. Norlie, *History of the Norwegian People in America* (Minneapolis, 1925), p. 533.

3. Numerous letters from the period in the possession of Peter Tjernagel Harstad prove this.

4. This section is based largely on Marie Tjernagel's *The Follinglo Tragedy* (Ames, 1993), a forty-seven page booklet containing her account of the tragedy and also many documents from the public press. Used here with permission.

5. Inez Waltman Bergquist, ed., *Tjernagel Family: 140 Years in the New World 1836–1966* (Eagen, Minn., 1966).

The American Land & Life Series

Bachelor Bess:
The Homesteading Letters of Elizabeth Corey, 1909–1919
Edited by Philip L. Gerber

Circling Back:
Chronicle of a Texas River Valley
By Joe C. Truett

Edge Effects:
Notes from an Oregon Forest
By Chris Anderson

Exploring the Beloved Country:
Geographic Forays into American Society and Culture
By Wilbur Zelinsky

The Follinglo Dog Book:
A Norwegian Pioneer Story from Iowa
By Peder Gustav Tjernagel

Great Lakes Lumber on the Great Plains:
The Laird, Norton Lumber Company in South Dakota
By John N. Vogel

Hard Places:
Reading the Landscape of America's
Historic Mining Districts
By Richard V. Francaviglia

Living in the Depot:
The Two-Story Railroad Station
By H. Roger Grant

Main Street Revisited:
Time, Space, and Image Building
in Small-Town America
By Richard V. Francaviglia

Mapping American Culture
Edited by Wayne Franklin and Michael C. Steiner

Mapping the Invisible Landscape:
Folklore, Writing, and the Sense of Place
By Kent C. Ryden

Pilots' Directions:
The Transcontinental Airway and Its History
Edited by William M. Leary

Places of Quiet Beauty:
Parks, Preserves, and Environmentalism
By Rebecca Conard

Reflecting a Prairie Town:
A Year in Peterson
Text and photographs by Drake Hokanson

A Rural Carpenter's World:
The Craft in a Nineteenth-Century New York Township
By Wayne Franklin

Salt Lantern:
Traces of an American Family
By William Towner Morgan